DISCARDED

D734 .N38 2015
Neiberg, Michael S
Potsdam

D0762361

Colorado Mountain College
Quigley Library
3000 County Road 114
Glenwood Springs, CO 81601

ADVANCE PRAISE FOR
Potsdam

"Ghosts and hopes informed the 1945 Potsdam Conference, which began a new era in European and world history. Michael Neiberg's comprehensively researched, smoothly presented analysis demonstrates that the statesmen who met at Potsdam were as much concerned with ending the era of total war that began in 1914 as with addressing the question of how best to go forward in securing peace and stability. *Potsdam* describes the processes and consequences in a perceptive work confirming the author's status as a leading scholar of the twentieth century experience."

—DENNIS SHOWALTER,
Professor of History at Colorado College

"A first rate account of a meeting that played a key role in defining the postwar world. Scholarly, thoughtful, and well written."

—JEREMY BLACK,
author of *Rethinking World War Two*

"The Potsdam Conference defined international relations in the second half of the twentieth century, and it continues to influence contemporary events in Europe and East Asia. This book offers a compelling account of the events that led to the conference, the personalities who dominated the conference, and the consequences of their decisions. Neiberg explains why Potsdam was more successful than the Versailles Conference at the end of the First World War, and he analyzes how Potsdam contributed to postwar peace. This is a powerful book with high drama—a must-read for anyone interested in global affairs."

—JEREMI SURI,
author of *Liberty's Surest Guardian:
American Nation-Building from the Founders to Obama*

POTSDAM

POTSDAM

The END of WORLD WAR II
AND THE REMAKING of EUROPE

Michael Neiberg

BASIC BOOKS
A MEMBER OF THE PERSEUS BOOKS GROUP
New York

Copyright © 2015 by Michael Neiberg

Published by Basic Books

A Member of the Perseus Books Group

All rights reserved. Printed in the United States of America. No part of this book may be reproduced in any manner whatsoever without written permission except in the case of brief quotations embodied in critical articles and reviews. For information, address Basic Books, 250 West 57th Street, New York, NY 10107.

Books published by Basic Books are available at special discounts for bulk purchases in the United States by corporations, institutions, and other organizations. For more information, please contact the Special Markets Department at the Perseus Books Group, 2300 Chestnut Street, Suite 200, Philadelphia, PA 19103, or call (800) 810–4145, ext. 5000, or e-mail special .markets@perseusbooks.com.

Library of Congress Cataloging-in-Publication Data

    Neiberg, Michael S.

    Potsdam : the end of World War II and the remaking of Europe / Michael Neiberg.

      pages cm

    Includes bibliographical references and index.

    ISBN 978-0-465-07525-6 (hardcover : alk. paper)—ISBN 978-0-465-04062-9 (epub) 1. Potsdam Conference (1945 : Potsdam, Germany) 2. World War, 1939–1945—Peace. I. Title.

D734.N38 2015

940.53'141—dc23

2015007545

10 9 8 7 6 5 4 3 2 1

For Sue and John, with love

CONTENTS

INTRODUCTION

O N JUNE 28, 1919, the same day that much of the rest of the world marked the signing of the Treaty of Versailles that officially ended the Great War, a US Army captain strolled down the aisle of his local church to marry his sweetheart. Although he had distinguished himself in the war and proven himself as a leader on the battlefield, he had little desire to make the military a career. Nor did he, at this point in his life, express any special desire to enter the world of politics. He and another veteran of the war had instead taken out a lease in order to open a men's clothing store. The war had ended. In the future, he hoped, he would spend his time thinking about his family and his business, not war. On this day of all days his thoughts were far from wars and the peace treaties that end them.[1]

Across the Atlantic Ocean on that same day, a controversial British politician was savoring a second chance. Having been humiliated and forced from office a few years before, he now had a dominant voice in Britain's defense policies as secretary of state for war and air. Anxious about the postwar world and fearful of the growth of Soviet-style Bolshevism, he had advocated an Allied operation to land British, American, and Japanese soldiers in northern Russia in support of the pro-czarist "Whites" in the Russian Civil War. He disliked the Treaty of Versailles, calling it "absurd and monstrous," in large part because he thought it weakened Germany too much. A dismantled Germany, he feared, could leave a deadly power vacuum in Europe that the Bolsheviks might seek to fill. Wanting to see Bolshevism "strangled in its cradle," he saw the Versailles Treaty as a missed opportunity to remake the postwar world. As early as 1920 he had begun to call for major revisions to the treaty in Germany's favor because of the "unreasonable demands" it made on the Germans, the only possible counterweight on the European continent to the potentially even more dangerous Russians. When the time came for him to write a postwar treaty, he would argue for rejecting the Treaty of Versailles as a model.[2]

The Bolsheviks then fighting the bloody Russian Civil War took little notice of the Treaty of Versailles. Their revolutionary ardor already anathema to the British, French, and Americans, the Bolsheviks had sealed their diplomatic isolation by surrendering to the Germans in the Treaty of Brest-Litovsk in March 1918. That surrender had given the Germans the resources they needed to launch the spring offensives in France that nearly won them the war that year. After the German surrender, therefore, the war's victors had seen no reason to invite the Bolshevik regime to the peace talks in Paris. To Bolshevik leaders, including the newly named People's Commissar for Nationalities, the issues surrounding the Treaty of Versailles paled in comparison to the life-or-death struggle they were waging against the czarist Whites. Only the treaty's formation of a new Polish state directly affected them. The ambitious commissar, however, took careful note of the attempts of the Western Allies to support the Whites; he had especially noted the menacing "strangle in its cradle" phrase one of the Western leaders had used. Years later, and under the radically different circumstances that a new war had created, he would have the opportunity to meet the man who made that statement and tell him in no uncertain terms his opinion of it.

Two of those three men—British Secretary of State for War and Air Winston Churchill and the Soviet Union's commissar for nationalities, Joseph Stalin—may well have foreseen themselves one day leading their nations in war and peace. Both men recognized the fragility of the new peace negotiated in Paris and had divined that Europe's period of peace would likely not last long. Ambitious men close to the centers of power in their respective countries, Churchill and Stalin knew that no treaty in and of itself could resolve the core issues of the murderous period of global conflict that had begun in that disastrous summer of 1914. The idea that in the next war they would fight shoulder to shoulder as allies likely would have struck them both as ludicrous in 1919, although they had each seen enough radical change in their lifetimes that perhaps nothing would have surprised them too much.

The third man, Captain Harry S. Truman, could have had no idea that the next time his country ended a major war, he would command not an artillery unit, but the entire nation. "Who the hell is Harry Truman?" demanded Franklin Roosevelt's chief of staff, Admiral William Leahy, when he heard that the Democratic convention of 1944 had selected the relatively obscure Missouri senator to run as Roosevelt's vice-presidential nominee. With only a high school diploma and no experience in foreign relations, Truman rose from failed businessman to president of the United States, marking one of the strangest career trajectories in the history of American politics. In July 1945, when he first met with Churchill and Stalin in the posh Berlin suburb of Potsdam, moreover, Truman knew that he had to take the place of a man he himself described as "impossible to substitute." He also knew that Franklin Roosevelt had kept him almost completely in the dark on the most critical matters of wartime policy. Truman arrived at the most important moment of his career woefully and astonishingly unprepared for the monumental task ahead of him. He had not even left the United States once since his return from the battlefields of France in 1919.[3]

THE TASK IN FRONT OF the three allied leaders and their staffs was nothing less than giving Europe peace and stability, something it had not known since the cataclysm of 1914. All three men, as well as their advisers, had had their worldviews formed in the crucible of the war of 1914–1918. For Stalin, the Russian Revolution and the bloody Russian Civil War that flowed directly from the Great War further proved the point that the transition from war to peace could present as many challenges as the battlefield itself. If the Big Three of Potsdam failed as the Big Three of Versailles had, then Europe would know not a future of peace but another age of strife, death, and more war.[4]

The three men had different postwar visions, based on the strategic interests and historical experiences of their nations in the first half of the twentieth century. Those years had seen astonishing, revolutionary changes. World War I had eliminated the most powerful monarchies of Europe and left in their wake a struggle between democracy, fascism, and communism to control the political and economic future of the continent. World War II took fascism out of the equation and also left such traditional powers as Germany, Italy, and France in tatters. Even Britain, nominally one of the war's great victors, sat on the edge of bankruptcy and at dire risk of losing the empire that had sustained its great-power status. In place of the traditional powers of Europe now came the United States and the Soviet Union. The former had largely turned away from Europe in 1919 and might still do so again in 1945. The latter, a revolutionary regime fresh from a bloody but triumphal victory, presented a terrible nightmare to some and an alluring future to others. In either case, the future of Europe no longer belonged exclusively, or even primarily, to Western Europeans themselves.

In the minds of the men who met in Potsdam in July 1945 to put the pieces of the world back together, the war that ended in 1945 had begun not in 1939 but in 1914. Men as diverse as British Foreign Secretary Sir Anthony Eden and French philosopher Albert Camus spoke not of two separate world wars, but one Thirty Years' War. The idea had a long heritage, beginning with the celebrated British war correspondent Charles Repington's appropriately titled 1920 bestseller, *The First World War*, in which he posited that the global troubles that began in 1914 would not end with the Treaty of Versailles; like many of his contemporaries, he fully expected a second world war. American soldier Alexander Clay echoed Repington and spoke for millions of his comrades on both sides of the lines when he remarked after the war: "I can truthfully say that without egotism we, the soldiers of World War I, predicted that within twenty-five to fifty years this war would be fought again. For we had a premonition that it was not entirely settled as it should have been."[5]

This thirty-year war encompassed not just two enormous world wars between great powers, but also the numerous civil wars and regional wars that emerged from the shattering of the old order in 1914. As Admiral William Leahy wrote in his diary at the end of the Potsdam Conference, "this means the definite end of the world war which started in 1914, had a temporary adjournment for further preparation [from] 1918 to 1939, and today comes to an end." Europeans saw less of an adjournment than Leahy did, given events like the Russo-Polish War (1919–1921) and the civil war in Spain (1936–1939), but however they parsed their history, the statesmen at Potsdam knew that the catastrophe they faced in 1945 had begun not with the German invasion of Poland in 1939, but rather with the events that followed from the assassination of a relatively obscure archduke on a street corner in a provincial Bosnian town in 1914.[6]

The delegates at Potsdam lived with ghosts that haunted the Cecilienhof Palace in the picturesque neighborhood where the meeting took place. The palace, built during World War I as a retreat for the German crown prince and his wife, served as a living reminder of the failures of statesmen at the end of that war. The Germans, so convinced of their imminent victory, built the palace while simultaneously devoting enormous resources to fighting an existential world war. The crown prince had been one of the most vocal militarists of the prewar years and had led an army group on the western front. The palace he never had a chance to inhabit thus stood as a reminder of the hubris of a once-powerful regime that had seemed so solid and so permanent before that fateful summer of 1914. Now, thirty years later, Germany had no government at all and sat at the mercy of its former enemies.

The ghosts of the Cecilienhof Palace paled in their power to haunt compared with the ghosts of the Palace of Versailles. Everyone at Potsdam saw the Versailles Treaty as a horrible warning from history of the failures of making peace. They all believed that the failures of 1919 had directly led to the outbreak of war twenty years later. The American president, Harry Truman, greatly admired one of the architects of that treaty, Woodrow Wilson; Truman had even taken his oath of office under a portrait of Wilson. Nevertheless, Truman saw the treaty as Wilson's greatest failure. He opened the Potsdam Conference by reminding his fellow statesmen of the "many flaws" that the treaty had produced and warned the delegates to learn from that experience or risk repeating it. No one at Potsdam disagreed with Truman on that score; nor did the president need to remind his fellow leaders that, if they did nothing else, they had to avoid a repeat of the Versailles disaster at all costs.[7]

That the statesmen of Europe had gathered for the second time in as many generations to negotiate an end to a catastrophic world war was proof enough of the futility of the Treaty of Versailles. Everyone, it seemed, brought his own criticism of the treaty, and the process that produced it, to Potsdam that summer. To some, the problem was the process itself. The treaty had emerged from a series of awkward compromises, trade-offs, and misunderstandings, but once committed to paper they brought with them the force of international agreement, even if most observers and participants could see the flaws inherent in them. Thus did many of the statesmen in 1945 come to Potsdam wanting the meeting not to produce a definitive treaty with specific policies for which they or their successors might later have to answer, but rather to be a symbol to the world that the Big Three stood together and would work in unison to produce a more just and peaceful future.

Moreover, several of the principles of the Treaty of Versailles already lay in tatters by 1945. Foremost among them was the Wilsonian ideal of national self-determination. In 1919 the great powers had moved borders in an ultimately futile attempt to match up political and ethnic boundaries. That process yielded not peace but a new round of irredentism and hyper-nationalism that produced repeated diplomatic crises in the 1920s and 1930s. As early as September 9, 1939, barely a week into the European war, Britain's *New Statesman* magazine argued that self-determination "has been a failure" and should not guide the peace process following the British victory the editors had already forecast. Their position reflected one held more generally; thus, national self-determination, a keystone of the 1919 negotiations, would play only a small role in 1945.[8]

A British Foreign Office assessment written in 1943 argued against another pillar of the Versailles Treaty, the League of Nations. The paper did not argue against the creation of an international organization per se, but it concluded that any future organization should not follow the democratic model of the League. Instead, the great powers should run it directly. Since, in the Foreign Office's estimation, only three or four great powers would exist at the end of the war (the United States, Britain, Russia, and maybe China), the design of any new international body should reflect their interests. France, Italy, Germany, and Japan would therefore not "be readmitted to the ranks of the Great Powers" at the conclusion of the war. Like other minor or regional powers, they would assure their future security needs through an international body that the great powers would firmly control. Stalin agreed, telling American envoy Harry Hopkins that "two world wars have begun over small nations." With the exception of the later elevation of France's status, one can see here the core of the idea that later became the United Nations Security Council.

American delegates at Potsdam had largely forgotten the stated reasons for the Senate's rejection of the treaty in 1919. Senators then had focused on the threats to American freedom of diplomatic maneuver. By 1945, few Americans remembered or cared about those seemingly ancient debates. To the American diplomats at Potsdam, the treaty's great flaw involved the financial aspects that forced a reluctant United States to assume the burden of Germany's reparations without receiving anything meaningful in return and without producing any positive steps toward a lasting peace. To the contrary, those same arrangements had created the conditions that had led to a global economic depression that had in turn led to the rise of the Nazis and the outbreak of war in 1939.

A few ideals from 1919, however, did survive. The idea that the victors would write the treaty without the direct participation of the defeated reflected the spirit of Versailles, as evident by the arrangements at Potsdam. The conquered Germans had no representatives; nor did the Italians; nor—much to their dismay—did the French or the Poles, who saw themselves as having been on the winning side, and therefore deserving of representation. The Big Three, however, disagreed. Potsdam, like Versailles, was to be a victor's peace, defined, yet again, by the great powers.

The British Foreign Office paper also included a study circulated in mid-1943 of the errors committed at Versailles. This insightful assessment warned that the situation at the end of the war would "be very different from that of 1918." It expected even greater hostility toward Germany than had existed in 1918, and also noted that this time, the Russians would surely play a large role in setting peace terms, whereas France likely would not. Unlike in 1919, in 1945 the Allies would need to occupy the whole of Germany and work with German officials, even though—or especially because—there might be no surviving government in that country. Nor could planners eliminate the possibility of German partisans fighting on even after the Nazi regime surrendered. Ending the war in Europe, moreover, likely would not end the war with Japan, meaning that the Allies would surely have limited resources for a long occupation and the rebuilding of Germany. Finally, it noted that the twin tasks of providing immediate relief and long-term humanitarian assistance likely would exceed those of 1918–1919 many times over.[9]

Although the British Foreign Office noted that "it is impossible to forecast how events will work out because there are so many unknown qualities," its analysts did a remarkable job of identifying the challenges ahead. In their critique of Versailles, they highlighted the failed economic mechanisms that devastated the very European economy that the great powers of 1919 had tried to rebuild. They also criticized David Lloyd George's bowing to the whims of British public opinion for an unduly harsh treatment of Germany, and the failure of the United States to ratify the treaty for "fatally affect[ing] its operation." This time, the Foreign Office argued, the British government must at a minimum secure the cooperation of the United States at any cost; force the Germans to acknowledge the magnitude of their defeat; and keep the Russians as far east as possible.[10]

The Western statesmen at Potsdam did all they could to dissociate their conference from the unmitigated disaster they all saw when they looked back at 1919. Whereas the men of that year had failed to establish the conditions for a lasting peace, the men of 1945 sought to build a Europe of stability and prosperity. Yet they could not escape the long shadows of Versailles. Whether they succeeded or failed at

Potsdam, they would all walk away anxious to tell themselves, and their peoples, that they had not repeated the mistakes of 1919.

Yet a third ghost haunted the villas and palaces of Potsdam that summer of 1945, the ghost of the appeasement of the 1938 Munich conference. Many American and British diplomats had already begun to see in Soviet behavior, especially the USSR's highly selective implementation of the agreements made at the Yalta Conference of February 1945, echoes of Germany's aggressive behavior in the 1930s. Invoking the Munich analogy to oppose concessions to the Russians (or, for that matter, the Japanese) immediately brought to mind all of the fears and failures of the period from 1933 to 1939. The Munich example carried with it a powerful reminder of the costs of appeasement, and to those who believed in the analogy, it implied that the Americans and British should use a firmer hand in their initial postwar dealings with the Russians.

WHETHER OR NOT ANY of these ghosts remained relevant to the problems the world faced in 1945, no one at Potsdam could avoid them. They reminded the delegates of the cataclysmic failures of the men who had gone before them. Virtually every decision the statesmen of 1945 made they made through the prism of events like the Paris Peace Conference of 1919 and the appeasement symbolized by the Munich Agreement of 1938. And these events did not come from a distant past. Unlike the men of 1919, who sometimes used vague historical understandings of the Concert of Vienna of 1815 as a rough guide, everyone seated around the conference tables, elaborate formal dinners, and social gatherings at Potsdam had personally watched the murderous events of 1914–1939 unfold. Some had even played key roles in them. Winston Churchill, of course, had staunchly opposed his own government's appeasement policy in the late 1930s, as had others in the British delegation at Potsdam. To them, especially, the ghost of Munich haunted the halls of Potsdam, as did the specter of an expansive Bolshevik Russia.

The new US secretary of state, James Byrnes, had attended the Paris Peace Conference of 1919 as a junior adviser to President Wilson; he may well have been the man who convinced Wilson to go to

Paris. He, too, felt the presence of the ghosts of the past weighing on the minds of the men at Potsdam. Byrnes concluded that the American delegation had made two critical mistakes. First, President Wilson had refused to bring along any Republican senators to the Paris Peace Conference, thus dooming the resulting treaty's prospects for ratification in the Senate. Byrnes, who had served for fourteen years in the House of Representatives and for ten in the Senate, ensured that both houses of Congress remained informed of the ongoing issues and discussions at Potsdam. Second, he argued that the United States had made too many commitments to solve the economic problems of Europe in the postwar years by essentially financing German reparations. That mistake, he believed, had contributed to the economic and political instability that had produced the Great Depression.[11]

The specters haunting the delegates at Potsdam thus seemed less like warnings from the distant past than present-day consequences of decisions from their own lifetimes. The Russians also felt them, even though they had not participated in the Paris Peace Conference. Thus in May 1945, two months before the Potsdam Conference began, Stalin warned Truman's envoy, Harry Hopkins, that he wished to avoid the Versailles model in his upcoming meeting with Truman and Churchill, although he did not elaborate on the specific problems he saw in that model. Nor did Hopkins think it wise to push him. On a separate occasion, however, Stalin told another American that he worried about the US Senate rejecting whatever the Big Three agreed to at Potsdam, just as it had rejected the Treaty of Versailles in 1920. The behavior of the Senate, a body foreign to Joseph Stalin's mind, caused the Soviet leader to wonder whether he could rely on any agreement he made with Truman.[12]

THIS BOOK AIMS TO get far beyond merely recounting what the statesmen at Potsdam said to one another during the conference meetings. Unlike the two previous histories of this conference, this book is consciously not a "then Truman said to Stalin" account of the daily events at Potsdam. Rather, it uses the meeting at Potsdam to explore at least three larger themes. First, although many scholars have examined the Potsdam and Yalta conferences as the opening shots that produced the Cold War, this book looks at Potsdam not as the start of a new era of history, but as the end of another. Although the participants at Potsdam all left with an understanding that tensions between the superpowers might well increase, they nevertheless still placed their bets on the ability of the United States and the Soviet Union to work together to manage the problems of Europe. They did not leave Potsdam convinced either of the imminence or the inevitability of superpower conflict.

Whatever responsibility the Potsdam Conference had for fueling the incipient Cold War (and that responsibility strikes me as rather small), the conferees thought much more in terms of Potsdam's role in ending the period of total war from 1914 to 1945. This book thus follows their lead in examining how the world's most powerful leaders understood that period and, no less significantly, how they sought to solve the problems of the world going forward. In other words, it seeks, as far as possible, to understand Potsdam by understanding the world as the leaders gathered there saw it.

Second, this book looks at how visions of history weighed on the conferees at Potsdam. Versailles and Munich loomed as the two most important historical models, but they were surely not the only ones. Some of the conferees understood history better than others, and some used history much more for political purposes than for intellectual ones, but they all acutely felt its weight. The Russians, of course, read history quite differently from the Americans and the British; for their part, most American and British observers did a poor job of understanding how Russian history made some options unacceptable to Stalin and his fellow Russians. How the statesmen understood the past inevitably conditioned the way they saw the present and the future.

Third, although the famous men of that year inevitably figure prominently in this book, strategic environments and historical understandings limited and shaped the range of options open to so-called "great men." Anne O'Hare McCormick, a reporter for the *New York Times*, wrote on the first day of the conference that "there are moments when the drama of our times seems to focus on a single scene." Potsdam was one of those scenes, she believed, because three men holding "in their hands most of the power in the world" had gathered to make potentially monumental decisions. But she also noted that the men were meeting near Berlin, once a symbol of a mighty world power but now a mere "graveyard." That graveyard, and everything that it meant to the men and women of 1945, set important limits on what the statesmen could accomplish. If anything, this book argues for some limits on the so-called "great-man" theory of history even though many powerful and important men appear in it repeatedly. The graveyard was as important as the men who had the responsibility of restoring it.[13]

In exploring this third theme, we will find that Potsdam offers a fascinating laboratory of sorts. In April 1945, Franklin Roosevelt died, leaving an enormous void in American foreign policy. Roosevelt had conducted most of the key elements of American wartime diplomacy himself, often shutting out his own State Department in the process. He also shut out his new vice president, Harry Truman, a man who badly needed as much help as Roosevelt could have given him. In the arena of foreign policy, the two men could not have been more different. Roosevelt, accustomed to making most of the key decisions himself, had a vast reservoir of knowledge and, much more importantly, the deep respect of statesmen across the globe. The neophyte Truman, by contrast, worried even those observers who came to like and respect him. William Leahy, who accompanied him to Potsdam and assumed much of the responsibility for helping him there, thought Truman so unprepared for his new role that he could not "see how the complicated critical business of the war and the peace can be carried forward by a new President who is so completely inexperienced in international affairs."[14]

The British government went through a similar process. British elections, with results tabulated in the middle of the Potsdam Conference, stunningly voted Winston Churchill's Conservative Party out of office in favor of the opposition Labour Party. Like Roosevelt, Churchill had a deep understanding of many of the key issues and enjoyed a reputation as one of the most powerful and influential men in the world. His departure mid-conference left the far less imposing Clement Attlee, who had served as Churchill's deputy prime minister in a coalition government, but had rarely been involved in key strategic decisions. Churchill liked to deride Attlee with characteristically witty insults, such as calling him a "sheep in sheep's clothing." Attlee, like Truman, came to Potsdam with far less of a profile on foreign affairs than his illustrious predecessor, having made his name as an advocate of the poor and working classes. Attlee's slogan, "With cake for none until all have bread," could not have sounded less Churchillian. As Truman brought a new secretary of state to Potsdam, so, too, did Attlee bring a new foreign minister, meaning that both delegations experienced almost wholesale changes in their foreign policy teams.[15]

Yet for all these fundamental changes in personality, the policies of the Americans and the British changed remarkably little. To the extent that the policies of Truman and Attlee differed from those of their predecessors, they did so mainly on the margins. Neither Truman nor Attlee made radical changes to their country's main positions. And neither inertia nor their own inexperience explains this remarkable stability. Rather, the continuity in policy only underscores the role that strategy and history play in the shaping of policy. Truman, Attlee, and the other members of the delegations at Potsdam, of course, all shared the same nightmares of their generation, namely World War I, the failed Treaty of Versailles, the Great Depression, the rise of fascism, and the outbreak of World War II.[16]

Of course, the Soviet Union did not go through a similar transition at the top. Joseph Stalin became general secretary of the Soviet Communist Party's Central Committee in 1922 and radically increased the level of control he exercised over the system after the 1927 assassination of the Soviet ambassador to Poland. The assassination increased Stalin's paranoia and his concern about not only his own hold on power, but his own mortality as well. Stalin did not leave the Soviet Union between 1913 and the Tehran Conference in 1943, in part because of security concerns. Stalin and the Russians remain the hardest element to read at Potsdam because of the opaqueness of the Russian system even today and the high level of paranoia within the system itself.[17]

Finally, this book makes no attempt to assess winners and losers at Potsdam; nor does it assign credit or blame for any events that later resulted from it. It certainly does not attempt to second-guess the leaders or suggest what they should have done differently. Rather, it seeks to explain the conference by placing it in the context not just of 1945, but of the entire period of war and conflict from 1914 to 1945. Thus, I hope that ultimately, this book goes far beyond what transpired over a couple of weeks at Potsdam. I hope it gives insight into the ways that wars end, the role of historical and strategic contexts in the shaping of decisions, and the sheer weight that history can exercise on the present. Although largely forgotten in our own time, Potsdam was surely about, as Winston Churchill described it to Harry Truman, "the gravest matters in the world," and there remains much that we can learn from it.[18]

"Jesus Christ and General Jackson"

THE SPRING OF 1945 witnessed massive transitions in American, European, and world history. Some of these changes, such as the final defeat of Nazi Germany, had long been anticipated. Others, such as the death of Franklin Roosevelt, came as a shock. Some seemed like terrible omens suggesting that the problems of the world might not yet be over. These crucial months changed the global strategic environment for the leaders who came to Potsdam that summer. So much change was concentrated into such a short period of time that understandings and assumptions made just weeks earlier now seemed irrelevant. As the end of the war in Europe finally became a reality, leaders began to face the immense challenge of reconstruction. They did so, however, in a different environment from the one that they had anticipated.

The imminent defeat of Germany set the context for everything that followed, but the process of rebuilding Europe and the world had already begun. On April 25, 1945, the United Nations Conference on International Organization opened in San Francisco for an inaugural two-month session. More than fifty nations sent representatives to hammer out the details for the new United Nations Charter. Unlike the League of Nations a generation earlier, the United

Nations got off to a strong start, in large part because the United States was fully committed to its success, as symbolized by the grand opening meeting taking place in California. This time, American leaders had repeatedly promised, the United States would not retreat into isolation, but would instead play a major role in shaping international solutions to the problems the world faced, with peace and reconstruction at the top of the agenda. This time, moreover, the nations of the world would meet before the war had even ended, in the hopes of smoothing the transition from war to peace that had proved so disruptive in 1918 and 1919.

On the same day, thousands of miles to the east, Soviet armies completed their encirclement of Berlin with perhaps the most powerful ground force ever assembled. The German capital had exhausted its final rations, and thousands of people were committing suicide every day out of fear for what the future might hold for their conquered country. Although much hard fighting remained, the noose around the German capital had begun to tighten. It was now a matter of when, not if, the Nazi regime would surrender, and of how much of the city the conquering Soviet forces would have to destroy in the battles to come.[1]

At the same time, near the small town of Torgau on the Elbe River northeast of Leipzig, American and Soviet forces finally linked up in a momentous meeting that made headlines worldwide. The event seemed symbolic of the impending end of the war. Soldiers celebrated with what one American officer likened to an Iowa picnic, with food, hugs, and even some celebratory gunfire. The photographs of smiling soldiers shaking hands were front-page news, and for many the day marked the definitive end of an old Europe and the birth of a new one—one where the Germans were defeated and the source of power had shifted. Notably, the French and the British were absent from the photos and the stories accompanying them. The great powers of 1914 no longer controlled the fate of Europe, which now lay largely in the hands of two new superpowers.[2]

But if the end of World War II seemed, at long last, finally to be coming into view (in Europe, at least), the shape of the new Europe was not. Circumstances had changed radically since the end of the

Yalta Conference just over two months earlier. Furthermore, no real consensus existed among the great powers about what they had agreed to at Yalta. That meeting, moreover, had been a wartime conference, aimed as much at the final destruction of the Germans as at the remaking of Europe. The chief agreements of Yalta—the occupation of Germany, borders for the new Poland, and reparations policy for the defeated powers—could all become irrelevant as the geopolitical situation changed.

PERHAPS THE MOST SIGNIFICANT change since Yalta had occurred far away from Germany in the sleepy little town of Warm Springs, Georgia, where Franklin D. Roosevelt died on April 12, 1945. Roosevelt had been so central to the American and Allied wartime policy and postwar vision that his death cast a pall over the joyous events of late April.

Roosevelt had been paralyzed ever since 1921, when he had contracted polio at the age of thirty-nine. He and his staff had gone to great lengths to hide his paralysis from the public, even though it remained one of the worst-kept secrets in Washington. His relationship with Congress showed increasing friction, but twelve years in the office had allowed him to centralize power and develop an effective method for running the executive branch, and he remained a popular president. With the impacts of his polio largely hidden from public view, the Roosevelt the American people saw still projected vigor and dynamism. It was not the polio that took him from the nation, however, but heart disease.

For those who were paying attention, it was not a complete surprise. Roosevelt looked much older than his sixty-two years. His delay in officially declaring himself a candidate for a fourth term as president in 1944 had fueled speculation that health problems might prevent him from serving four more years as the nation's chief executive. During the course of the 1944 election campaign, Roosevelt's health had increasingly become an issue of concern to those around him. In August, he had experienced serious chest pains while delivering a speech in Bremerton, Washington. He had been able to finish the speech, and tests run afterward had shown no abnormalities.

But after the Bremerton incident, Roosevelt often appeared notice-
ably tired. He made fewer public appearances, despite his intense
desire to defeat the Republican nominee, Thomas Dewey, a fellow
New Yorker whom Roosevelt had long despised. The president had
also lost weight, as much as twenty pounds, and he seemed, in the
words of the *Washington Post*, to have "lost his touch." The *Post* speculated that Dewey's youth (he was just forty-two years old in 1944)
would give him a vital edge in the last few weeks of the campaign,
and that it might even lead to the most shocking electoral upset in
the nation's history.

Researchers have since uncovered many of the details about
Roosevelt's heart problems and the inaccurate diagnoses performed
by some of the doctors who treated him. He was already becoming
easily fatigued by February 1944, several months before the Bremerton incident. He ran unexplained fevers and suffered sharp rises in
his blood pressure. His doctors hid the seriousness of Roosevelt's
condition, not only from the public but from those closest to the
president. Some of those who saw him in the summer of 1944 noticed the change. After meeting with Roosevelt in July 1944, General
Douglas MacArthur told his wife that he thought Roosevelt looked
like a "shell of the man" he had once known. "In six months," he
predicted, "he will be in his grave."

Rumors began to spread that the president had begun falling
asleep in meetings, and insiders became concerned that he might
not have the strength to fulfill a fourth term in office. The president's
physician nevertheless publicly pronounced him in excellent shape,
attributing his health problems to his recent recovery from a case
of influenza. In September, to assuage lingering concerns about his
health, Roosevelt delivered a fiery speech to kick off the final stage
of the presidential campaign. Then, in late October, he made a four-
hour tour through four New York City boroughs in an open car in
frigid weather. He capped his political barnstorming by speaking in
a freezing rainstorm to a crowd of 10,000 people at Ebbets Field in
Brooklyn.[3]

The New York City performance temporarily laid fears about
his health to rest, and Roosevelt won reelection handily in 1944. His

doctors publicly gave him another clean bill of health, and the press seemed more than willing to chalk up his previous appearance of ill health to the flu and the stresses and strains of trying to run a presidential campaign while fighting a war. That Roosevelt seemed older and more easily fatigued surprised few people, given the difficulty of the job he had. In private, however, concerns grew as Roosevelt's blood pressure continued to climb. His heart was beginning to shrink. Doctors who examined him disagreed on both the diagnosis and the proper way to treat his condition.

Those close to Roosevelt could see the decline of his health but seemed unable to envision a world without him. He had been president for longer than anyone else in American history, and he seemed indispensable to people the world over. Almost no one knew that his blood pressure had risen as high as 260/150, but many who saw him noticed the same decline that MacArthur had. Perhaps most ominously, Woodrow Wilson's widow, Edith, told Secretary of Labor Frances Perkins that "he looks exactly as my husband did when he went into his decline."[4]

The fearful comparison to Wilson came just two days before Roosevelt left the United States on a grueling trip to the Big Three conference at Yalta. Roosevelt, who had attended part of the Paris Peace Conference in 1919, had greatly admired Wilson, and he sought to restore Wilson's dream of having an international organization of nations to administer treaties and resolve disputes short of war. Wilson's tactical failures in presenting the Treaty of Versailles to the US Senate had led to a political fight that Wilson had taken directly to the American people in the fall of 1919. A fast-paced schedule amid fatigue and declining health had worn Wilson down. While in Pueblo, Colorado, Wilson had suffered a stroke, which was followed by a second, much larger stroke in Washington a week later that effectively ended his public career.

Roosevelt spent a great deal of time thinking about Wilson, whom he had served as assistant secretary of the navy. He liked to sit under Wilson's official White House portrait and contemplate the design of the United Nations that he hoped would fulfill Wilson's internationalist dream. Roosevelt had worked hard to lay the groundwork for the United Nations, and the war had seemed to prove the point that isolationism could not guarantee American security in the post-war world. In part owing to Roosevelt's efforts, in 1945 the United Nations enjoyed far more popularity than the League of Nations had in 1919. Roosevelt had also worked much harder than Wilson to ensure that the Senate and the American people would support full American participation in the new international organization. Roosevelt did not want a repeat of the Senate's refusal to join the League of Nations.

Wilson's stroke and the incapacitation that ensued haunted those around Roosevelt. Advisers close to Wilson, especially his wife and his doctor, had managed to keep his condition a secret not just from the press but also from many senior government officials. But 1945 was not 1919. The American people would certainly notice the absence of Roosevelt, a far more public figure than Wilson had been. If Roosevelt became incapacitated, as Wilson had, the media of 1945 would surely report the story. Roosevelt had already shown signs of decline and required far more rest than he had in previous years. A stroke like Wilson's would create an unprecedented and politically untenable situation.

At Yalta, several observers who knew Roosevelt well commented on the parlous state of his health. His son James thought his father "looked like hell" at the conference, and Lord Moran, Churchill's physician, observed that "the President had gone to bits physically." Reflecting MacArthur's warnings from a few months earlier, Moran thought Roosevelt might only have a few more months to live. On the journey back from Yalta, Roosevelt discussed his preference for funeral arrangements with his son. He had never raised the topic before, and no one else was privy to that discussion.[5]

Still, whether out of denial, or simply hope that the old master would come through, most people expected Roosevelt's health to improve after he was able to get some rest. His doctors ordered him to work less, smoke less, and alter his diet. These relatively minor recommendations—for a man who appeared so ill on the surface—may have led to a dangerous complacency among his advisers. Charles Bohlen, who translated for Roosevelt at Yalta, noted the president's "exhausted" state, but he remarked: "Although he did not look well, Roosevelt was not regarded by anyone whom I can recall, or have talked to since, as being critically ill then." Even once they were back in Washington, Bohlen saw little cause for serious alarm. "I was continually worried by Roosevelt's appearance, and it was now obvious to many that he was a sick man," Bohlen recalled about the weeks after Yalta. "But the thought did not occur to me that he was near death. . . . If those closer to Roosevelt considered the question of how to handle the President's illness, no one mentioned it to me."[6]

Others close to Roosevelt shared Bohlen's view that although the president was obviously declining, his condition did not pose a serious problem. George M. Elsey, one of Roosevelt's military aides, saw the president almost daily. He recalled noticing signs of the president's failing health, but not seriously worrying about it until just a week before his death. James Byrnes, an adviser who saw Roosevelt frequently, spoke to the president shortly before his death and concluded that he had recovered from the illnesses that had plagued him at Yalta. Byrnes thought he was "staging a 'comeback' as he had done on many previous occasions."[7]

UNABLE TO IMAGINE A WORLD without the man whom Chief of Staff Admiral Leahy had called "the captain of the team," those close to Roosevelt seem not to have worried much about who would succeed him if the worst should happen. The president's health was not a determining factor when the Democratic Party began the process of selecting Roosevelt's running mate in 1944. Most political insiders assumed that Roosevelt would win, but they did not want to take any chances at so crucial a point in history, and Roosevelt's personal animosity for Dewey drove his campaign staff even further.[8]

Issues other than Roosevelt's health dominated discussions among Democratic Party planners. Those on the party's more conservative wing had grown tired of Vice President Henry Wallace because of his pro-union and pro–civil rights positions. They had unsuccessfully opposed his nomination in 1940, and now they wanted to replace Wallace on the ticket as a way of both getting rid of him and reenergizing the campaign. But the obvious candidates to re-place Wallace all came with serious drawbacks.

James Byrnes, a Washington insider who had advised Roosevelt for years, emerged as one possibility. A former congressman, sena-tor, and Supreme Court justice from humble South Carolina origins, Byrnes had left the Supreme Court in 1942 at Roosevelt's request to run the new Office of War Mobilization. Despite its rather lackluster name, the office had vast powers over prices, wages, and the Ameri-can economy as a whole. Roosevelt gave Byrnes tremendous latitude to run the office and rarely questioned his decisions, thereby mak-ing Byrnes one of the country's most powerful men. Roosevelt called Byrnes his "assistant president" and relied on his experience on Cap-itol Hill to help him push through his legislative agenda. Byrnes had far more power—and more influence on Roosevelt—than Wallace ever did. To most conservative Democrats, Byrnes seemed the ob-vious choice for the vice-presidential nomination, even though the southern states where he was most popular sat safely in the Demo-cratic column.[9]

Byrnes certainly expected to receive the nomination, even if Roo-sevelt had not told him he would. Although becoming vice presi-dent would actually mean less power and influence than Byrnes had enjoyed in some of his previous positions, the honor would cap a distinguished career and make amends for the Democratic National Convention of 1940, when he had also expected to get the vice-presi-dential nomination before the delegates settled on Wallace. Byrnes's friend Harry Truman, a senator from Missouri, had offered to nomi-nate him at the 1944 convention in Chicago, in part to thank Byrnes for the fundraising help he had provided in Truman's senatorial elec-tions. In 1940, with Truman's campaign on the edge of bankruptcy, Byrnes had convinced financier Bernard Baruch to provide Truman with the infusion of money that his campaign desperately needed. With the anti-Wallace forces marshaling their efforts, Byrnes seemed to have the inside track for the slot.[10]

But Byrnes had his fair share of detractors. Democratic chances in the expected swing states of 1944—New York, New Jersey, Pennsyl-vania, Illinois, and California—would not improve with the addition of a southerner, even one who had supported the New Deal. Byrnes had staunchly defended segregation and had opposed a proposed anti-lynching law, positions that made him unpopular in those same swing states and among the liberals within Roosevelt's inner circle who wanted to keep Wallace or replace him with another liberal. Having an avowed segregationist like Byrnes on the ticket would not only cause difficulties in the campaign, but also make it harder for Roosevelt to tout American principles to the world after the conclusion of the war. Many of Byrnes's decisions at the Office of War Mobilization, moreover, had offended organized labor, whose leaders lined up in Chicago to argue against his nomination and show their support for Wallace.[11]

Still, had Roosevelt and his advisers been sufficiently worried about the president's health to seek a vice president who could step into the White House and immediately assume the responsibilities of the office, then Byrnes would have been the obvious, perhaps the only, choice. His flaws notwithstanding, he had experience in all three branches of government, had attended the Paris Peace Conference, and was on a first-name basis with almost all of the important people in official Washington. To be sure, Byrnes's conservative views rankled some Democratic leaders, but they did not disqualify him for nomination to the ticket. The decision to bypass him showed that the party bosses did not really believe they could be selecting the next president. Instead, they believed they were choosing the next man destined to sink into the obscurity of history, just like most other vice presidents, including John Nance Garner, Roosevelt's first VP (1933–1941), and Henry Wallace, his second (1941–1945).

By the time of the Chicago convention, the Democratic Party still had not yet decided on its vice-presidential nominee. Torn between the two poles of his own party, Roosevelt himself had declined to choose a running mate, leaving his advisers and the party bosses more than a little confused about his desires. Roosevelt's indifference also sent the subtle message that it didn't matter much who his running mate was. Like the others, Roosevelt did not seem to think it likely that the convention was selecting his successor. Adding to the confusion, no one told Wallace when Roosevelt finally did decide to replace him. Even after the convention had begun, Roosevelt remained aloof from discussions about the vice presidency, effectively ceding the decision to other party leaders. The confusion in Chicago led to intense infighting, with Byrnes and Wallace each certain that he would get the nomination even as the political winds were blowing against both of them. "Roosevelt and Byrnes" signs had begun to appear at the convention at the same time that the anti-Byrnes delegates were intensifying their efforts to find someone else. The United Press's Senate correspondent called the convention "The Battle of the Bosses," and until the last minute he still had no idea whom the bosses might select. Byrnes seemed too conservative, and Wallace too liberal.[12]

Needing a third option, the eyes of the party bosses turned to Harry Truman, a relatively unknown Missourian who brought little to the ticket, but who offended neither wing. Although he was just two years younger than Roosevelt, Truman projected an image of youth, vitality, and energy that Roosevelt no longer could evince. Truman only had a high school education, and he did not fit in well with the eastern Ivy League set that Roosevelt preferred, but he had none of the drawbacks of Byrnes or Wallace. His name had emerged in discussions about the vice presidency early on, but had then faded, both because of his inexperience and because of his apparent lack of desire for the job.

In selecting Truman, the Democratic bosses did not take Roosevelt's health into account. They did not assume they were selecting the next president. As Edward J. Flynn, a highly influential Democrat from the Bronx, noted, no one had really argued for Truman, he "just dropped into the slot" as other options fell by the wayside in the hothouse environment of a raucous party convention. Truman, who was then preparing to endorse Byrnes for the vice presidency, could hardly believe that the party leaders had selected him instead, and that Roosevelt had apparently agreed. "Oh shit," Truman said on hearing that Roosevelt would soon ask him to run as his vice president. "Why the hell didn't he tell me in the first place?" Not having prepared for the moment, Truman gave a one-minute acceptance speech absolutely bereft of policy discussion. Byrnes left Chicago furious with Roosevelt and none too happy with Truman.[13]

Although Truman probably did not win the ticket many votes, Roosevelt won reelection handily, giving him an unprecedented fourth term in office. The electoral vote was never really in doubt. Roosevelt fell from the lofty total of 523 that he had received in 1936, but he still won 432 electoral votes in 1944 to Dewey's 99. Truman later recalled the campaign as the easiest of his political career. On the campaign trail, Truman played it safe and stuck largely to the party line, making speeches urging the American people to support the administration's war policies and arguing against a return to isolationism after the war. As expected, Truman did Roosevelt and the Democratic ticket no harm.

The Democrats did well in the congressional elections as well. They picked up 20 seats in the House of Representatives to increase their majority to 242 to 191. In the Senate, they lost a seat, but still held a commanding 57 to 38 advantage. These results meant that Roosevelt would not face the problems Wilson had when the 1918 congressional elections, held just a week before the armistice, had resulted in both houses changing hands from his Democratic Party to the Republicans. The Democrats in 1945 would not quite enjoy the two-thirds majority in the Senate needed to ratify a peace treaty without the opposition party, but neither would Roosevelt have to do battle with an openly hostile Senate Foreign Relations Committee as Wilson had.

THE ELECTIONS HAD GONE WELL for Roosevelt and his party. Nevertheless, if Harry Truman balanced the ticket for the stretch run, he hardly seemed the man to move into the White House should death or illness befall Roosevelt. Nor was he a Roosevelt confidant. In fact, prior to being named to the ticket, he had not seen the president in more than a year. Roosevelt sent the new vice president a note on January 22, 1945, asking him to limit his communications with him to *absolutely urgent* items. Roosevelt also asked Truman to keep his messages "as brief as possible in order not to tie up communications." As Roosevelt made crystal clear, he had no intention of preparing Truman to take over the reins of government should illness incapacitate him.[14]

Truman, in any case, would have needed a great deal of help to be of service. He had not given much thought to foreign policy in his decade in the Senate. He had never met the secretary of state, Edward Stettinius, and although he had chaired important Senate committees overseeing how the federal government spent money for wartime projects, he knew far less than Byrnes—or, for that matter, even Wallace—about American foreign policy. Wallace had at least toured Russia in 1943 and had worked with Winston Churchill, although Churchill had come to dislike him.

Still, in 1943, Truman had uncovered unexplained expenditures for a massive project labeled S-1, also known as the Manhattan Project. When he asked Secretary of War Henry Stimson about the expenditures, Stimson told him only that they were for a "very important secret development," details of which he could not share, even with a US senator. Truman took him at his word, and the conversation lasted just a few seconds. When Truman later asked questions about expenditures for the construction of a facility near Hanford, Washington, the general in charge at Hanford told Stimson that Truman was "a nuisance and a pretty untrustworthy man." They decided to tell Truman nothing about the research into plutonium at Hanford, notwithstanding his chairmanship of important Senate committees. Truman had stumbled onto the project to build an atomic bomb, but he did not yet know it.[15]

Even after becoming vice president, Truman learned nothing of significance about military matters or foreign affairs. He met privately with Roosevelt just twice while he was vice president; on neither occasion did the two men discuss issues of substance. Truman noted the president's declining health, observing after one meeting that Roosevelt's hand shook so badly that he could not pour cream into his coffee. Still, Truman did not assume that he might soon have to take over for Roosevelt; nor did he ask that Roosevelt's advisers keep him better informed about the crucial issues of the day. Like the vice presidents who preceded him, Truman faded from public view in the shadow of the great man in the White House.[16]

Neither did the members of Roosevelt's inner circle see any reason to keep Truman informed. They kept Truman away from daily briefings and excluded him from the top-secret White House Map Room, the nerve center of wartime information. Roosevelt's aides did not share classified messages with Truman, and beyond a few routine cabinet sessions, he was not invited to top-level meetings. Roosevelt's Russian interpreter Charles Bohlen noted that Truman was "an obscure vice-president, who got to see Roosevelt much less than I did, and who knew less than I did about United States foreign relations." Neither Roosevelt nor Stettinius briefed Truman on the events of the Yalta Conference after their return. In fact, no one in the Roosevelt administration thought it necessary to tell the vice president what the United States had agreed to at Yalta.[17]

Truman's astonishing isolation from presidential decision-making defies easy explanation, especially since Roosevelt's health suggested that some serious preparation might well have been in order. As one White House beat reporter bemoaned, "Truman doesn't know what's going on. Roosevelt won't tell him anything." Truman appeared to need all the help he could get, yet he could not even see the secret transcripts of the Yalta discussions, and Stimson did not think that Truman's election to the vice presidency meant he should get a briefing on the Manhattan Project.[18]

Truman's isolation, combined with problems at the State Department, had the effect of further concentrating foreign policy making in the Oval Office. Like Woodrow Wilson, Roosevelt had preferred to handle foreign affairs himself. Late in 1944, he had replaced the ailing Cordell Hull as secretary of state with the uninspiring Edward Stettinius. A series of scandals had shaken the president's confidence in the State Department. At the Quebec Conference with British leaders in 1943, tensions between Hull and Undersecretary of State Sumner Welles had come to a head, with Hull accusing Welles of going over his head directly to Roosevelt on key issues. They had been feuding for months. At Quebec, Hull decided he had had enough of his subordinate's behavior.

Seeking a way to get Welles out of the State Department, Hull and William Bullitt, the first American ambassador to the Soviet Union and a Roosevelt confidant, began to circulate rumors on Capitol Hill that Welles had made homosexual advances to two African American railway porters. Knowing that Roosevelt would go to great lengths to keep such a scandal out of the newspapers, Hull went to the president to demand Welles's dismissal; if he did not grant it, Hull told Roosevelt, he himself would resign, with the threat to leak the scandal to the media left unspoken. Roosevelt exploded with anger at Hull, but he knew he could not risk the fallout from a scandal of that magnitude. He offered Welles an ambassadorship in Latin America as a consolation prize, but Welles declined. His resignation letter stated that he was leaving government service to care for his ailing wife. American magazines and newspapers hinted that there was likely more to the story, but they did not pursue it. The incident caused the breach between the State Department and Roosevelt to widen. Roosevelt stopped passing his correspondence with Churchill and Stalin on to the State Department, and he rarely relied on State Department personnel at the great-power conferences for anything but note taking and translations.[19]

ALL OF THIS TURMOIL, and Roosevelt's personal style of handling foreign affairs, complicated the process of shaping American goals for the postwar world. Like Woodrow Wilson, who had isolated his State Department and leaned on a personal emissary, Edward House, Roosevelt relied on advisers without portfolios, such as New Deal and Lend-Lease architect Harry Hopkins. Roosevelt used Hopkins as his personal representative to Great Britain and as a kind of unofficial ambassador, thus keeping the State Department in the dark. Hopkins saw Roosevelt more often than any other adviser; he had even lived in the White House until a 1943 scandal forced Roosevelt to insist on a bit of distance. Despite the scandal—which involved lavish gifts Hopkins's wife had allegedly received from British media barons—and Hopkins's debilitating battle with stomach cancer, he remained one of Roosevelt's closest advisers on matters of foreign policy.

Moreover, just as Woodrow Wilson had done, Roosevelt personalized American foreign policy, relying on his powers of persuasion and his near monopoly of sensitive information. Charles Bohlen, for one, found this style "a serious fault" in the shaping of foreign policy. Without State Department experts to guide him, and lacking a deep firsthand knowledge of many of the world's flashpoints, Roosevelt needed much more help than he was willing to accept. "A deeper knowledge of history and certainly a better understanding of reactions of foreign peoples would have been useful to the president," Bohlen observed as he tried to guide Roosevelt through a maze of problems similar to those which had bedeviled Wilson in 1919. But Roosevelt remained resistant to the advice of the State Department and even of area specialists such as Sovietologists Charles Bohlen and George Kennan.

Although Bohlen admired and respected Roosevelt, he became increasingly dismayed by his approach to foreign policy. "Helpful, too," he later wrote, "would have been more study of the position papers prepared by American experts, more attention to detail, and less belief in the American conviction that the other fellow is a 'good guy' who will respond properly and decently if you treat him right." When it came to the Russians, Bohlen believed that Roosevelt suffered a fatal flaw: he lacked "any real comprehension of the great gulf that separated the thinking of a Bolshevik from a non-Bolshevik, and particularly from an American." Roosevelt's rejection of Bullitt cost him one of his most important Russia experts. Consequently, the American delegation, led by Roosevelt, went into the great-power conferences as ill-informed on crucial topics as Wilson had been in Paris.[20]

Roosevelt did, however, have both power and principles to guide him. By the time of the meeting on the Elbe, the United States had developed an understanding of its economic power and of how to employ it on the world stage. The United States was far ahead of the rest of the world economically, and this gave the nation a window of opportunity that its leaders, in contrast to those of 1919, aggressively seized. In July 1944, the Americans hosted a conference at Bretton Woods, New Hampshire, involving forty-four countries, including the Soviet Union. With the United States clearly calling the shots, the conference produced the most sweeping changes in international economics in world history.

The global economic infrastructure that Bretton Woods created reflected American postwar goals—most notably, global free trade and the creation of worldwide markets. To stabilize international currency, Bretton Woods fixed global exchange rates, pegging them to the American dollar, which was in turn backed by gold at the prewar rate of $35 an ounce. As a result, the system of currency exchanges and purchases became more predictable. Not coincidentally, the agreements also shifted the international reserve currency from the British pound to the only currency backed by gold, the American dollar.

Bretton Woods saw the formation of new global institutions that were designed to deal with economic crises just as the United Nations was to deal with political ones. These included the International Monetary Fund (IMF) and the International Bank for Reconstruction and Development (IBRD), today called the World Bank. Each member state would contribute money to these funds in proportion to the size of their economies, meaning that the United States would emerge as the dominant voice in both institutions.

Few global leaders had any doubt that Bretton Woods represented a major shift of global power to the United States. Thereafter, the lion's share of the money needed to finance global development would come, in one way or another, from Washington and New York. British economist John Maynard Keynes, one of the attendees at Bretton Woods, saw parts of the new system, notably the banking innovations, as major improvements over the "ill-conceived racket" that had characterized the disastrous economic arrangements after World War I. He had famously criticized the World War I arrangements in his 1920 bestseller, *The Economic Consequences of the Peace*. The new system, moreover, by internationalizing credit and finance, would reduce the burden of European reconstruction on a nearly bankrupt Britain. It would certainly also end Britain's place at the financial center of the world economy.[21]

British officials bemoaned the change, but they knew how much they needed America's financial help, and it was far too much to object. Senior Bank of England officials called Bretton Woods a "swindle" and "the greatest blow to Britain next to the war." As one American financial official noted, "Bretton Woods is an acknowledgment of the fact that London has lost its position as the financial center of the world." Angry British officials fumed at America's strong-arm tactics, but Keynes, who knew he would have to ask the United States for more Lend-Lease aid in order to keep Britain afloat, did not complain. As a reflection of the parlous state of British finances, Keynes left Bretton Woods and went to Ottawa, where he lobbied the Canadian government to give Britain a stunning $655 million more in financial assistance.

Bretton Woods showed how far the United States had come from 1919. Wilsonian idealism remained at the core of America's worldview, but that idealism had been tempered by the American experience of the post–World War I world. In 1945, the Americans had a new sense of their own power, and they sought to back their ideals to a much greater degree with the new tools this power provided them. With Roosevelt leading the way, the United States would create a new world infused with American beliefs; but this time, unlike in 1919, the Americans would have the ability to enforce their will on both their former enemies and their allies.

But if Roosevelt and the Americans acted with a sense of their growing power, they failed to realize how little support there was for American idealism overseas. Few westerners understood how deeply the Soviet Union mistrusted American principles and America's insistence on applying them to European problems. Woodrow Wilson had proclaimed his belief in national self-determination in 1918; in Russian eyes, however, he had used it not for higher moral goals, but to contain the growth of Bolshevik Russia. Wilson had also used national self-determination as a means of creating a more powerful Poland, which served as part of a wider strategy for placing strong states on Russia's borders. Instead of welcoming what the Bolsheviks themselves called their democratic and anti-dictatorial revolution in Russia, Wilson had sent American troops to northern Russia, ostensibly to protect Allied supplies. The Bolsheviks, however, saw the deployment of Western and Japanese troops on Russian soil as part of a military scheme to deny the Bolsheviks victory in the Russian Civil War.[22]

Wilsonian idealism did not apply equally to all parts of the globe. In fact, Wilson, and the Americans more generally, had made it clear that the ideals he promoted for the rest of the world did not apply to America's backyard, Latin America. Nor, in practice, did they apply to the existing French and British empires, because the principle of national self-determination remained anathema in Paris and London. Even in East Asia, the Western powers had given the formerly German colonies in Shandong Province to Japan despite their overwhelmingly Chinese populations.[23]

The British and French, moreover, had used the defeat of the Ottoman Empire in 1918 to add even more colonies to their empires than they already had. Britain took Transjordan, Palestine, much of the Arabian Peninsula, and Mesopotamia, while France took Syria and Lebanon, as part of the secret Sykes-Picot Agreement of 1916. Imperial Russia had given its consent in exchange for much of eastern Anatolia. When the Bolsheviks seized power in 1917, they published the agreements, embarrassing the British and French governments by revealing their naked power grab.[24]

At the Paris Peace Conference, General Jan Smuts of South Africa had suggested calling the new territories "mandates" rather than "colonies." In theory, the Europeans would not annex these territories to their empires, but prepare them for independence. Adding the fig leaf of the mandate system, however, fooled no one, least of all the Bolsheviks, who criticized Western imperialism as a means of spreading the West's ostensibly anticolonial, but in reality blatantly capitalist, ideology. In Africa, the British and French divided the German colonies among themselves without even the veneer of the mandate system. To Russian revolutionaries like V. I. Lenin and Joseph Stalin, Western ideals stank of hypocrisy. They believed that all such arrangements were just the typical power grabs of an imperialist and capitalist system. For the Russians, America's quasi-colonial control of Latin America undermined American public statements opposing imperialism even further.[25]

Western conduct during World War II did not strike the Russians as any more principled than the mandate system agreements. The idealistic Atlantic Charter, issued by Roosevelt and Churchill in August 1941, seemed to fit right into the Wilsonian tradition. Although the charter pledged to support national self-determination and a lowering of international trade barriers, American leaders made clear that it would not interfere with American rights under the Monroe Doctrine to intervene in Latin America. Similarly, Churchill stated that the charter did not apply to the British Empire. Such conditions made it impossible for the Russians to take the charter and its ideals seriously; as a result, they never considered the charter as a model for Soviet behavior in Eastern Europe or anywhere else.

Allied policies during the war itself also seemed to undermine Western principles. If the West wanted to lecture Russia about its forced removal of suspected pro-German ethnic groups, such as the Tatars and the Chechens, the Russians could reply by citing the internment of Japanese Americans in US camps. If the British wanted to lecture Russia on its policies in Ukraine, the Russians could respond with allegations of British mistreatment of Bengal, where as many as 3 million Indians had died as a result of a famine—especially since the famine had been exacerbated by British policies that forced the export of Indian crops to the British Isles even in the midst of a worsening food crisis in India.[26]

Stalin rarely actually criticized Western policies, believing as he did that great powers involved in an existential war had the right to do as they wished, especially in their own spheres of control. Nor did the Russians genuinely care about the fate of Japanese Americans or Bengalis. But the apparent gap between the West's lofty ideals and its self-serving practices made the Russians extremely wary of pronouncements citing Western principles, which they saw not as real beliefs in the West but rampant Western hypocrisy. The Russians had little interest in idealism, especially when it came from the intellectual inheritors of the hypocritical Wilsonian tradition.[27]

The evils of imperialism, the Soviets concluded, had caused both world wars, and Western ideology therefore threatened the future peace and stability of Europe. The Russians had little interest in basing the postwar world on the principles touted in the West. Even on matters of strategy, the Russians were quick to point out what they saw as Western double standards. When Western leaders expressed their reluctance to modify the international agreements that gave Turkey control over the Dardanelles, for example, Stalin objected. He proceeded to point out the hypocrisy of the Western position, given American control over the Panama Canal and British control over the Suez Canal. To Stalin, the three passages had much in common, as each served as a vital waterway for a great power but was surrounded by the sovereign territory of another state. American and British reluctance to consider revising the international conventions on the Dardanelles, while keeping Panama and Suez under their exclusive control, struck the Russians as the basest and most obvious kind of Western hypocrisy. It also provided further proof to them that the West did not follow its own ideals except when Western ideals and Western interests overlapped.

ALL OF THESE PROBLEMS, and many more besides, were soon to fall on the head of the man who had found himself vice president almost by accident. On April 12, 1945, Truman went to the Senate to listen to a debate about a water-rights treaty with Mexico before going to the secluded room in the Senate known as the "Board of Education." Sam Rayburn, the Speaker of the House, often used the room to have a drink with colleagues at the end of the day. When Truman walked in, Rayburn told him that the White House press secretary was looking for him. Truman dialed the number and announced himself, then the others in the room noticed that all of the color left his face. "Jesus Christ and General Jackson," he said as he hung up the phone. Without saying another word, Truman then ran through the Capitol to get to the White House as quickly as he could. Waiting for him was the White House press secretary, with whom he had spoken on the phone moments earlier. Eleanor Roosevelt was also there. She approached Truman, placed her hand on his arm, and softly said, "Harry, the president is dead." "Is there anything I can do for you?" he asked. "Is there anything *we* can do for *you*?" she replied. "For you are the one in trouble now."[28]

Notwithstanding the signs of the collapse of Roosevelt's health, his death came as a genuine shock to people around the world. In Russia, Foreign Minister Vyacheslav Molotov seemed "deeply moved and disturbed," according to Averill Harriman, the American ambassador to the Soviet Union. Stalin grasped Harriman's hand for thirty seconds and seemed close to tears. From London, Foreign Minister Anthony Eden wrote to the British ambassador in Washington, "I still find it difficult to believe that our gallant friend is gone." The next day, Churchill told the British cabinet that he received Roosevelt's death as a "profound shock. [A] leap into the unknown." Even though Anglo-American relations, and the personal relationship between Roosevelt and Churchill, had cooled in recent months, Churchill knew that with Roosevelt's passing, he, and Britain more generally, had lost its most important ally.[29]

Even those closest to Roosevelt seemed unable to believe that he was gone. Presidential aide George Elsey noted that Roosevelt's death "came with no warning," even though some had noticed his decline. James Byrnes recalled being "stunned" by the news, and he must have thought about how close he had been to becoming the next president had the convention in Chicago gone differently. He recalled thinking of Truman and how "no new president ever faced a swifter pageant of great events" than his friend from Missouri. That Roosevelt had left him so inexplicably in the dark only made the weight of Truman's responsibility all that much greater. Admiral William Leahy, Roosevelt's chief of staff, confided to his diary both his anguish at the loss of the president he had served for so long and his fear that the new president would not be able to rise to the challenges he faced:

This world tragedy deprives the Nation of its leader at a time when the war to preserve civilization is approaching its end with

accelerated speed, and when a vital need for competent leadership
in the making and preservation of world peace is at least seriously
prejudiced by the passing of Franklin Roosevelt who was a world
figure of heroic proportions. . . . We are all at loose ends and confused as to who may be capable of giving sage advice and counsel
to the new leader in his handling of the staggering burdens of war
and peace that he must carry.[30]

The shock and consternation spread across Washington and the
nation. The United Press Senate correspondent, Allen Drury, wrote
that although he and his colleagues had covered Washington for
years, "still, we could not believe it." Franklin Roosevelt's decline,
in retrospect so easy to discern, struck the late president's contemporaries as a sudden and tragic event. Like so many in the nation's capital, Drury wondered how the "honest and simple" Truman could
possibly handle the challenges of a "black, sick century."[31]

Truman surely entered a strange White House, one whose occu-
pant since 1933 had suddenly disappeared. George Elsey, on duty in
the White House Map Room when the news of Roosevelt's death arrived, watched a surreal spectacle unfold. A senior naval aide, fresh
from the golf course, came storming into the room—which was still
off limits to Truman—and asked, "Do we know how to reach the
president?" Elsey and his colleagues exchanged blank stares "until
we realized he was asking about Harry S. Truman." The next day,
Elsey was in the East Room of the White House for Truman's first
day on the job. Out of custom, everyone in the room stood when
Mrs. Roosevelt entered, but no one stood a few minutes later when
Truman entered. Elsey noted that the White House staff had not intended disrespect. "Harry Truman," he noted, "was not yet felt, by
those present, to be the President, so great was the hold on their
minds of Franklin Delano Roosevelt." Getting out of the shadow of
Franklin Roosevelt was only one of the many challenges that now
fell to an obscure former haberdasher from Missouri.[32]

2

"The Most Terrible Responsibility Any Man Ever Faced"

HARRY TRUMAN TOOK the oath of office in the White House cabinet room underneath a portrait of Woodrow Wilson. With the architect of the failed League of Nations staring down at him in the same room where Franklin Roosevelt had contemplated the future of the United Nations, the relatively unknown Truman became the president of the United States the evening of April 12, 1945. The somber ceremony, with men dressed in dark suits—understandably, more appropriate to mourn the death of Roosevelt than to celebrate the inauguration of Truman—sent a sobering message of uncertainty for the future. Surviving photographs show no one smiling; the faces, Truman's included, betray a look of deep dread at what this surprising and unexpected changing of the guard might portend. "I felt as though the moon and a couple of planets had fallen on me," Truman himself said. "I have the most terrible responsibility any man ever faced."[1]

Those who had been in Roosevelt's inner circle wondered how the new president could possibly begin to deal with the ominous geopolitical situation confronting him. Henry Stimson, the secretary of war, who had so inexcusably kept Vice President Truman in the dark about critical military matters like the Manhattan Project, wrote in his diary: "I am very sorry for the President because he is new on his job and he has been brought into a situation which ought not to have been allowed to come his way." Stimson did not reflect on how he might have eased Truman's burden by helping to prepare him for the eventuality that he might, after all, have to govern. Instead, he noted that "it was very clear that [Truman] knew very little of the task into which he was stepping." Charles Bohlen agreed with Stimson's assessment, later recalling, "We in the State Department shared the concern of all Americans whether the 'Little Man from Missouri' could rise to the occasion." And what an occasion it was, with two major wars thousands of miles apart requiring critical strategic decisions, and a need to forge a vision for the postwar world.[2]

The world seemed to be sinking ever deeper into misery with each passing day. Even in Truman's first few hours on the job, the world situation changed for the worse. On the same day that Truman became president, the United States Sixth Armored Division liberated the first large Nazi concentration camp in the British and American zone of operations. The horrors of Buchenwald stunned the Americans who entered the camp. Although rumors, and some hard evidence, had reached Western leaders about Nazi crimes, American and British strategists had remained focused on the defeat of Germany, not on the liberation of the camps. Even the Soviet liberation of Auschwitz on January 27 had failed to change Western attitudes. Buchenwald forced the Allies to face the consequences of a strategy that ignored the Nazi killing machines. At Buchenwald the Allies saw tens of thousands of emaciated and dying victims and, for the first time, irrefutable evidence of a sophisticated system for the mass murder of human beings.[3]

Americans in Europe understood that the discovery of Buchenwald, and undoubtedly other horrors to come, would change attitudes about the postwar world. First, however, the news had to hit home. General Dwight D. Eisenhower, Supreme Allied Commander in Europe, spoke with American journalists, comparing notes on what the journalists had seen of the "hell camps" with what

American soldiers had seen. He then urged the reporters to ensure that "every American newspaper would print the story of German bestiality in detail." Edward R. Murrow, who entered Buchenwald shortly after its liberation, certainly did his part. He made one of the most eloquent commentaries of his distinguished career in an April 16 national broadcast on CBS News that ended with, "I pray you to believe what I have said about Buchenwald. I have reported what I saw and heard, but only part of it. For most of it, I have no words. . . . If I've offended you by this rather mild account of Buchenwald, I'm not in the least sorry."

Murrow noted that some of the recently liberated prisoners talked effusively about Roosevelt, equating him and the United States with their freedom. They did not know that Roosevelt had died just as they had regained that freedom, leaving Harry Truman with the awesome responsibility of taking up his mantle. The following month, war correspondent Martha Gellhorn followed Murrow's account of Buchenwald with an article in *Collier's* about another recently discovered camp. Entitled "Surely This War Was Made to Abolish Dachau," it called on the peacemakers to create a better world or face the awesome consequences of the failures of their actions. "If we ever again tolerate such cruelty," her article ended, "we have no right to peace." In the weeks and months to come, more stories, each seemingly more horrifying than the last, would appear in the American and British media.[4]

Although no one could predict what the liberation of the camps might mean for the postwar world, their discovery changed the tenor of debate about Europe's future overnight. Even a world shocked and numbed by the horrors of a generation of total war now had to face an entirely new level of barbarity. For the Americans, especially those government officials who had tried to ignore the evidence they had of the camps, the mass murder of millions of people complicated an already overwhelming set of problems for the reconstruction of the postwar world.

ESPECIALLY GIVEN THE ENORMITY of the challenges he faced, Truman did not exactly inspire confidence in those around him.

General Omar Bradley observed that the new president "did not appear at all qualified" for the breathtaking responsibilities ahead. Presidential aide George Elsey watched with a combination of sympathy and concern as Truman, finally admitted into the top-secret Map Room, struggled to make sense of it all. He could not even find strategically important places like Rangoon on the maps, and, much to everyone's dismay, no one could find the official copies of the minutes of the Cairo, Tehran, and Yalta proceedings. Truman therefore had no official record of those conferences to guide him. Those close to him generously offered their help, but they, too, voiced concerns and fears. James Byrnes noted that Truman was understandably "overwhelmed by the responsibilities suddenly thrust upon him"; Roosevelt's press secretary remarked that on his first day in office, Truman looked like "a very little man as he sat waiting in a huge leather chair." Former President Herbert Hoover offered a much more blunt assessment about the new president, calling Truman "really dumb" in private correspondence to a lower-level official.[5]

In his own diary, Truman bemoaned his lack of familiarity with the major issues of the day, especially the agreements Roosevelt had made with the nation's wartime allies on the nation's behalf. The absence of the official minutes further complicated the problem, requiring Truman to rely on officials' conflicting memories of what Roosevelt had agreed to do, sometimes in closed-door meetings that they had not personally attended. The shake-ups at the State Department left the new president further in the dark. Truman likened becoming the president in such a fashion to being struck by lightning. He confided to a friend, "You don't know how difficult the thing has been for me. Everyone around here that should know something about foreign affairs is out." To another friend, he said, "I'm not big enough. I'm not big enough for this job."[6]

Not having attended college, Truman lacked the formal education of Roosevelt and his aides. He thus struck many Washingtonians who had known the Roosevelt White House as, to say the least, rustic. He had not traveled much and had had no substantive discussions with any of the leaders or ambassadors of America's allies. He had only met Winston Churchill in passing, and he had never had a reason to think carefully about global problems; about other countries, such as China or Poland; or about postwar imperatives, such as economic reconstruction. The State Department, in particular, worried about Truman's lack of polish and his unfamiliarity with major foreign relations issues. But Truman had a quick mind, and he read voraciously. He knew how to deal with the condescension of the eastern elite. And he did not shy away from making important decisions.[7]

Although not everyone warmed quickly to him, Truman began to impress many of those who watched him face his new responsibilities. A reporter for the Kansas City *Star* who had known Truman for years relayed to Eisenhower in late April that from what his sources in Washington had said, Truman "hasn't done anything wrong to date"—faint praise indeed. The reporter also told Eisenhower that Truman carefully followed the advice of the highly respected army chief of staff, General George Marshall, and that he would "be a fine president" once he had a chance to learn his new role. Leahy and others close to Truman also grew in their admiration of him as they watched him tackle his many challenges with energy and honesty. Whether he could learn fast enough remained anyone's guess.[8]

In his first few days in office, Truman made all the necessary public pledges to uphold the policies and the spirit of Franklin Roosevelt. On just his second day in office, he sent a message to Winston Churchill that read: "You can count on me to continue the loyal and close collaboration which to the benefit of the entire world existed between you and our great president." In reality, Truman had no choice but to pledge to fulfill Roosevelt's policies, even if he did not fully know what those policies entailed. His words helped to reassure allies in London, Moscow, and elsewhere while also sending the signal that even an event as massive as the death of Franklin Roosevelt would not change key American positions on matters such as the upcoming San Francisco conference on the United Nations or the Bretton Woods economic agreements made a few months earlier. Lacking any other guiding principle, Truman would follow the status quo, for the time being at least.[9]

Harry Hopkins assured British leaders that Truman, "a real country boy," would follow Roosevelt's policy of close Anglo-American cooperation. Being "completely ignorant of foreign [affairs]," he assured British Ambassador Lord Halifax, Truman could do little else. Halifax in turn advised British Foreign Minister Anthony Eden that neither he nor Churchill should come to the United States for Roosevelt's funeral, because American leaders would not yet be ready to talk about issues of substance, given Truman's complete lack of information about them. Truman, Halifax warned, would not be in a position to discuss serious issues for several weeks. Nevertheless, Halifax reassured London that Truman seemed "honest, capable, methodical," and far more willing to use official channels than Roosevelt had been. The last point must have seemed like music to Eden's ears, as the personal one-to-one system of communications that Churchill and Roosevelt had used often left him as much in the dark as his American counterparts.[10]

Truman leaned heavily on Admiral William Leahy, Roosevelt's chief of staff, and Roosevelt adviser James Byrnes to help him get quickly up to speed. Byrnes's aide, Walter Brown, talked with his boss en route to Roosevelt's funeral, later noting in his diary, "By all rules of the game, he [Byrnes] should now be president and not Truman. We both knew Truman was a weak man." He would thus need all the help Byrnes could provide. Byrnes and Brown agreed that Byrnes had to find a way to become the secretary of state, "to save the peace," because they both viewed Secretary of State Edward Stettinius as part of the "dead wood" among Roosevelt's closest advisers. "There were no brains down there," Brown recalled about Roosevelt's cabinet. Byrnes especially despised Roosevelt's reliance on informal emissaries like Harry Hopkins and Joseph Davies in lieu of his own State Department.[11]

Byrnes moved quickly to cement his influence on the new president. After Truman took the oath of office, the two men met for an hour to discuss details of the Tehran and Yalta conferences. Then Byrnes stayed while Truman discussed some of those same topics with Stettinius and Russia expert Charles Bohlen. Byrnes returned to the White House early the next morning for more discussions about

Yalta. He quickly became Truman's most trusted confidant, even if tensions between them remained just below the surface. For his part, Byrnes started off by calling Truman "Harry" as he always had, but soon switched to "Mr. President," however much Byrnes must have thought about how close he had come to having the title apply to him.[12]

Lacking much help from the State Department, which often found itself as ill-informed as Truman himself, the new president had to lean temporarily on Roosevelt advisers like Leahy, Hopkins, and Davies, as well as on the US ambassador to the Soviet Union, Averill Harriman. They gave Truman conflicting advice about the Russians, with Harriman and Leahy being the most pessimistic about the future of cooperation with the Soviets, and Hopkins and Davies the most optimistic. Truman also learned how deeply Byrnes polarized Roosevelt's inner circle. Leahy did not shrink from calling Byrnes a "horse's ass." Harriman was normally too diplomatic to use such language, but he also despised and mistrusted Byrnes.[13]

Nevertheless, formalizing Byrnes's position at the senior level of the new administration became one of Truman's most important personnel changes. Privately, Truman wondered how long he and Byrnes could work together, but publicly he had nothing but praise for Byrnes. Hopkins recognized as early as April 16 that Byrnes would likely become secretary of state as soon as Truman could arrange it, and news of the impending change made the rounds of the American newspapers. Most of the newspapers, as well as Washington officials, thought the move ideal, and even Leahy privately called it "the best appointment made by Mr. Truman since his accession to the presidency," despite Leahy's own negative view of Byrnes as a person.

On paper, Byrnes indeed seemed an excellent choice, just as he had seemed for the vice presidency. He had attended the Paris Peace Conference of 1919 in addition to Tehran and Yalta, even though Roosevelt had largely ignored him at the latter. Byrnes had a wealth of government experience, and Truman, at least at this point, trusted him, notwithstanding the awkward and uncomfortable events of the Chicago convention. Most importantly, Truman needed Byrnes's knowledge of world events, especially in the absence of an agreed-upon official record of the major conferences.[14]

Even before his official appointment to head the State Department, Byrnes began to assume some of the functions of a senior cabinet official. He urged Truman to get rid of most of Roosevelt's cabinet, despite the new president's initial belief that he had neither the right nor the authority to force sitting officials confirmed by the Senate to resign their posts. Truman complained to Byrnes, according to Byrnes's aide, Walter Brown, that "if a dog came in and shit on his office floor he could not tell him to get out," leaving Byrnes "feeling very low because he feared for his country" in the hands of such a weak-willed man. Byrnes sought to provide that will. He edited Truman's speeches, isolated informal advisers like Hopkins and Davies, urged Truman to make personnel changes, and even hosted a foreign policy meeting with Anthony Eden and Lord Halifax, the British foreign secretary and ambassador, respectively. Stettinius, still serving as secretary of state, did not receive an invitation to that meeting. The *New York Times* reported on the meeting's significance by announcing that "the new administration would be built around Byrnes."[15]

Byrnes also provided much-needed experience in government, especially in the Senate, which could block or force modifications to any treaties Truman negotiated. The memory of Woodrow Wilson's ugly fight with Senate Foreign Relations Committee Chairman Henry Cabot Lodge cast a long shadow. Truman himself remained a welcome face in the Senate, but no one knew how long his status as a popular alumnus of the body would continue to be an asset, now that he had changed roles. Byrnes could therefore serve as a useful conduit into Senate back channels.

Byrnes's experience solved a constitutional problem for Truman as well. Until the passage of the Twenty-fifth Amendment in 1967, if the vice president became president due to the death in office of a sitting president, the vice presidency remained open. This oversight was a curious statement by the framers of the US Constitution about the importance (or lack thereof) of the office. Should anything befall Truman while in office, the presidency would pass to the secretary of state. Few people in official Washington wanted the lackluster Stettinius, a man who inspired little confidence, and had never held an elected office, sitting just a heartbeat away from the Oval Office.

Truman thus made clear early on that he wanted Byrnes to be his secretary of state, and therefore to succeed him as president should it become necessary. Changing secretaries would also shake up the State Department, which Truman distrusted as much as Roosevelt had. State Department officials were among those most likely to look down on Truman's background and his lack of formal education. Although he occasionally used them in due course, Truman saw Roosevelt's most trusted diplomatic advisers—men like Cordell Hull, Harry Hopkins, and Joseph Davies—as "old and physically incapacitated." He therefore needed a functional State Department.[16]

Byrnes also bolstered Truman's growing desire to get rid of old elites like Treasury Secretary Henry Morgenthau, a man the new president said "didn't know shit from apple butter." Under the rules in place in 1945, the secretary of the treasury sat next in the line of succession behind the secretary of state. With Truman and Byrnes likely to head to Europe together, Morgenthau, a man Truman said he would not appoint as a dog catcher, would become president should anything befall Truman and Byrnes overseas. Byrnes or one of his associates may have been behind a press leak about Truman's lack of faith in Morgenthau, who privately asked the new president for a public statement of confidence for the media. When Truman refused to provide it, Morgenthau offered his resignation, which Truman accepted with relief.[17]

Truman continued to seek new advisers, especially in the State Department, which he believed had been less than truthful with him. In the first few days of May, Truman confided to his diary, "Evidently, some of the State Department boys believe nobody not even the President of the United States. Ain't it awful? Must make some changes." Three days before he wrote this diary entry, the State Department had neglected to pass along a message from Stalin disapproving of the American announcement of Germany's surrender on May 8. The timing of the entry suggests that Truman had now found out. Because the Germans had surrendered only to the Americans and the British at the time of the announcement, Stalin thought the American celebrations were premature, and he viewed this as a much more serious breach than the State Department apparently did. The Soviet Union, Stalin had tried to remind the president, remained technically at war with Germany, and the three powers had agreed in 1943 that they all had to consent to the terms of any German surrender. The formal German surrender to the Soviet Union came in due course—in fact, just hours later, at a ceremony in the Berlin neighborhood of Karlshorst. But the State Department's decision not to tell Truman about Stalin's message nevertheless likely raised some eyebrows in the White House.[18]

Truman's changes began at the top, with Byrnes becoming secretary of state on July 3, just three days before they set sail for Potsdam. Byrnes likely would have had the job much sooner if his supporters in the Senate had not tried to force his nomination through the confirmation process with a bit too much enthusiasm, thereby offending senators who insisted on following proper procedure. In the end, the Senate confirmed Byrnes with only a perfunctory voice vote. Byrnes, who had a background as humble as Truman's, never did gain the trust of the career men at the State Department, but he did not seem to care. As one journalist noted, Byrnes "emphatically determined to be the real Secretary of State, and not to be run by his subordinates— as he observed Stettinius being run by his subordinates at Yalta and elsewhere. He will be the boss."[19]

At least for the first few months of their tenure, Byrnes and Truman formed an effective team. The new secretary of state ended the practice Roosevelt had used whereby the president met most often with Bohlen, who then transmitted information to Stettinius. Until the rift between them began to widen near the end of the year, Byrnes met with Truman personally as often as possible. Truman, too, seemed pleased with the arrangement. Four days after he formally nominated Byrnes, he wrote in his diary: "The smart boys in the State Department are against the best interests of the United States. . . . But they are stymied this time. Byrnes and I shall expect our interests to come first."[20]

With Byrnes encouraging him, Truman quickly got past his initial reluctance to make changes at the cabinet level. He gave the senior advisory team that Roosevelt had built almost a complete overhaul. Henry Morgenthau, the secretary of the treasury and a former Hyde Park neighbor of the Roosevelts, left soon after the Potsdam Conference, although Truman had stopped listening to him long before. Truman called Stettinius, the first cabinet officer he targeted for removal, "as dumb as they came." By the end of July, Truman had also replaced the secretaries of war, labor, and agriculture, as well as the attorney general. Only one of the new advisers came from the Northeast, and only one had an Ivy League degree.[21]

The aristocratic British ambassador to the United States, Lord Halifax, described Truman's new team, and Truman himself, as "provincial." They were, as a group, more straightforward and less diplomatic than Roosevelt's team, and they were fonder of poker and bourbon than of bridge and champagne. To some, the transition seemed like a step backward into a world of machine politicians and populists. To others, Truman brought a refreshing willingness to say what he thought; the man who popularized the saying "The buck stops here" also made decisions and stood by them as often as a politician can.[22]

In contrast to the cabinet members, Truman's uniformed military advisers remained in place. He kept Admiral Leahy close at hand and considered him for cabinet positions as well. Leahy had diplomatic experience, having served in the challenging role of ambassador to Vichy France in the difficult years of 1941 and 1942. He had also served as governor of Puerto Rico, and during his time as Roosevelt's chief of staff he had transformed the office into a powerful advisory role. He stayed on Truman's staff until his retirement in 1949. Truman also listened with near-worshipful attention to Army Chief of Staff George Marshall, whose judgment Truman rarely questioned. When Byrnes finally left the State Department in 1947, Truman selected Marshall as his replacement.

With new advisers in place, Truman impressed people with his attitude and his approach to his newfound responsibilities, even if he obviously still had much to learn. Wallace Deuel, a reporter for the *Chicago Daily News* (and also an agent for the Office of Strategic Services, or OSS, the forerunner of the Central Intelligence Agency), found him more "orderly and business-like" than his predecessor. Truman, he thought, "has a lot of sense," and unlike Roosevelt, didn't "make talk," presumably meaning that he got straight to the point. Charles Bohlen also found Truman much more focused than Roosevelt, noting that he "rarely philosophized," and instead stuck to the practical matters at hand. Everyone who met him realized, however, that Truman had a great deal to learn in a short period of time.[23]

Truman also had to build relationships from scratch with America's allies. He met Lord Halifax on day three of his presidency, leaving the British ambassador convinced that "we shall have in him a loyal collaborator" who would value the "unity and understanding between our two countries." Halifax told Foreign Secretary Anthony Eden that he was "much heartened by this first conversation." Truman might not bring the personal closeness that had once characterized the relationship between Roosevelt and Churchill, but neither did he seem tainted by the drift in that "special relationship" that had become evident at Yalta. Perhaps, then, Truman's accession offered an opportunity not only to resuscitate the former closeness of Anglo-American relations, but also to open a new, more productive chapter.

As Eden, Halifax, and others knew, good relations with the Americans were the key to Britain's future. Thus did Halifax write to Eden on April 22 saying that he hoped to convince Truman to make an early trip to Britain, or to agree to a major three-power conference, ideally to be held in Europe soon after the German surrender. British statesmen would then have the chance to explain their interpretations of major agreements to Truman and impress upon him personally their views of a postwar situation that seemed to them increasingly worrisome with each passing week. The British also took heart from the selection of Byrnes as secretary of state, viewing him as more reliably pro-British than either Stettinius or others rumored for the job, such as Admiral Leahy.[24]

Truman's new team worked with him to bring him up to speed as quickly as possible. Truman complained of eye strain from reading thousands of memoranda and reports, but he worked hard and listened carefully. His willingness to read and think deeply represented a change in style, if perhaps not as much in substance, from the more intuitive and impulsive Roosevelt. Truman also seemed more willing to listen to expert advice than his predecessor had been, although he clearly had much ground to cover.[25]

IN SOME WAYS, American goals for the postwar world as articulated by Roosevelt in 1944 and Truman in the spring of 1945 differed little from those of 1919. In neither case did the American people want to play the role of global policeman or maintain a permanent military infrastructure in Europe. Furthermore, American leaders knew full well that their postwar goals were not identical to those of their European allies. The "special relationship" with Great Britain was more rhetorical than real. Roosevelt's distancing himself from Churchill at Yalta had sent the message that the British could not expect the Americans to maintain a permanent commitment to British goals, as a number of disagreements over postwar strategy and British imperial policies clearly demonstrated.

The same questions about America's role in the world that had confronted Wilson in 1919 remained for Truman and his team in 1945. The failure of American foreign policy in the years in between complicated matters even further. World War I and the subsequent economic problems of the interwar years had left a sour taste in American mouths. Truman's advisers disagreed on many of their foreign policy assumptions and recommendations, but they unanimously opposed a re-creation of the 1920s financial schemes by which the United States had financed German reparations to the British and French in the hopes that the British and French would in turn pay off their debts to the United States. That cycle had, from Washington's perspective, destabilized the international economic system and contributed to the onset of the Great Depression.[26]

The rhetorical American commitment to anti-imperialism also remained from the World War I era. Europeans often criticized America's position in Latin America, backed up by the Monroe Doctrine, as a form of quasi-imperialism, but Roosevelt nevertheless had held firm to policies and rhetoric opposing imperialism. His own Good Neighbor Policy toward Latin America, and a 1936 statement supporting independence for the American colony in the Philippines, backed those words with action, even if Roosevelt intended for the Philippines to remain firmly inside an American orbit after independence. During the war, some of the sharpest disagreements between the Americans and the British had come from the American refusal to support British military operations that the Americans viewed as extending the power and cohesion of the British Empire. Not for nothing did the Americans belittle the British-led Southeast Asia Command (SEAC) as "Save England's Asiatic Colonies."

Roosevelt's views on imperialism hardened even further during the war. He had spoken sharply against French imperial policy, announcing that the United States would seek a postwar international trusteeship in Indochina rather than help the French to reassert their control in the region. After Yalta, he had also announced American opposition to Britain returning to the status quo ante in India. Although he belittled Indians as "the brown people in the East," he also noted sympathetically that "our goal must be to help them achieve independence," because India was "ruled by a handful of whites and they resent it." As Wilson had done in Paris in 1919, Roosevelt and then Truman prepared to contest the expansion or resumption of European imperialism in the postwar world on philosophical, moral, and economic grounds, regardless of any opposition from the European powers themselves.[27]

Like Wilson and Roosevelt, Truman did not expect the American people to favor a semi-permanent military mobilization. He anticipated that once the war ended, the American people would react as they had in 1919, demanding a return to peacetime conditions, an end to conscription, and a lowering of defense spending. Increased global responsibilities notwithstanding, Truman and his advisers believed the United States would need to plan for steep reductions in its commitments to global security.

In other ways, however, the position of the United States in the final months of World War II differed greatly from its 1919 position. On the strategic level, the United States still had a war to conclude with Japan. For many American leaders, settling scores with the nation that had attacked Pearl Harbor was more important than trying to work out permanent diplomatic arrangements in Europe. In practical terms, the question centered on how many military assets the United States would move from Europe to Asia after Germany's surrender. The more assets the Americans transferred, the less leverage they would likely have in Europe, especially against the Russians, who would certainly not demobilize as quickly as the Americans or the British. With expectations of a costly war with Japan continuing into 1946 or 1947, few American strategists wanted to leave a disproportionate number of men, tanks, and airplanes half a world away in Europe.

American attitudes toward its nonmilitary instruments of national power had changed drastically since 1919. Whereas Wilson had relied primarily upon his idealism and the power of his vision, the Americans of 1945 wanted to back idealism with economic power. Knowing, or at least assuming, that America's postwar military power would wane after the war, as it had in 1919, American planners aimed to make economics a primary means of national influence. Even more so than at the end of World War I, America would emerge from World War II as the world's greatest economic power. Not only had the United States avoided the horrific infrastructural damage that had befallen nearly every other advanced economy, but it had invested billions of dollars into its economy while also increasing personal savings through war bonds. Those savings, plus thoughtful legislation like the GI Bill, would likely fuel the postwar economy, or, at the very least, help the United States avoid sliding back into depression-like conditions once the federal government stopped its high level of wartime spending. Although the postwar economy had its share of risks, perhaps no other country in history had ever emerged from a war with such a favorable relative economic advantage.

The question remained how best to use it, but whatever they did, the Americans would clearly act in a more determined manner than in 1919. They sought nothing less than a chance at the redemption of Woodrow Wilson's failure of a generation earlier. This time they would not miss the opportunity that the triumphant end of a war provided. As Will Clayton, the State Department's senior economist, noted in an influential speech in May 1945: "For the second time in this generation, our country is faced with the responsibilities and opportunities of participation in world leadership. At the end of the First World War we stepped aside and the mantle fell to the ground. This time, the mantle is already around our shoulders, and a devastated and terrified world is hopefully looking to us to help them back to peace and life." Clayton, who was later named to chair the reparations committee at the Potsdam Conference, warned that only the worldwide expansion of democracy and free enterprise, backed by American power, could prevent a third world war.[28]

The Americans had enjoyed an economic advantage in 1919 as well, but Wilson either would not or could not translate that economic power into political power. Even as America demobilized its army, such that the nation's influence over other great powers would henceforth depend primarily on economic instruments, Wilson remained reluctant to base his policies on economics. His commitment to economic liberalization notwithstanding, he remained far more comfortable using appeals to moral principles than economic leverage to get what he wanted. American leaders a generation later pledged not to make that same mistake. They sought nothing less than the complete reform of the world economic system, both to follow the principle of free trade and to take advantage of the immense power of the American economy.[29]

The United States had supported the notion of free trade for decades, often in the form of self-serving concepts like the Open Door Policy in China. Woodrow Wilson saw free trade as more than an economic policy, linking free trade to the pursuit of international peace. The third of his Fourteen Points called for "the removal, so far as possible, of all economic barriers and the establishment of equality of trade conditions among all the nations consenting to the peace and associating themselves for its maintenance." Equal access to trade and raw materials had also featured prominently in the Atlantic Charter that Roosevelt and Churchill had issued in August 1941. At their most benign, free trade policies called for linking states together through commerce and making their economies interdependent, thus, theoretically, reducing the risk of war. Free trade also theoretically reduced the friction caused by the global competition for markets by leveling playing fields. Most American economists argued for free trade as an alternative to the high tariffs and quests for autarky that had greatly exacerbated the effects of the Great Depression.

Critics, and not just those in the Soviet Union, countered that a free trade system would inevitably benefit the one world economy that had grown significantly since the start of the war. American corporations were perfectly positioned to take advantage of free trade conditions, as they had in the 1920s. The end of World War II, however, promised conditions far better, particularly if the European economies could recover enough to provide demand for American goods. American money and free trade policies, the Americans argued, held the key to global recovery from thirty years of war and depression. Without that recovery, most of Truman's team believed, Europe would likely experience conditions conducive to another round of political extremism. But the recovery itself would undoubtedly make the United States even stronger.[30]

None of these issues necessarily meant increased conflict with the Soviet Union. Truman's own inexperience seemed to be the most imposing barrier to progress in relations between the two superpowers. The new president, who by his own admission had little knowledge of foreign affairs, needed to meet the key players and start to shape American policy. He therefore invited Soviet Foreign Minister Vyacheslav Molotov to stop in Washington on his way to San Francisco for the opening of the United Nations Conference on International Organization in late April.

Truman and his advisers disagreed on how best to handle this first meeting with a senior Soviet official. It would be the first conversation of any kind that Truman had ever had with a Russian. Ambassador Harriman, who warned Truman of the possibility of a new "barbarian invasion" from the east in the form of the Soviet Army, urged Truman to confront the difficult and explosive Molotov. The Americans, Harriman argued, had leverage over the Russians, because the Russians would need American money in order to re-build. He worried that the Russians, who believed in "power politics in its crudest and most primitive form," were not living up to their agreements at Yalta. The meeting with Molotov, he argued, provided an opportunity for the new president to get tough and show the Russians that he meant business.[31]

Former ambassador Joseph Davies, who held much more moderate views toward the Russians, urged caution. A harsh first meeting, he warned, might send the wrong signal to the Russians, whose help the United States needed. The Russians, he warned, had the option of dropping out of the United Nations, thus ruining Roosevelt's dream, or "go[ing] it alone" by canceling its international agreements. Neither outcome, he argued, served American interests. Nor did Davies want the new president to get off on the wrong foot with the Russians at such a critical moment. Truman's daughter Margaret, who was twenty-one years old when her father became president, watched as her father struggled to get a handle on his awesome new responsibilities. It was difficult for him, she later said, to reconcile the conflicting advice of hardliners like Harriman and Secretary of the Navy James Forrestal with the softer approach recommended by Davies, Secretary of War Henry Stimson, and Treasury Secretary Henry Morgenthau.[32]

Truman chose the hard line, warning Molotov during an April 23 meeting that Russia's failure to implement the Yalta agreements as the Americans interpreted them would "cast serious doubt upon our unity of purpose in regard to postwar collaboration." Truman interrupted Molotov on at least three occasions when the Russian tried to explain his country's position. The meeting ended with Truman curtly dismissing Molotov, who rose and said to Truman, "I have never been talked to like that in my life." Truman replied, "Carry out your agreements and you won't get talked to like that."[33]

The Americans initially saw the meeting as a great success. Truman bragged to Davies that he had delivered a "one-two, right to the jaw!" The president's advisers thrilled at the president's performance. Leahy marveled at Truman's directness, noting that the president spoke to Molotov "unadorned by the polite verbiage of diplomacy." Charles Bohlen, who had a front-row seat for the show, later recalled "how I enjoyed translating Truman's sentences! They were probably the first sharp words uttered during the war by an American president to a high Soviet official." The difference, Bohlen noted, lay less in the substance than the tone. Roosevelt, he thought, would have conveyed the same message, but in a fashion "more diplomatic and somewhat smoother." Even Harriman, who had urged Truman to stand firm, was "taken aback" by the harshness of the president's tone.[34]

Molotov, too, was taken aback. The Americans had not fully taken into account the context within which the Russian foreign minister would read Truman's directness. To Molotov, the meeting meant that the era of cooperation with the West had ended. As he told both the Americans and Stalin, the "basis of collaboration" between them had been the assumption that "the three governments had dealt as equal partners and there had been no case where one or two of the three had attempted to impose their will on the other." Full cooperation and open dialogue among equals, Molotov warned, "was the only [basis of cooperation] acceptable to the Soviet government."[35]

Valentin Berezhekov, who had accompanied Molotov on the trip to Washington, later recalled the president's behavior as "harsh" and "threatening." Although Molotov had had the diplomatic courtesy not to mention it to Truman, he told Berezhekov that he knew of Truman's June 1941 comment in the *New York Times* in which Truman had said that, "if we see that Germany is winning we ought to help Russia, and if Russia is winning, we ought to help Germany, and that way let them kill as many as possible." This first meeting with Truman therefore confirmed in the minds of the Russian delegates that, in Molotov's formulation, "Roosevelt's policy [had] been abandoned" in favor of a new one that saw the Russians as enemies or rivals rather than partners. American policy, Soviet officials concluded, had changed, and the Russians would need to change with it. For his part, none of the conciliatory words Molotov heard American diplomats use subsequently erased this impression of, in his mind, unwarranted American hostility to an ally.[36]

Predictably enough, the Russians reacted to the Molotov-Truman meeting with actions the Americans read as hostile. Stalin sent Truman a message confirming the Soviet desire to exercise control over postwar Poland, noting icily that the Russians had not interfered with British and American occupation policy in France, Belgium, or Greece. He thus implied that he expected no Western interference in Poland, no matter what the Big Three had agreed to at Yalta. Once in San Francisco, Molotov dug in his heels on Poland, insisting that only the pro-Soviet Lublin delegation could serve as the representatives of the Polish people at the United Nations conference. The Americans and British supported a different group, called the London Poles, but had assumed that the Russians would not introduce the touchy issue at San Francisco. American officials in Soviet-occupied Austria, Bulgaria, and Romania then reported that the Soviets had introduced tough new measures further limiting their freedom of movement. Most days, they could not leave the capital cities where they were stationed without a Soviet escort. Davies responded by urging the president to reconsider his hard line and to arrange a meeting with Stalin to clear the air.[37]

The Soviets were not Truman's only problem. The gaps between American policy and British policy had widened as well. One of the most important involved the placement of British and American troops in liberated Central Europe. At Yalta, the Allies had agreed to occupation zones that placed the cities of Berlin, Prague, and Vienna clearly inside the Soviet zone. Due to the intense nature of the fighting in the east, however, the British and the Americans had the opportunity to push further into the Soviet zone and occupy more territory than they had agreed to at Yalta.

Churchill fully supported plans to move Allied armies further east, hoping at least to use future troop withdrawals out of the Soviet zone as a bargaining chip with Stalin and Molotov. The farther east the Allies had troops at the end of the war, Churchill argued, the more influence they would have in Germany, Austria, Czechoslovakia, Yugoslavia, and elsewhere. About a week before Roosevelt's death, Churchill had sent him a memorandum urging the president to support a renewed Anglo-American push on Berlin in the hopes of capturing it before the Russians did. "If they also take Berlin," Churchill asked in another of his philosophical flourishes, "will not their impression that they have been the overwhelming contributor to the common victory be unduly printed in their minds, and may this not leave them in a mood which will raise grave and formidable difficulties in the future?"[38]

Leaving aside Churchill's astonishing unwillingness to recognize that the Russians surely *were* the overwhelming contributor to the victory over Germany, the Americans had no interest in Churchill's scheme. General Omar Bradley, whose army group would have to do the fighting, estimated that taking Berlin might cost the United States 100,000 casualties, "a pretty stiff price to pay," he judged, "for a prestige objective." General Eisenhower agreed, telling Army Chief of Staff George Marshall in late March that Berlin itself was "no longer a particularly important objective." Especially with a war against Japan still ongoing, Eisenhower opposed risking American lives for a city the Americans would have to return to the Russians in any case if they were to uphold their end of the Yalta accords. Marshall, who certainly had both Roosevelt's and later Truman's ear, agreed with Bradley and Eisenhower.[39]

As it turned out, Bradley had underestimated the price of Berlin. It cost the Russians not 100,000 casualties, but 300,000 casualties. Even the lower estimate, however, had scared Roosevelt enough to dismiss the idea of a drive on Berlin, especially when the War and State Departments could not agree on American policy regarding the German capital. Roosevelt also saw no reason to antagonize the Russians so soon after the Yalta Conference had produced agreement on lines of demarcation in Germany. Nor did he want to force a change in ongoing American military plans in northern Germany, or, in the most horrific of scenarios, risk creating a situation where American and Soviet troops fired on one another, either intentionally or accidentally. Roosevelt had thus responded to one Churchill memorandum on the subject with a curt "I do not get the point."[40]

After Roosevelt's death, Churchill tried to resurrect the scheme with Truman. American troops would then have had a difficult time capturing Berlin, but other key objectives lay within their reach, and the American commander in the area, General George S. Patton, seemed willing enough to try to capture them. Still, Truman refused even to discuss the matter, and his senior military advisers supported him. Truman saw upholding the Yalta agreements as far more important than pushing east to capture objectives of dubious strategic importance. The British reacted with alarm. Churchill wrote to Truman: "I view, with profound misgivings, the retreat of the American Army to our own line of occupation in the central sector, thus bringing Soviet power into the heart of Western Europe and the descent of an iron curtain between us and anything to the Eastward. I hoped that this retreat, if it has to be made, would be accompanied by the settlement of many great things which would be the true foundation of world peace."[41]

More alarmingly, the British learned of plans for US troop withdrawals from Europe to Asia not through official channels but from the newspapers. The withdrawals appeared to be significantly larger than the Americans had suggested they would be in recent staff talks. Anthony Eden complained to Lord Halifax, after reading a report in his morning newspaper of large US troop withdrawals to Asia scheduled to begin in early summer, "What are we to do? Great pressure will soon be put on us to demobilize partially. In a very short time our armies will have melted, but the Russians may remain with hundreds of divisions in possession of Europe from Lübeck to Trieste." He also noted the departure of half of the US Air Force for the Pacific as well as an announcement by the Canadian government to bring its troops home at the earliest possible date.[42]

The Americans refused to budge no matter what arguments the British used. Truman in particular did not want to be the first leader publicly accused of violating either the letter or the spirit of Yalta. American generals also questioned British motives, suspecting them of wanting to use US troops to extend British influence into Central Europe and the Balkans, where the British had a particular interest in the future of Greece. For this reason, Leahy had blocked a British proposal for a joint Anglo-American operation in Syria. These disagreements reveal not only the divergence of American thinking from British thinking, but also the consistency in American policy from the Roosevelt administration to the Truman administration, as well as the nature of American goals heading into the Potsdam Conference.[43]

Truman knew, however, that in one critical, top-secret respect, his position differed from Roosevelt's at Yalta, and certainly from Wilson's at Paris. Of the advisers who went to Potsdam, only Byrnes, Leahy, and Stimson knew as much about the secret Manhattan Project as Truman now did. Truman had written in his diary about a month before he left for Potsdam that he had experienced "some very hectic days." A small number of scientists and select senior military officials had briefed him on a weapon that could cause damage "beyond imagination." Truman, at long last, knew the details of the S-1 project he had uncovered as a senator two years earlier. In the weeks leading up to the Potsdam Conference, Truman and the slowly growing group of officials who were in the know would wonder not only if the atomic bomb would work, but also what they might do with it if it did.

3

May Days

THE VIEWS OF THE three victorious Allies diverged even further in the days following the German surrender. Churchill and the British continued to push the Americans to maintain their troops in place in Europe rather than retreat back to the lines agreed to at Yalta. To withdraw would mean giving back to the Russians thousands of square miles of territory that the Western Allies now held, most of it in Germany, Austria, and Czechoslovakia between the agreed dividing line and the Elbe River. Churchill saw no reason to give that land back voluntarily, especially since so much of it held strategic value. In a May 11, 1945, letter to President Truman, Churchill argued passionately that a decision to withdraw British and American forces to the agreed lines would "be one of the most melancholy in history" and "an event in the history of Europe to which there has been no parallel and which has not been faced by the Allies in their long and hazardous struggle." In Churchill's mind, the issue of the troop withdrawals represented his country's single most powerful "bargaining counter," but he needed American help to use it.[1]

The debate over the placement of Allied troops shows the differing views of the postwar world in London and Washington as well as the way in which power had tilted toward the latter. The Americans continued their vigorous opposition to keeping troops on the line of the Elbe. American diplomats did not understand how the

United States could possibly argue one day for keeping their troops in places not agreed to at Yalta, then accuse the Russians the next day of not themselves honoring the Yalta agreements. General Eisenhower agreed with the State Department's position, writing that "to start off our first direct association with Russia on the basis of refusing to carry out an agreement in which the good faith of our government was involved would wreck the whole co-operative attempt [with Russia] at its very beginning." The American officials also pointed out that at least so far, the Russians had upheld their side of the bargain by not getting involved in the civil war brewing in Greece. Continued good relations with Russia struck many Americans as being just as important as good relations with the British, and perhaps even more important.[2]

Still, the more the United States opposed the idea of keeping troops outside the Yalta agreement line, the more Churchill dug in his heels. He argued for the line of the Elbe on historical grounds, moral grounds, and economic grounds. His arguments became so emotional and so inconsistent that Admiral Leahy wondered if "the great Englishman was not in vigorous health" to make such a fuss when he was "plainly wrong . . . on this matter."[3]

Churchill was not the only British leader calling for the Allies to keep troops in Eastern Europe. Foreign Minister Anthony Eden thought the issue of "a settlement with Russia before our strength has gone" seemed to "dwarf all others," and he wondered openly whether the issue would open another "period of appeasement" that would, like the last one, lead not to peace but to world war. Moving the troops back to the lines agreed to at Yalta, the British argued, threatened to put the Russians that much closer to the heart of Western Europe. Moreover, if the United States could not guarantee the security of Europe—and Russia seemed to Eden to threaten that security—then British strategy would have to depend on a new alliance with France, even though, as he saw it, France was "weak and difficult to deal with." Thus, the placement of Western military forces as far east as possible seemed to him a reasonable and rational response, regardless of what the great powers had agreed to do at Yalta.[4]

Eventually, Churchill and Eden ran out of arguments, no matter how strongly they believed the Americans did not understand the seriousness of the situation. To General Lionel "Pug" Ismay, Churchill complained that his American allies failed to see how the withdrawal could turn into "a fateful milestone for mankind." As he later did at Potsdam, he yelled, cajoled, and made emotional appeals, but eventually saw that he had to yield. After the Americans told him that they would not support a British plan to drive onto and hold Vienna (part of the Russian zone agreed to at Yalta), Churchill noted that "this struck a knell in my very breast, but I had no choice but to submit."[5]

Churchill tried other tactics to cement the United States to Great Britain. He proposed a scheme to Truman whereby the American and British air forces would share reciprocal basing rights. Truman turned him down, leaving Churchill to note that trying to interest the United States in such projects was like proposing marriage to a woman who would "always be a sister to him."[6]

Churchill thought he might do better if he could meet with Truman and Stalin and present his country's views in person. Hoping to use his powers of persuasion, in May he proposed a Big Three conference as early as possible, preferably in late June. He argued that he needed to finish the conference before the British parliamentary election on July 5. But the logic failed to carry the Americans, who wanted to postpone the conference into July or even August, both to give Truman more time to prepare and, possibly, to give the Manhattan Project scientists in New Mexico a chance to finish their work. Churchill's desires for an early conference centered on his belief that time favored the Russians as the Americans demobilized their army or shifted it to Asia. Shortly after receiving Churchill's request for a June meeting, Truman countered with July 15, disappointing the prime minister yet again.[7]

The flirtation, the courtship, and the jilted love continued, with the British trying to rekindle the romance despite not having the money for flowers or wine. When their advances failed to have the desired effect, they often acted hurt and disappointed, hoping to woo the Americans back with any tactic, even guilt. As plans for the

Big Three meeting began to take shape, Churchill wrote to Truman, in an almost pitiable missive, "I see reports in the papers that you propose to stop in Paris and see [French General and President of the Provisional Republic] General [Charles] de Gaulle before coming on to the conference at Berlin. President Roosevelt promised me on several occasions that he would not visit France before he visited Britain. I am sure that you will bear this in mind in any decision you may take." In fact, Truman had no intention of visiting France, but he did meet with the French ambassador without informing the British; reports of that meeting further upset Churchill. Truman did leave open with Churchill the possibility of visiting London after the conclusion of the Potsdam Conference, but soon after the conference began, an aide told Truman's head speechwriter not to worry about writing speeches for the trip, because the president had no intention of making it.[8]

Truman's accession to the White House left joint Anglo-American policy toward the Soviet Union in a state of flux. Churchill had urged a stronger line against the Russians with Roosevelt in his last days, but the president had sent back mixed messages. In his final message, sent from Warm Springs, Georgia, just one hour before he died, Roosevelt had told Churchill: "I would minimize the general Soviet problem as much as possible because these problems, in one form or another, seem to arise every day and most of them straighten out." But in the same message Roosevelt also said: "We must be firm, however, and our course thus far is correct." Churchill could be forgiven for wondering exactly what that course involved, and whether Truman knew the contents of Roosevelt's mind any better than Churchill himself did. Furthermore, no one in London knew whether Truman would continue to have a harsher policy toward Russia, as indicated by the meeting with Molotov, or begin to listen to his more conciliatory advisers, such as Joseph Davies.[9]

Exaggerating the Russian menace served as another ploy on Churchill's part as he tried to draw the Americans closer to the British viewpoint. Churchill's anti-Russian rants grew much worse after Roosevelt's death, and worse still after the German surrender. This harsher line served both a domestic and an international function.

Overseas, he hoped to present the Americans with a view of a world fraught with danger that only a continuation of the Anglo-American coalition could prevent. At home, he hoped to keep the minds of British voters off of economic problems and on the global arena, where he had a clear advantage over his rivals.

At Yalta, Churchill had had his suspicions about Russian intentions, but he had kept them largely in check, full in the knowledge that the British needed the Russian Army's help on the battlefield to tie down German units in the east, while the British and Americans advanced in the west. At that point, he had also been, in the recollections of one British diplomat, buoyed by "drinking buckets of Caucasian champagne which would undermine the health of any ordinary man," and this helped him to remain lively and in good spirits in Russian company. In the weeks following Yalta, Churchill continued to speak highly of Stalin personally; to Eden's dismay, he put great faith in his ability to forge an understanding with the Russian leader notwithstanding the wide gulf between British and Soviet visions of the postwar world. The differences between British and Soviet views on Poland alone, Eden believed, might be enough to sink Anglo-Soviet postwar relations, especially if the United States did not see the world as the British did.[10]

By May, with the war in Europe over and an election approaching, Churchill had grown much more morose and pessimistic about the future of Anglo-Russian relations. His drinking, always an issue of concern, had markedly increased, and this had begun to worry many of those around him. He also seemed subject to more violent mood swings. These conditions may have affected his temper when he met with senior Soviet officials. On May 18, he harangued the Soviet ambassador, Fedor T. Gusev, about Soviet policy in Poland, Vienna, Prague, and Trieste, Italy, in such undiplomatic language that Gusev felt compelled to write a complaint to Moscow. Churchill, he said, had been full of "threats and blackmail." He also suspected that Churchill lay behind the increasingly anti-Soviet tone in the British press. "We should recognize that we are dealing with an adventurer who is in his element at war," Gusev wrote in a missive to Molotov that contained more than a grain of truth. Gusev also reported his concern that Churchill was meeting more often with military officials, such as General Eisenhower and British Field Marshal Bernard Montgomery, than he was with diplomats, even now that the fighting had ended, raising Soviet suspicions that perhaps the prime minister did not yet see the war in Europe as over.[11]

Churchill went on a similar rant to President Truman's envoy Joseph Davies during the latter's visit to Britain in June on the president's behalf. He told Davies, formerly the American ambassador to the Soviet Union, that the only hope for Europe was for the United Nations to serve as a "united front" led by the United States and Great Britain, exactly the sort of scheme Davies knew that the Soviets most feared. Churchill railed with such ferocity against the Soviet Union that Davies asked him if he "was now willing to declare to the world that he and Britain had made a mistake in not supporting Hitler, and had bet on the wrong horse." Churchill, Davies reported, seemed "tired, nervous, and obviously working under great stress." Still, Churchill hoped that Davies would impress upon Truman that the United States and Great Britain shared a common interest in standing up to the Soviets at the upcoming conference at Potsdam. "It would fall to a very few men," he told Davies, "to decide in the next few weeks the kind of life that would confront several generations to come."[12]

A final meeting between Davies and Churchill, held at Chequers, the prime minister's country house, brought matters to a head. Davies informed Churchill that Truman might want to meet alone with Stalin at Potsdam before meeting with Churchill in order to clear the air about the confrontation with Molotov in April. The news sent Churchill off on two rants. In the first he used "his brilliant vocabulary" to express his anger at the mere thought of any meeting between Truman and Stalin happening without him being present. He accused Davies and Truman of trying to "pull a deal" with the Russians at British expense. He later wrote to Truman saying, "I should not be prepared to attend a meeting which was a continuation of a conference between you and Marshal Stalin."[13]

Churchill then began another anti-Soviet rant that left Davies puzzled and angry. "During his castigation of our Russian ally,"

Davies later recalled, "I thought I was listening to Goebbels, Goering, and Hitler." As he had done a few days earlier in London, Davies challenged Churchill to defend his statements, and Churchill calmed down. But the damage had been done. Eden already despised Davies for his pro-Russian sentiments. After the meeting at Chequers, the ill feeling spread to Churchill, who privately called Davies "a vain amateur." About the same time, Truman was complaining that Churchill gave him as many problems as Stalin did.[14]

Notably, Davies also concluded that the problems between Churchill and Stalin had far less to do with geopolitics or personality than with their respective roles after World War I. Davies, who had met often with Stalin during World War II, thought the Russians still held a grudge against Churchill for his early anti-Soviet policies and his advocacy of an Allied intervention in northern Russia on the czarist side during the Russian Civil War. Britain, Davies also concluded, needed the United States far more than the United States needed Britain. If necessary, he argued, the United States could, and perhaps should, ignore British wishes in the hopes of a rapprochement with the Russians that could avoid either a showdown between the superpowers or "an armaments race that would probably bankrupt us." If Churchill had hoped to impress upon Davies the importance of future Anglo-American cooperation, he appears to have left the exact opposite impression.[15]

As Britain and the United States drifted further apart, the British began to reconsider their bargaining position for the upcoming conference. Eden revealed the evolution of his thinking in a memorandum to Churchill outlining the "cards we hold for a general negotiation with the Russians." Although he did not say it outright, Eden let it be known that he did not like the look of his hand. He saw just four potential trump cards, the first of which, an extension of financial credits to the Soviet Union, the British could not effect by themselves, because Britain, too, needed money. The Russians, he admitted to Churchill, "would not be interested in credits from us of a size that we could afford to give." Only the Americans could provide reconstruction funds on the enormous level that the Soviet Union needed.

The other three cards in the British hand would hardly take the trick. Britain had possession of most of the German merchant fleet, and 70 percent of Germany's steelmaking capability sat in the British zone of occupation, but the recent agreements on a joint occupation policy promised that economic assets would be more or less shared. As to the merchant fleet, the Russians might like to have part of it, but German merchant ships hardly formed the core of Russian maritime strategy, except insofar as they would help Russia move military assets from Europe to Asia for the final fight against Japan. The second card, therefore, was hardly more powerful than the first.

That left just two cards in the hand, both of them relatively weak. For some reason, Eden thought that the Russians might want the secrets in the Nazi archives that the British had captured badly enough to barter for them. He could not have held out much hope on that score, given that the Russians had captured Berlin, and with it, presumably the most valuable archives. The Russians also had control of most of the German scientific assets in the Berlin area, most notably the Kaiser Wilhelm Institute in the Berlin suburb of Dalhem. Finally, Eden told Churchill, the British could use the United Nations to try to block any revision of the diplomatic agreements that governed the Dardanelles, a strait in northwestern Turkey that the Russians had long seen as vital to their strategic interests. Next to the size of the Russian Army and the likelihood that it would remain mobilized, the British hand could hardly have intimidated Stalin.[16]

Eden appreciated the need for American support, but he had far less faith than Churchill did in American abilities. He had no doubts about America's military prowess in the hands of men like Dwight Eisenhower and George Marshall, but, like Churchill, he knew that that prowess would melt away as the Americans moved the bulk of their forces out of Europe, leaving power mostly in the hands of the diplomats. Eden had far less respect for American statesmen, whom he called "deplorably weak," especially on sensitive matters like Turkey and Poland, where American understandings were thin. To many British and American observers, the smartest and most experienced American diplomats were either now gone, like William Bullitt and Sumner Welles, or not in Truman's inner circle, like Charles

Bohlen and Sovietologist George Kennan. Among those who came to Potsdam, few impressed Eden.[17]

PROBLEMS CONTINUED TO GROW between the United States and the Soviet Union as well. Soviet ideas about the West remained rooted in traditional Russian fears and suspicions, which were now dramatically amplified by the traumatic experiences of two world wars. As Stalin told the Yugoslav partisan Milovan Djilas in 1944, "perhaps you think that just because we are allies of the English that we have forgotten who they are and who Churchill is. They find nothing sweeter than to trick their allies. During the First World War they constantly tricked the Russians and the French." Events during the Second World War such as the long Anglo-American delay in creating a second front in France, and Western unwillingness to pressure Franco's Spain, which sent 47,000 men to the Russian front as part of the German Army, only increased Russian suspicions.[18]

Suspicion turned to something bordering on paranoia after Roosevelt's death. Stalin had deeply respected Roosevelt; the president's death left him, in the words of former ambassador Joseph Davies, who delivered the news to Stalin, "more disturbed than I had ever seen him." The Russians had also relied on Roosevelt to curb some of Churchill's wilder ideas, such as an Anglo-American invasion of the Balkans. Harry Truman was virtually unknown in Russia outside of his well-publicized 1941 comments from the *New York Times*.

Roosevelt's death, and a series of controversies that quickly followed, increased the Soviet Union's sense of uncertainty. Shortly after the German surrender in May, the bombastic American general George Patton made headlines by telling an undersecretary of war, in full view of journalists, that the United States should begin preparations for a war with Russia. He urged as a first step that the United States should not demobilize its army or shift too many men to the Pacific: "Let's keep our boots polished, bayonets sharpened, and present a picture of force and strength to these people. This is the only language they understand and respect. If you fail to do this, then I would like to say to you that we have a victory over the Germans and have disarmed them but have lost the war." Statements like these not only failed to grasp the realities of the geopolitical situation but also reinforced the Russian dread of imminent betrayal or another invasion of Russian soil by the West, as had happened at the end of the previous world war.[19]

American diplomats tried to assuage Russian fears by dismissing comments by men like Patton as rash and unrepresentative of official opinion, but the actions of the US government itself fed Russian paranoia. Around the time of Roosevelt's death, Soviet intelligence officers had learned of meetings in Bern, Switzerland, between American spymaster Allen Dulles and a senior general in the Nazi paramilitary group the SS to discuss surrender terms. Stalin instinctively suspected a double-cross by the United States. The meetings had in fact taken place with the support of the State Department and the knowledge of Roosevelt and Churchill. They fell apart when the Allies held to their demands for an unconditional surrender of all German forces, a condition agreed to at the Casablanca conference of January 1943, in part to convince the Russians that the Allies would not deal separately with the Germans. Churchill had nevertheless supported the Bern meetings and wanted to explore the option of local German surrenders to British and American forces. Truman's team, however, had insisted on the Americans holding to their position of unconditional surrender, even if it might make the Germans fight on to the bitter end.[20]

The Bern incident infuriated Soviet officials. Soviet Foreign Minister Vyacheslav Molotov called the discussions "utterly incomprehensible" and accused the Americans of hatching a plot with the German general Albert Kesselring whereby the Germans would stop fighting Allied armies in Italy so that the Allied forces fighting there could redeploy to block Soviet advances in Germany itself. Stalin raged at Joseph Davies, saying that if the Americans and the British "did not wish to deal on a friendly basis, the Soviet Union was strong enough to look after itself."[21]

What the Americans saw as a simple misunderstanding, the Russians, looking through the prism of 1918–1919, read as evidence of impending betrayal. Confusion and misunderstandings escalated, with Stalin directly accusing the United States of offering to stop its advance in Italy in order to allow the Germans to shift three of their divisions to the Berlin area to halt Russian progress there. To the Russians, the Bern meetings symbolized all of the treachery they had long suspected from the West. In the final days of his life, Roosevelt, angry at Russian accusations of his government's betrayal of its Casablanca promises, did his best to dissipate Russian fears, but he found it hard to understand why Stalin needed those reassurances at all. Stalin remained convinced that the West had betrayed Russia yet again. As he told Harry Hopkins, the incident made it seem "as though the Americans were saying that the Russians were no longer needed." That the betrayal seemed to come from a man Stalin had trusted only made the situation that much more disconcerting. Now he would have to deal with a man in whom he had far less trust, making the future all that much less clear.[22]

In part because of growing Anglo-American strategic disagreement, Western leaders still had not agreed on how to deal with Stalin and the Russians. Although the Western leaders had no illusions about Stalin's brutality, none of them mentioned details on that topic in their private or public correspondence in the weeks before Potsdam. Even the hardliners, who could have used that information to make a case for standing firm against the Russians, failed to do so. The information may have been such common knowledge that mentioning it seemed unnecessary. More likely, however, Western leaders might still have been dealing with the cognitive dissonance it must have entailed to rely so heavily on one murderous dictator in order to defeat another murderous dictator. Newspaper articles and propaganda in both the United States and Great Britain still routinely referred to Stalin as "Uncle Joe"; in the glow of the victory in Europe, the Russians received far more positive press in the West than negative press. Charles Bohlen later noted that Western journalists remained enthralled by the Soviets and their astounding sacrifices on the way to victory. Reporters did not want to hear, let alone print, the negative impressions that Bohlen and others had developed about the Soviets and their intentions for the postwar world.[23]

While not forgetting the sins of his past, Western leaders did still have a mostly positive view of Stalin and the Russians more generally. In late 1944, Churchill had expressed his optimism for the future by saying about Stalin, "I like him the more I see him." Churchill concluded that if he could have dinner with Stalin once a week, "there would be no trouble at all." The prime minister had come a long way from 1941, when he had made his famous defense of helping the Russians in their war with Germany: "If Hitler invaded hell," he had said then, "I would make at least a favorable reference to the devil in the House of Commons." By February 1945 he had changed his tune, saying, "Poor Neville Chamberlain believed he could trust Hitler. He was wrong. But I don't think I am wrong about Stalin."[24]

Had Churchill known how much Stalin despised and belittled him, Churchill might well have felt differently, but as late as May he remained optimistic about his ability to negotiate directly with Stalin. For his part, Stalin spoke positively about Churchill when it suited his interests, but he deeply mistrusted Churchill as the consummate capitalist and imperialist. He criticized Churchill as a petty thief and relished reports about Churchill's weaknesses, such as one relayed to him by veteran Soviet diplomat Andrei Gromyko that described Churchill being so enthralled with Russia's female security guards in their "marvelous uniforms" at Yalta that he dropped cigar ash all over his suit. More importantly, Stalin saw Churchill and the entire British delegation as representatives of a formerly great power on the path of inevitable decline.[25]

American leaders shared Churchill's double vision when it came to Stalin. Just after the Yalta Conference, Harriman, who counted himself among the hardliners, described Stalin as "better informed than Roosevelt, more realistic than Churchill, and in some ways the most effective of the war leaders. At the same time, he was, of course, a murderous tyrant." As this offhand comment suggests, Harriman had a grudging admiration for Stalin while acknowledging the brutality of his reign. Truman's senior aides were often even more effusive. James Byrnes, the new secretary of state, said just before Potsdam, "The truth is he is a very likeable person." More amazingly, Davies remarked in 1938 that "a child would like to sit on his lap and a dog would sidle up to him."[26]

Patton's impolitic outburst at the end of the war notwithstanding, American military men generally believed that they could work with the Russians in developing a joint occupation plan for postwar Germany. Generals Dwight Eisenhower and Lucius Clay both spoke in positive terms about the level of cooperation between American and Russian forces after their well-publicized handshake on the Elbe River in April. Clay and his Soviet counterpart, Marshal Georgi Zhukov, had established a good working relationship, and they reached agreement on most points fairly quickly. Working throughout May and June, they had agreed on the framework of a four-power occupation with joint policies on the press, education, and coal distribution. Command of the occupation, with France added as the fourth power, would rotate every two weeks. Each power would maintain law and order in its own zone, but remain in constant consultation with the others. The Soviets had even offered the Americans the use of two airfields in their sector, although they did limit the Americans to just one railway into the city. No one at the time thought that the arrangement might lead to a permanent division of Germany into two states.[27]

Most senior American officers had a healthy respect for the Red Army and what it had accomplished, even if they remained suspicious about Soviet intentions in the postwar period. When Lucius Clay's deputy, Brigadier General John Whitelaw, overheard two American officers belittle the Red Army as "stinking Cossacks," he shot back, "Those same stinking Cossacks with all of their poor staff work made the teeth of the Wehrmacht rattle when we were playing around in Tennessee with wooden weapons." More senior officers, such as Eisenhower and Marshall, knew how powerful the Red Army was and how much the Americans might need that power in the Far East, even if the atomic bomb experiment worked. For that reason, Marshall had judged Truman's tough stance against Molotov in the White House in April unwise. Disagreements with the Soviets, he concluded, did not justify underestimating them or needlessly provoking them.[28]

The most pessimistic voices came from Americans on the periphery of power, but, tellingly, also from some of the men who had the most experience working closely with the Russians. From the American embassy in Moscow, George Kennan had presciently warned that the Russians would hold out the lure of cooperation at the upcoming conference, offering smiles and lavish hospitality, but in the end they would not yield an inch on any issue of substance. They would, however, cry foul if the Americans or British did not honor their commitments in full. Kennan warned that American politicians would not be able to win the Russians over with "games of golf or invitations to dinner," as they did with fellow American politicians and businessmen. Ambassador Harriman warned both Roosevelt and Truman that, with the Russians, "you have to buy the same horse twice," because the terms of the deal always changed at the last minute.[29]

Similarly, presidential adviser and interpreter Charles Bohlen, who had tried in vain to warn Roosevelt about the difficulty of negotiating with the Russians, tried to do his best to temper the enthusiasm of Truman, Eisenhower, and others. Bohlen told Lucius Clay that Clay's confidence in the Russians would fade, and that he would change his tune on the Soviets within a year of working with them. Although Bohlen did not completely agree with Kennan on the best way for the United States to deal with the Russians, the two friends did share a generally negative view of the Russians and their leadership. "Anyone who started with too many illusions about the Soviets," Bohlen warned Clay, "came out totally disillusioned."[30]

Mistrust built, both as a result of differing goals and because of the confused nature of those chaotic weeks of transition in late April and early May. On May 11, Ambassador Harriman convinced Truman, who had been in office for less than a month, to cancel American Lend-Lease aid to the Soviets. Legally, Harriman had a solid case. With the end of the war in Europe three days earlier, the Soviets could no longer make use of aid meant specifically for prosecuting the war against Germany. He and Leahy convinced Truman that the move would put more pressure on the Soviets to join the war against Japan as quickly as possible. Once the Soviets were legally at war again, Lend-Lease supplies could flow as they had before. Harriman, who had long said that the United States should demand concrete concessions from the Soviets in exchange for Lend-Lease aid, presented the case to Truman so convincingly that the new president signed the order without reading it. The order even called for ships then at sea to return to American ports.[31]

Harriman rather tactlessly failed to inform the Russians of the change in American policy. They reacted with confusion and anger when the ships failed to arrive as scheduled. Stalin called the decision "scornful and abrupt," then issued a warning. If the Americans intended to threaten or soften up the Russians by moves such as these, they were making "a fundamental mistake" that put future great-power cooperation at risk. For his part, Stalin favored the Soviets entering the war against Japan, but he resented the use of Lend-Lease to extort them into doing it on an exclusively American timeline.[32]

Joseph Davies, who was far more sympathetic to the Russian position than Harriman, convinced Truman that he had made a serious mistake and talked him into rescinding the order. He argued that taking too strong a position against the Russians at this point put at risk any future Russian cooperation on larger issues, such as Poland and reparations for Germany. The Soviet Union might also withdraw from the United Nations, he argued, using as a pretense one of the many issues of disagreement in the details of the organization that had arisen in San Francisco. Molotov had already cried foul over American support for charter membership for the "fascist" government in Argentina. Hardliners in both Washington and London blasted Davies, whose pro-Russian attitudes had already made him a clear target. Eden called Davies "a born appeaser" for his advice to Truman, saying that Davies "would gladly give up all Europe, except perhaps us, so that America might not be embroiled" in a future European war. Davies, in his view, displayed "all the errors of Neville Chamberlain substituting Russia for Germany."[33]

Many American advisers agreed, citing Davies's bestselling 1941 book *Mission to Moscow* (which was made into a movie starring Walter Huston two years later) as proof of Davies's pro-Soviet attitudes. Still, Truman saw the wisdom of toning down American rhetoric until he had a chance to divine Russian intentions in person at the upcoming Big Three meeting. Lend-Lease supplies soon resumed, and Truman sent a conciliatory note to Stalin through Harriman. The administration publicly blamed the Lend-Lease disruption on a bureaucratic misunderstanding, but that explanation failed to convince the Russians, who saw in the move further proof that the Americans did not see them as future partners.

American attitudes toward the Soviets by late May thus spanned a range from attraction to revulsion, with most of the senior leaders still generally optimistic about their future dealings with the Soviet Union. Harry Hopkins had noted that after Yalta, "there wasn't any doubt in the minds of the President [Roosevelt] or any of us that we could live with them and get along with them peacefully for as far into the future as any of us could imagine." Events like the tumultuous Truman-Molotov meeting, the Bern incident, and the cancellation of Lend-Lease made much more of an impression on the Russians than they did on the new American team. Most of the Americans still had faith that they could smooth over the bumps once they sat across a table from their Russian counterparts.

RUSSIA'S LEADERS WERE far more pessimistic about the future and not at all as impressed with the Americans, especially their new president. Stalin initially saw Truman as "vulgar" and, perhaps informed of Truman's 1941 statement to the *New York Times*, suspected him of a strong anti-Soviet bias. In sharp contrast to Roosevelt, Truman, he thought, was "neither educated nor clever." Molotov agreed, belittling the new president as "far from having Roosevelt's intellect," although his impressions might well have been conditioned by the testy exchange in Washington.[34]

Meeting in person, some thought, could help to smooth all of these rough edges. Stalin had first indicated his support for a three-power conference in a May 23 message to Churchill that followed a tense exchange on the future of Poland. In one of those messages, Churchill had written a bit presumptuously to "my friend Stalin" that a meeting could help the leaders of "the English-speaking democracies" explain to the Russians "how they look at life." The wording, of course, was intended to present to Stalin the picture of perfect Anglo-American unity toward the future, not just of Poland, but of the world. Churchill strongly advocated a meeting of the Big Three as early as possible.[35]

Some Americans, mostly the hardliners, wanted to make the Russians, as Charles Bohlen recalled, "come over to meet us" for the first major postwar conference. Having ventured to Tehran and Yalta to meet with Stalin, they wanted the next meeting to take place in Washington, or, as Truman floated as a compromise, Alaska. But Stalin instead insisted on meeting somewhere in the area of Berlin, the German capital, which his armies had captured at great human cost. In late May, he reminded presidential adviser Harry Hopkins that at the end of the Yalta Conference, he and Roosevelt had toasted the idea of a major postwar peace conference in Berlin itself. Hopkins and Roosevelt had discussed the idea further on their flight back from Yalta. A conference in Berlin would therefore seem to fulfill one of the dead president's final wishes.[36]

A meeting in the Berlin area carried political meaning as well. Not only would it drive home to the Germans the cold reality of their defeat, but it would underscore the magnitude of the Soviet contribution to that defeat. Remembering German denial at the end of the last world war, the great powers wanted to leave no doubt in the minds of German citizens that they had lost the war—and not only that they had lost, but also that their enemies had completely vanquished them. For this reason, the Soviets later built two enormous and conspicuous war memorials in Berlin, one of them just outside the famous Brandenburg Gate, well within sight of the Reichstag. This time, no future German leader would do what Friedrich Ebert had done in December 1918, when he had welcomed home German soldiers from the western front by telling them that they had returned "undefeated on the field of battle." Nor would German leaders looking for revenge be able to perpetuate a "stab in the back myth" to fuel another German military revival. The Germans of 1945—above all, those in the capital—would know the totality of their defeat, which would be symbolized by their former enemies determining Germany's future not in a luxurious Paris or a distant Alaska, but in an occupied and shattered Berlin.[37]

Not coincidentally, a great-power conference in Berlin would also force Churchill and Truman to see the ruins of the city and of Germany more generally with their own eyes. President Wilson had stubbornly refused to spend much time in the towns and cities that the Germans had destroyed in Belgium and France in World War I, for fear that the sites would make his heart grow hard. Wilson wanted his principles, especially his quest for a "peace without victory," to remain uncorrupted. He had therefore strenuously resisted French and British pleas that he tour the front. Stalin did not want a repeat of that scenario. He wanted to be sure that Truman acknowledged the destruction the war had caused.

The Russians had every reason to think that such a tour might have a beneficial effect on the new American president, just as it had had on Roosevelt several months earlier in the Crimea. On seeing the damage in and around Yalta, Roosevelt had bitterly remarked that seeing Russia with his own eyes made him "more bloodthirsty in regard to the Germans." Such un-Wilsonian words must have been music to Russian ears. "I had read about Warsaw and Lidice and Rotterdam and Coventry," the president had noted. "But I saw Sevastopol and Yalta. And I know that there is not room enough on earth for both German militarism and Christian decency." Kathleen Harriman Mortimer, the perceptive and intelligent daughter of the American ambassador to the Soviet Union, remarked after the trip from Moscow to Yalta, "We saw enough war damage to last me a lifetime. My God, but this country has a job on its hands just cleaning up." Bringing the Big Three conference to Berlin would reinforce the brutality of the war to the new American leadership and boost Russian demands for heavy reparations and a brutal postwar treatment of Germany.[38]

Joseph Stalin, the Soviet Union's vaunted "Man of Steel," also hated to fly. He hated to travel for any reason, but he especially hated airplanes. He had flown just once, in 1943 to attend the Tehran conference. The turbulence en route to Tehran had been so rough that the passengers had spent most of the flight holding onto their arm rests for dear life. Stalin complained for a week afterward of ringing in his ear. Stories soon spread throughout the West that Stalin didn't fly because he didn't trust his own pilots, his paranoia for security having overcome his need to travel. Legend had it that he would assemble three airplanes on an airfield, then either select the most trustworthy aircrew or, if he did not like the looks of any of them, cancel the trip. The truth was far simpler: his first flight had terrified him so much that he had sworn never to get into an airplane again.[39]

Having survived a rise to power in an era marked by political assassination, Stalin had a nearly maniacal obsession about his own personal safety. When it came time to find a location for the next Big Three meeting, Stalin again expressed his desire that it be within the zone the Soviet Union controlled, so that he could travel to it by train. He then ordered new uniforms made to reflect his recent appointment as marshal of the Soviet Union. Stalin would travel to Potsdam, but he intended to do so as a conqueror.

On May 29, Churchill replied favorably to Stalin's suggestion of a meeting in "what is left of Berlin" as soon as it could be arranged, perhaps in mid-June. Stalin continued to resist suggestions of other meeting places, indicating to Churchill his exclusive preference for Berlin, which Churchill had little choice but to accept. Churchill's proposed timing did not suit Truman, who demanded that the conference not begin before mid-July. As a consequence, Stalin selected the location of the conference, and Truman selected its timing. All that fell to Churchill was to give the conference its code name, Terminal, an indication of his hopes that the conference would avoid the problems of 1919 and set the conditions for stability that both Britain and the world so badly needed. Fittingly, the White House's official historical reports for the Potsdam Conference noted that Truman and Leahy accepted Churchill's choice of Terminal as the codename "just to please Churchill's ego." The other main decisions regarding the conference were made in Washington and Moscow.[40]

4

"Our Troubles Might Not Yet Be Over"

WITH THE CONFERENCE'S PLACE and date set, the great powers began making their final assessments of their situations and setting their strategies. For the second time in as many generations, British leaders faced the immense task of making peace after the conclusion of a destructive world war. In 1945, as in 1919, they believed that Britain had entered a war in order to prevent an aggressive continental power from dominating Europe; they also believed that their nation's sacrifices had destroyed a regime that had committed terrible crimes against civilians. In both cases the hegemon had been the same country, Germany, meaning that the British would have to find a way, in concert with their allies, to solve the German problem once and for all. If they did not, a third bloody war on the European continent might result.

Also as in 1919, British strategists worried that one of their wartime allies, in this case Russia instead of France, might emerge from the war in too strong a position, which could lead to a future imbalance of power. In just the few short weeks since Yalta, the Russian position had grown far stronger. Such an imbalance on the continent, the British feared, could lead to a new continental war. The peace process in 1945 would therefore require Britain to pursue policies that would contain the power of both Germany and Russia, even while acknowledging that Britain sat in a potentially weaker relative position than it had in 1919 or 1939.

At the end of World War I, Prime Minister David Lloyd George had to face the reality that although Britain had emerged victorious, it had also ended the war in desperate financial straits. As a member of the winning coalition, it had achieved the negative goal of denying Germany its bid to dominate the European continent, but it had not set conditions necessary for a positive lasting peace; nor had it added anything of real value to Britain, other than some colonial gains in Africa and the mandates in the Middle East. The latter, especially the mandate in Palestine, provided far more headaches than they were worth. As all Britons realized, moreover, none of the gains from 1919 made good even a fraction of British losses from 1914 to 1918.

Now, twenty-six years later, the British faced a similar situation. Once again, they had stopped Germany from dominating Europe, and once again they had defeated a terrible regime that had engaged in horrific practices. As the images coming out of the concentration camps showed, the effort of 1939–1945 had undoubtedly been necessary for the greater good of human civilization. Whether British leaders could redeem their sacrifices in a way that would prevent a third world war remained an open question, especially with the obvious failure of the Paris Peace Conference looming ominously in the shadows.

Little about that conference suggested a way forward for Great Britain. Some of the harshest critics of the Treaty of Versailles were in fact British, and several still held important policy positions in the government in 1945. Most famously, John Maynard Keynes's 1920 bestseller, *The Economic Consequences of the Peace*, blasted the treaty for destabilizing postwar economic structures. David Lloyd George himself criticized the treaty even though he had been one of its chief architects. As the 1920s and 1930s began to show the cracks in the Europe the treaty had made, Britain had faced the challenge of confronting Germany or appeasing it through modifications to the Versailles system. British policymakers had wavered until 1939, when they had made the decision to fight rather than accommodate Germany any longer. Churchill, of course, had led that fight. Now, at the end of the war that he had directed with such energy and dedication, he faced the responsibility of ending it on terms favorable to the British.

Thus British policymakers in 1945 knew that they once again faced the challenge of redeeming the sacrifices of their people. Their situation resembled that of 1919, but in some ways British policymakers had even fewer options. Britain in 1945 emerged from war weaker in a financial sense, with far more infrastructure damaged or destroyed, and, most alarmingly, much more dependent on the strategic goals of a senior partner, in this case the United States. Britain's other strategic partner from the war, Russia, appeared to many Britons as the next potential rival and European hegemon. Britain, however, had less flexibility in 1945 than it had enjoyed in 1919, even as the challenges seemed greater.[1]

In 1919, the British at least thought they saw some attractive pieces on the global chessboard to take as compensation. The imperial situation at the end of World War II presented far fewer options, in large part because of stiff American resistance to the resumption of the prewar British and French imperial models. Whereas Woodrow Wilson had resisted the expansion of empires on idealistic grounds, Harry Truman and his advisers in 1945 could stop even Britain's reacquisition of its former colonies by cutting off the credits upon which Britain so badly depended.

Even if the Americans did provide some financial support or stood indifferent on the imperial question, the attitude of most of Britain's colonial subjects had changed so radically since 1919 that the British faced local obstacles to imposing the status quo ante. In the Far East, the British faced the enormous task of returning to places where Japanese armies had humiliated them, such as Hong Kong, Burma, and Singapore. The war had also undermined British prestige and power in Egypt, where local leaders, especially in the army, had proven sympathetic to the Germans. This development had complicated Britain's hold on the Suez Canal, one of the most strategic places on the globe for British policymakers.[2]

In India, the British had faced not one, but two wartime movements aimed at forcing Britain out of its longtime colony. India was one of Britain's most vital sources of wealth. Nevertheless, the British had fueled both movements with their brutal wartime treatment of India, especially in the eastern state of Bengal. The more frightening of the two movements, in British eyes—at least during the war years themselves—was Subhas Chandra Bose's Indian National Army and the Azad Hind political movement. With Japanese help, Bose had formed the nucleus of an army out of Indian prisoners of war serving in the British Army who had been captured by the Japanese in Singapore and other locations in the East. Bose hoped to lead that army back to India and get India its independence by force, or at least spark an anti-British uprising. Although his plan failed, Bose remained a key figure, both for the power he held and for the prestige he commanded among Indians. That prestige continued even after his death in a plane crash on August 18, 1945.

India posed a seemingly unresolvable problem for British leaders. Few of them thought that India was ready for independence, or that Britain was in a financial position to let it go. The success of Bose's movement, and the eagerness with which millions of Indians rallied to him, sent a frightening message to British leaders. Wartime Deputy Prime Minister Clement Attlee later recalled that Bose's movement had sent the signal that the entire edifice of British rule in India had suffered "a severe jolt" from which it would likely not ever fully recover. Although Attlee's Labour Party disagreed with the Tories on many domestic issues, their similarities on imperial issues outweighed their differences. On India, Attlee had said in October 1944 that he was "frankly horrified" at the mere thought of giving India to a "brown oligarchy."[3]

Bose's efforts had undermined British prestige and power in India, perhaps irreparably. So, too, had the Quit India movement led by Mohandas Gandhi. Begun in 1942 as a response to Britain's increasingly ruthless handling of wartime India, Quit India, in the eyes of Churchill and other British leaders, had grown into a menace to the health of Britain itself. Churchill saw it as nothing less than a Japanese fifth column working to hand India over to Tokyo at the first opportunity. The British replied with a wave of arrests, including that of Gandhi himself, and the imposition of tougher measures on India that helped to trigger one of the twentieth century's worst famines.[4]

The coming end of the war forced the British to reconsider their policy on India. In June 1945, the British released many of Quit India's leaders from the jails where they had languished for three years. Thousands of Indians, however, remained in jail under wartime emergency acts; they, too, would need to be released upon the end of the war and the concomitant end of martial law. Between 1942 and 1945, the famine and the increased British brutality only raised the level of hostility Indians felt toward Britain. Jawaharlal Nehru and other leaders of the Quit India movement left their jail cells determined to lead strikes, demonstrations, and protests against Britain to end the odious colonial period once and for all. Not all of them had made the commitment to nonviolence that Gandhi had.

Here, too, a ghost of 1919 reemerged. In April of that year, a British Army unit had reacted to a peaceful protest at Jallianwala Bagh (also called Amritsar, and located near the modern India-Pakistan border) with horrific violence. Although the numbers remain disputed, most scholars accept estimates of 400 dead and 1,100 wounded, many of them women and children who had gathered at Jallianwala Bagh for the festival of Vaisakhi. The massacre undermined British control and prestige in India in the years following World War I. Now the Quit India movement and the continued activism of Bose's followers held out the possibility of resistance on a far greater scale. Religious tensions in India and the demands of Muslims for a separate state also presented problems for British strategists as they looked at Britain's global role following World War II.

The British therefore faced an even more unsettled geostrategic environment in 1945 than they had in 1919, and they had fewer resources with which to face it. The permanent loss of Singapore, Egypt, or even parts of India would cause severe, perhaps irreparable, damage to the British economy, as well as to Britain's international standing. On that point both the Conservatives and Labour agreed. Although the world of 1919 had presented challenges, the world of 1945 seemed, if anything, to present even greater uncertainty and the specter of future conflict across the globe.

Thus did General Lionel "Pug" Ismay, one of Britain's senior military leaders, recall the muted response in Britain to the announcement of the German surrender in May: "There was none of the unrestrained enthusiasm which had broken all bounds on November 11, 1918. The general mood seemed to be one of immense relief and infinite gratitude, tempered by the realisation that Japan was still unconquered and the feeling that all our troubles might not yet be over." Lord Ismay reflected the general sense among British leaders at the end of the war that Britain might still have its greatest challenges in front of it. He found Winston Churchill, like most of the rest of the British leadership, "filled with forebodings about the future." Churchill had confided his fears in a morose letter to Franklin Roosevelt sent in January 1945 that read, in part, "The end of this war may prove to be more disappointing than was the last." Foreign Minister Anthony Eden wrote to Churchill just before the Potsdam Conference to share his "gloomy" outlook on the world and Britain's place in it. Eden did not expect that Britain could gain much at Potsdam, given its paucity of resources and the number of demands on those resources. Nor could the British hope for any American aid whatsoever to help them solve their postwar imperial problems, even in areas like Suez, Singapore, and India, which the British saw as strategically vital.[5]

When Harry Truman's envoy Joseph Davies met with Churchill in June 1945, he found the prime minister depressed, nervous, and tired. Churchill ranted against Charles de Gaulle, fretted about problems in the Balkans, and seemed overwhelmed by his lack of power to solve his country's problems. Davies reported that Churchill seemed "bedeviled by the consciousness that his Government no longer occupies its position of power and dominance in the world." Churchill had also come to realize that the differences between British and American postwar goals likely spelled the end of any special relationship between the two countries. That second-class world status might be the price Britain had to pay to win two world wars struck Churchill forcefully. "I could not escape the impression,"

Davies told Truman, "that he was basically more concerned over preserving England's position in Europe than in preserving peace."[6]

Churchill was far from alone in his dark moods. John Maynard Keynes, the chief British economist at the Paris Peace Conference of 1919 and later its most devastating critic, was among the most pessimistic of British officials. Having watched helplessly as the failed financial arrangements of the peace of 1919 slid the world toward depression, he again saw instability coming out of the economic arrangements of 1945. He had reluctantly supported the financial strings that came along with accepting American Lend-Lease aid out of short-term necessity, but he saw those strings as extremely damaging to the long-term health of the British economy. He argued that the United States, although still showing goodwill to the British in general, had used Lend-Lease to "see that the British were as near as possible to bankruptcy before any assistance was given." He did not share the view of some hardliners in London that the Americans sought intentionally to reduce a prewar trade competitor to penury, but he saw better than most officials the cumulative effect of American wartime financial policy on his own country.

Far from being the "most unsordid act" that Churchill had once lauded, Lend-Lease, Keynes believed, was a mechanism that would eventually result in near-complete British dependence on American largesse. He noted that the United States had treated Britain "worse than we have ever ourselves thought it proper to treat the humblest and least responsible Balkan country." The US Treasury Department had tried throughout the war to leverage Lend-Lease aid into control of British monetary reserves, especially the gold that would serve as the basis for US currency, and thus the global trade system. The US State Department had also used monetary policy and Lend-Lease assistance as a crowbar to pry open the "imperial preference system" that had once put American firms at a competitive disadvantage when trading inside the British Empire.[7]

Keynes saw the arrangements at Bretton Woods as another blow to British power. Although he had helped to negotiate the Bretton Woods protocols in 1944, and had agreed to them out of dire necessity, he knew it would require "blind faith" to see them as anything but another step in Britain's increasing dependence on America. He knew that, thereafter, global trade would be conducted in dollars; even trade between two parts of the British Empire would likely use dollars, not sterling. Thus would the City of London's dominance in world financial markets come to a crashing end, as would trade barriers that had kept firms from the United States and other nations out of imperial trade.

At the end of the war, Britain would be, in Keynes's words, "financially at the mercy" of its senior partner. Churchill, too, saw the problem, but given Britain's bankruptcy, British leaders felt they had little choice. Not only did they have to accept whatever conditions the Americans demanded, but they had to do it with a smile in order to ensure future goodwill on any terms the Americans wished to impose. As an exasperated Churchill once said to US Treasury Secretary Henry Morgenthau, when the Americans threatened a reduction in Lend-Lease aid, "What do you want me to do? Sit up on my hind legs and beg like Fala?" The comparison to Roosevelt's faithful Scottish terrier may have hit a bit too close to home, but, as Churchill knew, it was not so far off the mark, either.[8]

Britain's dependence on the United States reduced its strategic options going into the Big Three conference, as its leaders well knew. British statesmen found themselves arguing that the Americans should forgive or refinance British debt because of the sacrifice in blood that the British people had made in the common quest for victory. British leaders a generation earlier had scoffed at the exact same argument when French statesmen had made it in 1919, but now it seemed to be the only argument that the British, in a strikingly similar strategic situation, could possibly make. British statesmen knew that without some level of forgiveness or restructuring of debt, Great Britain's role as a first-class power stood at great risk. Although Churchill had declared in 1942, "I have not become the king's first minister in order to preside over the liquidation of the British Empire," he now faced exactly that possibility.[9]

Failing some help from Washington, Great Britain would emerge from World War II more than $20 billion in debt, a heavy burden for a victorious power. The staggering sum portended a bleak future of belt-tightening austerity and a greatly reduced global role. As Keynes quipped, Britain could not afford to police half the world while remaining deeply in debt to the other half. From a purely financial perspective, he argued, half hypothetically and half hopefully, that the best scenario for Britain involved a quick end to the war with Germany, but a prolongation of the war with Japan. British expenses in the war with Japan were far less than those in Europe, but as long as the war continued somewhere, the British could secure the Lend-Lease aid on which they depended. If peace in Asia came too quickly, the British would have to go back to the Americans hat in hand. Thus did he write, half sarcastically, one hopes, that he hoped "the Japanese would not let us down by surrendering too soon." With all of these challenges in front of them, British leaders of both parties approached Potsdam with a sense of foreboding.[10]

NOT SO JOSEPH STALIN, whose political life had been formed in the crucible of World War I. Stalin prepared for Potsdam informed by the belief that the West had both depended upon and discounted Russian sacrifices as part of its strategy to win both world wars. Differences of ideology mattered far less to the West, he believed, than did the sheer size of the Russian Army—first under Czar Nicholas II and then under the Communists—and its ability to absorb the majority of German combat power. Like Russian leaders before him, Stalin remained highly suspicious of the West's willingness to, as the saying went, fight the war to the last drop of Russian blood. The Americans and the British had, in Russian eyes, delayed opening a second front in France in large part to force more of the human costs of the war onto the Russians. Churchill had ventured to Moscow personally in 1942 to talk with Stalin and explain the Anglo-American decision to invade North Africa rather than France. "I am sure that the disappointing news I brought could not have been imparted except by me personally without leading to serious drifting apart," Churchill had written boastfully to Roosevelt. But if Churchill genuinely believed in the power of his own rhetoric to win over Stalin, he had deluded himself.[11]

Although it was widely celebrated in the West, not even the dramatic D-Day invasion of Normandy in June 1944 fully won Russian confidence. In public, the Russians welcomed Operation Overlord as, in Stalin's official pronouncement, "a brilliant success." Yet in private Stalin ridiculed the operation in front of the Yugoslav partisan Milovan Djilas, who happened to be in the Kremlin when the news arrived. The US military liaison to the Soviet Union, General John R. Deane, noted that both Russian officials and the people he met on the streets of Moscow were generally dismissive of the landings, though they were still complimentary and supportive. Deane's British counterpart made the same observation. Perhaps the operation seemed small to the Russian officials because they were comparing it to what they themselves had in store for their German enemies.

The Russians launched their own offensive on June 22, 1944, the third anniversary of the German invasion of the Soviet Union. That operation, codenamed Bagration, dwarfed Overlord, involving 1,254,000 soldiers supported by 4,000 tanks and almost 6,000 airplanes. A dramatic success, Bagration led to an estimated 500,000 German casualties and put Russian forces at the gates of Warsaw by the end of July. Thus, although the Russians expressed gratitude for the material assistance the Americans had provided through the Lend-Lease program, they felt they had no reason to cede credit for Germany's defeat to the Americans, the British, or anyone else.[12]

A British or American statesman need not have sympathized with the Soviet Union's Bolshevik ideology or ignored its brutal treatment of its own citizens to grasp how badly scarred the war had left the Russians. An observer with even a superficial historical understanding could see that the recent war marked the third time in a century and a half that Russia had faced a massive invasion from the West. In this context, a Russian quest for security at almost any price should have struck both the British and the Americans as rational, if not exactly welcome. Also in this context, Eden and Churchill should not have been surprised by Russian hostility or suspicion toward Western leaders critical of the Soviet Union, including Churchill, who had once said that he wanted Bolshevism "strangled in its cradle," and Truman, whose 1941 *New York Times* comments were well-known in Moscow. Only the most naïve statesman could have presumed that the Russians would have forgiven or forgotten rhetoric like that.[13]

Perhaps more remarkably, British (and some American) statesmen suggested that with the end of active fighting, Russia's positions on its security would change. They badly underestimated the Russian desire for revenge against the Germans, despite the abundance of such rhetoric in Russian sources that were commonly read in London and Washington. Russian writer Vasily Grossman, a Jewish reporter for *Red Star* who lost his entire family to Germany's death camps, for example, had a wide audience in the West during the war. His 1944 article "The Hell of Treblinka" was one of the first eyewitness accounts of a concentration camp to reach the West. It cried out for revenge and later became part of the case against German officials at Nuremberg.[14]

The famous Soviet writer Ilya Ehrenburg, a World War I veteran and a frequent guest at the Moscow home of the American ambassador, captured the prevailing spirit by noting that "until we reached Germany's borders we were liberators. Now we shall be judges." And judges they became. Grossman noted that the Red Army "changed for the worse" as soon as it entered German soil, bringing with it a deep and burning hatred for Germany not shared in the West. General Ivan Chernyakovsky told his men on crossing into Germany that the soldiers of the Red Army should burn "with hatred and thirst for revenge. The land of the fascists must be made into a desert, just like our land that they devastated. The fascists must die, like our soldiers died." Or, as Ehrenburg put it: "We shall not speak any more. We shall kill. If you have not killed at least one German a day, you shall have wasted that day." Berlin, the *Red Star* observed in January 1945, would pay "for the sufferings of Leningrad."[15]

No one should have expected these feelings to disappear as soon as the guns fell silent. Churchill's clarion call, "In victory, magnanimity," carried little weight with the Russians in June 1945. Soviet behavior in the lands they had occupied reflected a spirit of vengeance, not magnanimity. In October 1944 the Russians had entered East Prussia, the heartland of traditional Germany, and razed the town of Nemmersdorf. In the course of a single night in the small town, the Russians killed seventy-two women, crucifying some on church doors, and raped others, some as young as twelve, others as old as eighty-four. The Russians also murdered children, including infants, several of whose skulls they allegedly shattered during a night of astonishing violence.

Nemmersdorf represented not a single bloody act of catharsis but the tip of an iceberg and the start of a brutal pattern of revenge. As the Russians advanced, they continued to wreak their awful vengeance, sinking two hundred unarmed ships transporting German civilians across the Baltic Sea, and killing thousands of refugees in the process. They also used artillery to break up the ice on frozen rivers in order to prevent other civilians from fleeing. Word quickly spread of both the appalling Russian behavior and the propensity of some Russian officers not to restrain their men but to encourage them or even join them. Western diplomats and journalists reported widely on the behavior of the Russians in East Prussia, but most of them failed to understand what exactly it meant for the future of Eastern Europe. They also failed to grasp that Russian desires for revenge in 1945 would far exceed those of the French in 1918 and 1919.[16]

Acts of vengeance had, in fact, just begun. Most Soviet soldiers saw their actions in Germany not as war crimes, but as justifiable acts. Avenging the deaths of loved ones served as the primary motivator for Soviet soldiers. "I was furious," noted Yevgeni Khaldei, a Soviet combat photographer who entered Germany early in 1945. "The fascists killed my father and three sisters and they didn't just shoot or hang them. . . . They threw them down into a pit and 75,000 people were thrown alive into this pit. How could I forget a thing like that?" Another Russian soldier claimed a "moral and legal right" to strip Berlin bare, both to atone for the German crimes of the past and to prepare Russia for an uncertain material future.

Two massive Russian army groups converged on Berlin in mid-April with what may have been the greatest concentration of firepower yet assembled in human history: 41,600 artillery pieces, 6,250 tanks, and 7,500 aircraft to support 2.5 million Soviet soldiers. The

Red Army dedicated 70,000 of these men, organized into "trophy brigades," to plundering the German capital, a city that cost them 81,000 dead to capture. The Russians boasted of their triumph, which was immortalized by the iconic photograph of an enormous hammer-and-sickle Soviet flag flying over the smoking ruins of the Reichstag. The Soviets made no secret of their plans for Berlin. When Churchill's personal physician, Lord Moran, arrived there in July 1945, he saw a large banner that read, "For Stalingrad and Leningrad and All the Ruined Cities of Russia We Bring Back Our Hate to Germany."[17]

The behavior of Soviet officials encouraged excess. Soviet tribunals rarely convicted any soldier accused of rape who could recount a story of his own family's suffering at the hands of a German, and every Soviet soldier had such a story. Stalin himself saw the estimated 2 million cases of rape in Germany not as crimes worthy of prosecution but as a natural response to the conditions of war: "Imagine a man who has fought from Stalingrad to Belgrade—over thousands of kilometers of his own devastated land, across the dead bodies of his comrades and dearest ones. How can a man react normally? And what is so awful about his having fun with a woman after such horrors?" Although Soviet officers had the legal power to shoot their men on sight to prevent them from raping German women, most Soviet officers reacted as Yevgeni Khaldei did, arguing that the women accusing Soviet soldiers of rape had instead given themselves up willingly in exchange for food, cigarettes, or money. American soldiers in Berlin knew otherwise, having seen evidence of rape with their own eyes. British officer J. E. Rhys saw it, too, having met German women of all ages who had applied a concoction of "paste and crushed grain" to their faces in the hope that it would result in horrible scars that would make them less appealing to the predations of Russian soldiers.[18]

The Soviet tribunals did not prosecute soldiers for property crimes, either. Russian officers instead encouraged their troops to take whatever they could find, both to impoverish Germany and to enrich Russia. Everything from wristwatches, fountain pens, and light bulbs to power stations and entire factories disappeared. Rhys watched Russian soldiers steal bicycles, an object few of them had seen before, from terrified Germans, then turn furiously angry when they could not ride them, assuming that the Germans had tricked them into looking foolish. Other Russians, having never seen indoor plumbing, used German toilets to wash their clothes, assuming the devices to be washing machines. American soldiers watched in amazement as the Russians stole soap, then ate it, assuming it to be food. The contrast between the seeming opulence of Germany and the vast poverty of Russia only infuriated the Russians all the more. One Russian recalled: "Our soldiers have seen the two-story suburban houses with electricity, gas, bathrooms, and beautifully tended gardens. Our people have seen the villas of the rich bourgeoisie in Berlin, the unbelievable luxury of castles, estates, and mansions. And thousands of soldiers repeat these angry questions when they look around them in Germany: 'But why did they come to us? What did they want?'"[19]

Like many other experienced and intelligent diplomats who would come to the Potsdam Conference, Anthony Eden read Russian behavior not as a response to real suffering, but as a manifestation of behavior that called to mind Germany's in the 1930s. These diplomats committed the cognitive error of analogizing Russian behavior to the most available historical example rather than seeing it as a product of distinct historical conditions. Eden and many others dismissed or downplayed Russian suffering for self-serving reasons as well, in the hopes that doing so might mitigate Russian claims at the upcoming conference. To acknowledge the level of Russian suffering would also require acknowledging the disproportionate role of the Russian Army in winning the war and, subsequently, giving disproportionate attention to Russian demands.

Eden and others saw a need to stop what struck them as a new round of appeasement, this time of the aggressive Russians. Eden had not forgotten the two years during which Britain fought Germany nearly alone because of Russia's signing of the 1939 Nazi-Soviet Pact. "Russian policy now," Eden told Churchill just before the conference began, "[is] one of aggrandisement. This is undoubtedly true." Downplaying the human cost of Russia's contribution to victory, and by extension to Britain's own victory as well, allowed Eden to play tough and urge Churchill not to give in to what he suspected were Soviet ambitions in Persia, the Moroccan port of Tangier, Turkey, and Lebanon ("quite the last place where we want them," Eden noted). Any mention of Russian rights of access to the Mediterranean at Potsdam, Eden cautioned, would only lead the Russians to demand more. Thus did Eden's reflexive fear of repeating the mistake of Munich condition his view even of Russia's enormous wartime losses.[20]

The Russians certainly seemed to Eden and others to have aggrandizement on their minds. On that point, Eden merely reflected the consensus of the American and British diplomatic communities. Few of them doubted that the Russians would seek to remain in Eastern Europe in some capacity, probably through the deployment of their armed forces or the establishment of puppet regimes in Poland, Hungary, and Romania. Most diplomats also expected the Russians to demand revision of the 1936 Convention of Montreux, which gave Turkey control over the Dardanelles. The issue of the straits was a touchy one for strategic reasons, because it related to Russia's desire for access to the Mediterranean Sea. Eden therefore feared a Russian presence in Lebanon. It also was a touchy subject because of the 1915 landings on the Gallipoli peninsula, which the British had carried out in part to sustain Russia during World War I. The Gallipoli operation and its disastrous outcome was like a ghost haunting Potsdam—it reminded Churchill of his greatest failure.[21]

Reading Russia remained as difficult for the West in 1945 as it had been in 1939, when Churchill had famously described it as "a riddle wrapped in a mystery inside an enigma." George Kennan, who had devoted as much of his life as any westerner to trying to understand Russia, also used the word "enigma" in an assessment in 1944, proving that even a career of study could not unlock all of Russia's mysteries. In its worldview, its political ideology, and, perhaps most importantly, its history, Russia differed so much from the West that Western leaders could neither comprehend nor empathize with the Russian experience. James Byrnes, the new US secretary of state, and others made facile analogies to political experiences they understood. "I know how to deal with the Russians," Byrnes said on taking office. "It's just like the United States Senate. You build a post office in their state, and they'll build a post office in our state." But, as Byrnes would soon learn, the Soviet leadership had quite different motives and priorities from those of the American politicians with whom Byrnes had worked for fifteen years, and they wanted much more than post offices, even metaphorical ones.[22]

Western leaders were far from alone in finding it difficult to comprehend the nature of the Soviet system, especially the mindset of its leaders. One of the few people outside the inner circle to get a glimpse into Stalin's thinking, Yugoslav partisan Milovan Djilas, noted that Stalin "regarded as sure only whatever he held in his fist." He and his senior advisers had developed a worldview, built in the cauldron of thirty years of struggle and shaped by their reading of Karl Marx, in which the world was a "horrible unceasing struggle on all sides. Everything was stripped bare and reduced to strife which changed only in form and in which only the stronger and more adroit survived." In the Soviet mindset, Djilas said, "there was no choice other than victory or death." Djilas met with Stalin after the Yalta Conference and heard Stalin express not his happiness over the coming victory in the current war, but his belief in the inevitability of another great-power war to come in the next fifteen to twenty years.[23]

FOUR DISTINCT, AND OCCASIONALLY overlapping, ways of understanding the Russians emerged in Western minds in the weeks before Potsdam. Truman's initial instinct led him to presume that the problems between the Western Allies and the Russians had resulted from miscommunications between diplomats during the confusing weeks between Roosevelt's death and the German surrender. A fresh start, with new diplomats on the American side—and a reassurance from Truman himself of the value the Americans placed on their relationship with the Russians—would set matters right.

Truman hoped to deal with Stalin as he had dealt with the men of the Pendergast political machine in Kansas City, by looking them in the eye and cutting a deal that fit the interests of both parties. Shortly after his inauguration as president, he had sent New Deal veteran and Lend-Lease architect Harry Hopkins to Moscow to talk to Stalin and lay the groundwork for such a deal. Hopkins had been one of Roosevelt's informal advisers on both domestic and foreign affairs; although Truman did not want him in his cabinet, he saw the value of sending someone Stalin trusted to open negotiations. Dealing with the Russian leaders, Truman assumed, would be like dealing with any other group of politicians.[24]

Even after it became clear that the differences between the West and the Soviets might run more deeply than Truman thought, he still persisted in the belief that he could easily overcome them in face-to-face encounters with Stalin. Truman's diaries and private papers are full of historical references to the corrupt nature of human beings, but he also had an inherent optimism that human beings could work through their imperfections. Truman, an avid poker player, chose to place his bets on his ability to sit across the table from just such a human being in Joseph Stalin and reason with him.[25]

Few of the Western diplomats preparing for Potsdam shared the president's optimism. A second set of views read Soviet behavior as an extension of the traditional behavior of the Russian czars. Truman himself held some of these views, noting that Soviet desires for the Dardanelles resembled those of "all the czars before him," and that Soviet imperialism wasn't "much different from czarist imperialism." At another point, he observed that "the Communist Party in Moscow is no different in its methods and actions toward the common man than were the czar and the Russian noblemen." By this reading, the Western Allies could expect the Soviets to make demands relating to the traditional ambitions of the Russians—most notably control of Poland, a recovery of lands in the East lost to Japan in 1905, and some form of guaranteed access to the Dardanelles. Advocates of this position, however, saw no justification for Eden's fears of a Soviet power play for south Persia, Tangier, or Lebanon.[26]

British officials most often thought in terms of a third explanation of Russian behavior: their desire to spread communism. Eden worried about allowing Russia any gains in the Middle East in part because he saw the region, "with its rich Pashas and impoverished Fellahin," as "ready prey to communism." Churchill agreed, seeing the Russian threat as global and the Western position as growing weaker with every passing day. In a June 11 meeting with his military advisers, Churchill gave what the chief of the Imperial General Staff, Field Marshal Lord Alan Brooke, called "a long and very gloomy" appraisal of the strategic situation. "The Russians were further west in Europe than they had ever been except once," Churchill had said, and "they were all powerful in Europe," with influence in Greece, Italy, France, Germany, and elsewhere. The Russians had already shifted twenty divisions from Europe to Asia in anticipation of invading China, either to rid that country of the Japanese or to play kingmaker in the ongoing war between the Nationalists and the Communists under Mao Tse-tung. Churchill finished the meeting "by saying that never in his life had he been more worried by the European situation than he was at present," and this at the moment of what most Britons considered their nation's greatest victory.[27]

Although American opinion remained divided on how much of a threat the Russians posed, the hardliners in Washington saw the situation largely as Eden and Churchill did. The hardliners included Admiral William Leahy, who thought that Roosevelt had given the Russians too much at the Yalta Conference. Leahy confided to his diary that he, along with the irascible chief of naval operations, Admiral Ernest J. King, and veteran American diplomats such as Charles Bohlen, Secretary of State Edward Stettinius, and Secretary of War Henry Stimson, believed that "the time had arrived to take a strong American attitude toward the Soviet [sic]" before it was too late.[28]

For the hardliners, Russia quickly replaced Germany as the new threat, its Bolshevik ideology perhaps even more menacing than Nazism. To them, even though Germany now lay defeated, the lessons of Munich had never seemed more relevant. As a group they argued for taking a firm stand against the Russians and treating them not as future partners but as potential future rivals. Even if they lost the struggle to keep the Russians from dominating postwar Poland or reducing Germany to penury, the West would still benefit by showing its mettle to the Russians and by making it clear that the West would respond in meaningful ways to Russian aggression anywhere, even in places as far-flung as Persia and Lebanon.

A fourth reading of the Soviets analyzed their behavior in light of Russian history, especially the cataclysm of the past three decades of revolution and total war. This school's most thoughtful advocate, the perceptive American Sovietologist George Kennan, argued that the war had reinforced the worst features of the Russian system, most notably its paranoia, its sense of insecurity, and its willingness to act cruelly to others in order to guarantee its security. The Soviet state, which Kennan described in a June 1945 memorandum as "a regime of unparalleled ruthlessness and jealousy," had emerged from thirty-one years of nearly continuous struggle. The Soviet Union was now more confident in its ability to shape its own future, yet at the same time more fearful of another invasion. "Determined that no outside influence shall touch them" ever again, the Soviets saw areas like Poland as absolutely essential to their survival. Now in control of those regions, Kennan warned, they would make any British or American efforts to reduce their control over Eastern Europe prohibitively expensive. They would not, however, seek to incorporate Poland or any other new "indigestible" territories into the Soviet Union itself, because to do so would antagonize the already difficult Soviet nationalities problem.

As a result, Kennan argued, the Americans and British had little choice but to accept postwar Soviet domination over the areas then under their control. He advocated submitting to the de facto division of Europe into two spheres of influence, with the Americans and British on the one hand, and the Soviets on the other, each doing as they wished in their sphere. The Soviets would accept this arrangement, Kennan argued, because it would allow them to "hold the conquered provinces in submission" and bankrupt them in the process. Eastern Europe would then have to depend upon the Soviet Union for security and economic development.[29]

Any direct Western challenge to the core Soviet sphere, Kennan argued, would elicit a swift response. America would have to recognize that it could do little for Eastern Europe until conditions changed. Better, he argued, to "muster up the political manliness" by strengthening those areas the Americans did control and standing firm where possible. Failure to find a modus vivendi with the

Russians would make another world war "inevitable," this time, with "civilization faced with complete catastrophe." Kennan discounted Truman's faith in personal relationships, which he felt the Russians used as merely "a series of illusions" designed to mollify Western leaders and feign Soviet interest in Western ideals. Kennan's views did not yet dominate American or British policy, but they attracted growing interest from his peers and would form the basis of the ideas he advanced in February 1946 as part of his so-called Long Telegram.[30]

The difficulty of reading Russian intentions only increased Western uncertainty as the Potsdam Conference approached. The Soviets had begun to limit the freedom of movement of American officials in Eastern Europe, and the restrictions in turn limited the information they could gather and report to London and Washington. Churchill had already used the phrase "iron curtain" in a May 12 memorandum to Truman. He was referring not to a political division of the European continent, but to an information blackout by the Soviet Union to prevent the West from gaining intelligence on the conditions in areas under Soviet control.[31]

Although Kennan probably came closest to understanding the Soviets, none of these four ways of thinking fully captured the mindset of the Soviet leadership. Most Russian leaders calculated that time was on their side. Deeply influenced by their Bolshevik worldview, they assumed that the capitalist states would quickly turn to fighting among themselves for access to colonies and postwar markets. The working classes of Europe would, in the coming decades, become disillusioned with the West, and would therefore voluntarily support communism. At the end of the war, Stalin said: "The social conflicts in America are increasingly unfolding. The Labourites in England have promised the English workers so much concerning socialism that it will be hard for them to step back. They will soon have conflicts not only with their own bourgeoisie but also with the American imperialists." By this logic, the Soviets had more to lose than to gain by confronting the West or actively trying to foment revolution in Europe.

As the Big Three conference neared, moreover, Russian prestige was rising as a result of the Red Army's role in liberating Eastern Europe from the Germans. That prestige, combined with the imprisonment or death of most fascist leaders, seemed to guarantee communism a bright political future in the East for years to come. In any event, Soviet leaders reasoned, Russia would need twenty to thirty years of peace and recovery before it could even consider another war. The upcoming conference gave them a chance to get those years, if they played their cards right.[32]

5

"A Vast Undertaking": Coming to Potsdam

HAVING PREPARED FOR the conference as well as they could, the statesmen of the great powers began to converge on Potsdam, just southwest of Berlin. The time had come to convert ideas into reality. The delegates remembered the seven months between the November 11, 1918, armistice and the June 28, 1919, signing of the Treaty of Versailles. They knew that these deadly months had been consumed by influenza, war in Eastern Europe, and paramilitary violence on the streets of German cities. They hoped to avoid a repetition of that mistake, first by reaching key decisions on the future of Europe, and then by implementing them quickly. The devastation of Germany convinced them all the more of the necessity of beginning the process of reconstruction immediately; it also convinced them of the immense difficulty of the task ahead of them. Realities they had been able to postpone having to face while the war still raged now appeared starkly before them. The men of 1945 would have to face the consequences of their own actions—as well as the actions of statesmen from a generation earlier.

Just days before leaving for the Potsdam Conference, British Foreign Minister Sir Anthony Eden handed a revealing memorandum to Prime Minister Winston Churchill. Potsdam, he told Churchill, would take place under circumstances quite different from the past two great-power conferences. Conditions had changed dramatically owing to the German surrender on May 8: "At previous meetings such as Tehran [November 28–December 1, 1943] and Yalta [February 4–11, 1945] we have met in the knowledge that Russia was bearing a heavy burden in this war and that her casualties and the devastation of her country were worse than anything that we or the Americans were suffering. But now all this is over. Russia is not losing a man at the present time. She is not at war with Japan."[1]

Eden's assessment reflects an astonishing lack of understanding of the Soviet war, especially for a man who had spent the war years as Britain's foreign minister. Eden acknowledged Russia's "heavy burden," yet he managed to downplay it at the same time. He shouldn't have. Although statistics are an imprecise and impersonal measure, and there remains some doubt about the Soviet figures, the discrepancy between the wartime casualty numbers of the Soviet Union and of the Western Allies bears deep consideration. Current estimates place the number of British battle deaths at 383,800, and American battle deaths at 416,800. These numbers, although enormous by the historical standards of their place and time, absolutely pale in comparison to the Russian figures, which current estimates place at somewhere between 8.8 million and 10.7 million. Even the range of uncertainty between these figures (about 1.9 million human beings killed) is more than two and a half times the number of battle deaths suffered by the British and Americans *combined* (800,600). Expressed another way, the Soviets had more men killed in battle in the three weeks of intensive fighting from January 12 to February 4, 1945, than the Americans had on two fronts in the entire war.[2]

The difference in the numbers of civilian deaths puts the case even more starkly. The British lost 67,100 civilians in the course of the war, while the Americans lost 1,700 civilians. The British continue to keep their civilian dead close to their historical understanding of the war, as reflected in monuments to those killed during the Blitz and the omnipresence in British memory of the Battle of Britain, which Churchill famously called Britain's "Finest Hour." Compare that figure, however, to the estimated 14.6 million Soviet civilians who died. Eden correctly noted that Russian sacrifices were "worse than anything that we or the Americans were suffering," but he failed to comprehend the full magnitude of the Soviets' suffering. World War II had cost Russia an astounding 13.9 percent of its prewar population. By contrast, the British lost 0.94 percent and the Americans 0.32 percent. Such enormous numbers often fail to make the point or become confusing by their sheer enormity. As Stalin himself once said, "one death is a tragedy—a million deaths is a statistic." Sometimes smaller numbers tell the story better. To cite one poignant example, the city of Stalingrad, which had a prewar population of 850,000, had just nine children with both parents still alive at the end of the war.[3]

Other numbers, too, stagger the imagination. In four years, the Soviet Union lost 1,710 towns, 70,000 villages, 32,000 factories, 65,000 kilometers of rail lines, 100,000 farms, and an estimated 30 percent of its national wealth. The war also left the nation with approximately 25 million people homeless. The standard of living of the average citizen, a 1947 Soviet report noted, was "the lowest imaginable."[4]

Eden's attitude as he prepared to go to Potsdam is revealing, and many other Western leaders shared this mindset. One might forgive Eden's failure to understand the full burden that such losses put on Soviet citizens and their leaders. The magnitude alone beggars the imagination. But his failure to recognize that such a burden would persist after combat ended, or that such an astonishing level of human suffering would play a profound role in the attitudes and behaviors of the Soviets at Potsdam, requires some explanation. Eden and others who shared his views knew that unlike Britain and the United States, the Soviet Union had faced the full fury of invasion and genocide as part of the deliberate German policy of *Rassenkampf*, or racial struggle. Millions of Soviet citizens died not as a result of battle, but simply for being Slavic or Jewish. World War II, moreover, occurred at the end of a murderous three-decade-long period in Russian history that included the Russo-Japanese War, World War I, the Russian Civil War, and the nearly genocidal policy of the brutal Stalinist regime in Ukraine and elsewhere. Yet Eden still resisted taking these basic facts into account when assessing the Russians or the positions they would likely advocate in the coming negotiations.

Eden's selective reading of both recent and more distant history reflected those of the Americans and British more generally. Few of them fully understood what the war, and the 1914–1945 period, had done to the psyche and the attitude of the Russians, even though they knew in a general sense about the depths of Russia's losses. As the Polish poet Czeslaw Milosz wrote at the end of the war, "The man of the East cannot take the Americans seriously," because "they have never undergone the experiences that teach men how relative their judgments and thinking habits are." Because neither the Americans nor the British had suffered as Eastern Europe had, Milosz concluded, "their reluctant lack of imagination is appalling."[5]

FOR CHURCHILL AND EDEN, the pressures of an election contributed to the problems of formulating strategy for the upcoming conference. Throughout the war, Britain had functioned with a coalition government of national emergency. Churchill had invited Labour Party leader Clement Attlee to join the cabinet and had kept him well-informed and involved in many key decisions. Still, there were cracks in the system, as in any political coalition. Churchill came to despise Attlee, frequently deriding him with classic Churchillian wit. Most cuttingly, he had once observed that Attlee was a very modest man who had much to be modest about. He also said on at least one occasion that he had fought the war against two enemies, Hitler and "Attler."[6]

Just as in 1918, the end of the war meant that the British government would call for elections. Few people expected much difficulty for Churchill and his Conservative Party after the successful prosecution of a war. Nor did Attlee have any of the traits that so marked Churchill as a figure of national prominence, including the latter's magnetic charisma, his grasp of international affairs, and his successful run as a wartime prime minister. Even Attlee seems to have hoped only that his party would be able to do a bit better than in the last elections and maybe gain a few seats in Parliament. He had even rented a cottage on the shore for August in anticipation of not having much to do once the Conservatives no longer needed him.

The government scheduled the election for July 5, although tabulation of the results would not begin until July 26, in order to allow for the inclusion of the ballots of overseas servicemen and women. The first general election since 1935, it held out the promise for Churchill of consolidating his Conservative Party's hold on British policy. With 386 parliamentary seats to Labour's 154 (and the Liberal Party's 21), the Tories had a solid majority that they hoped either to extend or at least to hold. Success in 1945 could end the need for a coalition and give Churchill even more command of British policy both at home and abroad. David Lloyd George had successfully used the Khaki election of December 1918—so-called because of the number of soldiers who voted and stood for office—to increase his power after World War I. He then attended the Paris Peace Conference able to boast of having received a clear mandate to speak for his people.

The 1945 election thus mattered greatly to Britain's future, although it also provided an unfortunate distraction to Churchill and the government at a sensitive point in history. Some of those around Churchill thought it seemed to force him into harsher public stands against Germany than many in his own government advocated. Like his onetime friend and mentor David Lloyd George in 1918, Churchill now played up British anger at the Germans and promised that he would redeem British losses with German money, even though British policymakers had not yet finally decided on reparations policies. Many, such as Keynes, strongly opposed the same harsh economic terms for Germany that Churchill publicly supported in the weeks before the election.

Several observers, including the American Joseph Davies, thought that Churchill played up fear of the Soviet Union as a ploy to keep the election focused on foreign affairs, where he had a presumed edge over Attlee. His campaign rhetoric, however, threatened to increase Anglo-Russian tensions going into the Potsdam Conference, especially given Russian concerns about the United Nations and anger over alleged backroom deals, such as the discussions at Bern. Additionally, the focus on Russia may well have undermined Churchill's political strategy by depicting him as out of touch with

British voters, who wanted solutions to problems at home, not ominous warnings of another conflict abroad.[7]

Churchill also used Attlee's Labour politics to frighten British voters with the Soviet bogeyman. Against the counsel of his closest advisers, Churchill made a controversial radio address on the BBC in June that demonized Attlee and his party, claiming that, if elected, they would threaten the freedom of the British Parliament just as the Gestapo had threatened the Reichstag in 1933. He referred to Attlee not as a Labour politician, but a Socialist, with the implication that the term meant a close association with Soviet policies. "A free Parliament," Churchill said in a loaded comparison, "is odious to the Socialist doctrinaire." He seems to have quickly realized that he had overplayed his hand, telling his wife that he ought to have deleted the phrase as she had advised him to do. Clearly, on this occasion his classic gift for oratory let him down.[8]

Attlee answered with a calm and measured address of his own that was heard by about half of the people in Britain. Churchill, Attlee sarcastically responded, "feared that those who had accepted his leadership in war might be tempted out of gratitude to follow him further. I thank him for having disillusioned them so thoroughly." The speech received a warm reception in Britain, although as Churchill, Attlee, and the British delegation headed to Potsdam, few thought it would make much difference to the expected Tory victory.[9]

Perhaps Churchill had lost his touch. He certainly appeared less focused than he had been at the height of the war. Eden thought he looked "unwell and tired" in these critical weeks, although no one was suggesting that Churchill had begun a permanent decline of the type that befell Roosevelt. He did, however, spend the weeks between the end of the war in Europe and the start of the Potsdam Conference drinking more than his usual copious amounts of alcohol. To the great dismay of his advisers, he stopped reading official memoranda with the same gusto he had for them during the war. He had begun to run cabinet meetings in a disconcerted and confusing way that baffled and worried his own cabinet officers. Some of them, most importantly Anthony Eden, had begun to lose faith in him, although in an election season his supporters kept those views largely contained to the inner circle of government.[10]

Still, Churchill soldiered on. Reflecting British policy more generally, he and his advisers sought to use the upcoming meeting to get closer to the Americans. He had planned to come to Washington for Roosevelt's funeral, in large part to meet Harry Truman and make his pleas for a renewal of the special relationship. At the last minute he canceled his plans, giving those close to him no explanation, and baffling his biographers to this day. Possibly, he could not face the death of the man to whom he had once been so close and on whose friendship he had gambled the future of his country. Perhaps he had been strongly influenced by the letter from Lord Halifax, the British ambassador to the United States, saying that Truman would be in no position to discuss matters of substance. In any case, he looked forward to Potsdam to get the measure of the new American president and begin a new chapter in the special relationship he had formed, at least rhetorically, with Truman's predecessor.

The interval between the British general election and the start of the conference left Winston Churchill with almost two weeks of precious time. He used it to take advantage of an admirer's offer of his house in Hendaye on the southwestern coast of France near the Spanish border. There Churchill hoped to enjoy a restful break before heading to Potsdam. He brought with him his paints, plenty of provisions in case the markets in France had not yet returned to form, and a staff of thirty-five aides, valets, bodyguards, and advisers.

The advisers hoped that Churchill would make good use of the time to review the imposing stack of official papers that his cabinet officers had prepared for him on a wide range of critical topics. Given the weak position his country would have at the conference, preparation and study, they thought, might provide Britain its only advantage. Instead, Churchill drank even more than usual at Hendaye. He ignored the stacks of papers on his desk, and he spent the lion's share of his time painting. Those with him in France found him difficult, short-tempered, and unable to focus on crucial matters of state.

Few people begrudged Churchill a few days of rest after the conclusion of five and a half grueling years of war in Europe. At Yalta, he had seemed almost as tired as Roosevelt. Those close to him worried that Britain would suffer at Potsdam if Churchill did not come to the conference better prepared. But Churchill did not seem ready for his role. Anthony Eden had grown particularly dismayed by Churchill's lack of focus in the previous few months, and he openly doubted that his tired colleague was up to the task that he now faced. "It was foolish to try to win on Winston's personality," he later recalled. Britain needed a prime minister who was fully prepared to engage with other world leaders on the substance of the issues, but Churchill had not prepared himself for that role.[11]

While Churchill was trying to relax and recharge, military representatives from the victorious powers were meeting in the Berlin area to decide on joint-occupation policies. They made decisions quickly, both to begin the reconstruction of the city as rapidly as possible and to show the diplomats that a basis for cooperation existed among the victors. Although theoretically, the Berlin discussions were supposed to be coequal among Britain, France, the Soviet Union, and the United States, there were three dominant voices: that of Marshal Georgi Zhukov of the Soviet Union, and those of the American generals Dwight Eisenhower and Lucius Clay. The British, having already lost the debate with their American allies about the placement of forces east of the line agreed to at Yalta, were in no position to argue about occupation policy; the French, whose occupation zone had to be carved out of the British and American zones, also sat in a clearly secondary position. If, however, Churchill performed well at Potsdam, he might be able to win at the Big Three conference what the British had been unable to attain thus far.

CHURCHILL RETURNED TO London from Hendaye only long enough to meet Eden and Deputy Prime Minister Clement Attlee so that the senior members of the British delegation could travel to Potsdam together. Given that the outcome of the election still lay in doubt, British leaders wanted to send as clear a message as possible that the British leadership stood together no matter what that outcome might reveal. As it turned out, those three men between them would hold the position of prime minster from 1940 to 1957, showing a greater political consistency than any of them might have thought possible as they left together for Potsdam.

Neither on the way back to London nor on the way to Potsdam did Churchill stop in Paris to meet with the leader of the Provisional Government of the French Republic, Charles de Gaulle, even though many British diplomats had come to the realization that Britain might need French help if the Americans rapidly demobilized their forces in Europe. Churchill had had enough of de Gaulle's posturing and his demands for a greater share of influence in the postwar world. Although Churchill spoke warmly about the French people, he told American envoy Joseph Davies that he had run out of patience for de Gaulle. "He ought to be 'brought up,' sharply," Churchill told Davies, and he should not have the authority to make any political or military decisions outside the borders of France without British and American approval. French officials, indeed, had begun to push for an expanded French occupation zone in Germany and Austria, a dominant voice on policy in Italy, and a senior role on the reparations committee. They also wanted a seat at the Potsdam Conference itself, and several British diplomats supported them, based both on the hope that France would line up with Britain on most issues and the presumption that no postwar peace agreement could possibly last without French participation.[12]

Still, the British and the Americans knew that bringing de Gaulle to Potsdam would likely create more problems than it solved. The Russians would likely claim that France did not merit a seat at the table, having collapsed in 1940, thereby allowing the German Army to redirect its forces east in order to invade the Soviet Union the following summer. The Soviets could also plausibly claim that several of the smaller states in Eastern Europe had suffered more at German hands than France had; if France claimed a seat, why not Hungary, Poland, or Romania, states well under the control of the Red Army in 1945? No one wanted to repeat the Paris Peace Conference's mess of forty-four states being represented. Admitting France might well open a Pandora's box.[13]

De Gaulle, furthermore, did his characteristic best to annoy both the British and the Americans. Demanding far more for postwar France than anyone in Washington or London—to say nothing of Moscow—thought its due, and arrogantly protesting any minor decision made without his consultation, he promised to be as difficult an ally at the peace table as he had been during the war. The fact that France had not participated in either the Tehran or the Yalta accords posed another problem, as those accords specified only a three-power reparations committee for Germany. For his part, Truman called de Gaulle an "SOB" for the way he had treated Roosevelt and said sharply that if he wanted to see de Gaulle at Potsdam, he would send for him just as he would the Poles. Thus the Big Three decided not to become the Big Four, prompting the appearance of the French ambassador at the White House just before Truman sailed for Europe to lodge a final futile protest. Churchill, not wanting to face de Gaulle at such a sensitive time, opted to get about as far away from him as he could while still being on French soil.[14]

Churchill's time off at Hendaye seemed not to have done him much good. Once in Germany, he struck those close to him as even more out of touch than he had been in France. He told one traveling companion that hearing the cheers called out to him by German civilians had buoyed his spirits and dissolved some of the hatred he felt for the German people. No one had the heart to tell him that the men cheering him were not German civilians, but British sailors and Royal Marines close enough for Churchill to hear, but too far away for him to have properly identified. The British officers who escorted Attlee to Potsdam and then through what remained of Berlin's Tiergarten noticed that the British soldiers cheered more loudly for Attlee than they did for Churchill, although no record exists of any of Churchill's advisers having had the nerve to tell him that, either.[15]

The British brought an enormous delegation to Potsdam. Churchill had 17 staff members dedicated to him personally; the Foreign Ministry had 34 staffers; the War Office had 20; and the communications section had 29, including 26 telephone operators. Many of the latter had also attended Yalta, Tehran, or both. The British also brought 39 people to take photographs, interpret, and record the discussions. In all, the British delegation added up to 260 people, including their protocol director, Joan Bright, who was legendary inside the British government for always ensuring the smooth operation of the social and practical sides of conferences and state dinners.[16]

Attlee attended the Potsdam Conference despite his anticipated defeat in the upcoming election, and despite his not having been fully included in much of the preconference planning. Churchill knew the possibility existed that Attlee might take over the government in mid-conference and, as he told Truman, "the United States and the Soviet Union have a right to know that they are dealing with the whole of Britain whatever our immediate party future may be." Of course, should the election return a strong Conservative majority, Churchill would expect Attlee and his colleague Ernest Bevin, who was then serving as minister of labour and national service, to return to the United Kingdom.[17]

The elections thus created a bizarre diplomatic arrangement. Although the British saw it as demonstrating unity, the Russians found it peculiar for the British to have a prime minister, a deputy prime minister, and two other cabinet members at the conference. They thought the British were trying somehow to secure an extra seat at the table for Attlee, thereby doubling the number of British votes. "But Mr. Attlee was so subdued and terse a figure," Eden noted, "that this hardly seemed possible." That Attlee had no staff of his own at the conference reassured the Russians somewhat, although Eden noted that they remained "perplexed," even as they also remained "convinced that Mr. Churchill and I really had come to stay," because the Conservatives would doubtless win the election. The vagaries of Western democracy baffled Soviet leaders throughout the conference.[18]

The British took great care to assure the comfort of their delegates. They flew in their own food and wine along with British cooks and waiters, although they seem not to have shared the Russian fear that some of the German food suppliers might try to poison them. The British brought an entire Westminster in miniature with them to Germany. They even flew in British milk to help Anthony Eden recover from a recent bout of ulcers that had left him, in his own words, "haggard in fact as in looks." They also sent back to England for Yorkshire hams when Churchill expressed his distaste for the hams served to him in the opening days of the conference.[19]

The exact location of the British delegation's housing remained a closely guarded secret outside the members of the delegation and a few members of the British press. Churchill, Attlee, and Eden all moved into villas on a block of Babelsberg's Ringstrasse, which had once been owned by the magnates of the German film industry. Russian security controlled the roads into Potsdam and neighboring Babelsberg up to the ironically named "Friendship Bridge" that led into Babelsberg itself; once the British were across, the Russians did not let anyone go back the other way without a special pass, ruining the effect the bridge's name might have implied. The restrictions made many of the British delegates feel like they were living in a comfortable but heavily guarded prison colony. The Russians observed, with some trepidation, that senior British diplomats wore nothing to distinguish themselves from their staff, which in turn meant that clearing Russian checkpoints took more time. Churchill's house had six British uniformed guards on it at all times; the houses of Attlee and Eden had three guards each. A patrol of six more guards marched along the Ringstrasse around the clock. No vehicle could drive on the Ringstrasse unless it boasted one of the special red passes handed out by the Russians. The British delegates prized these, but only a few obtained them. Only that pass could gain a delegate unquestioned passage over the Friendship Bridge.[20]

Although the British took responsibility for their own security, the Russians still controlled the sector. They assigned the British a protocol officer from Moscow, who spoke excellent English, to serve as a liaison to the Russian protocol office. They also took "unlimited trouble," in the recollections of one British officer, to see that the houses were in "perfect style" and lacked no comforts whatsoever. In fact, the Russians had taken furniture and other items from German civilian homes to replace items looted from homes in Potsdam and the adjacent town of Babelsberg; thus did British delegates sometimes complain about the eclectic style of decoration that it seemed to them the German middle-class must prefer. Despite the relative level of comfort and the big smiles on the faces of the Russian guards, one British colonel observed that the members of his delegation "never felt at ease" at Potsdam, even in their own sector. "An unexpected Russian would appear or one would find an armed sentry on the other side of the door," ostensibly to check on accommodations or security. They all seemed to speak English, leading the British to presume that they had been sent to eavesdrop.[21]

The British also suspected that the Russians had intentionally assigned men from the "hordes of Asia" to serve as security in the British sector, although this impression may well have reflected their own racial views. Nevertheless, a British general recalled the Russian guards as "Kazaks, Uzbegs, Turkomens, shades of Genghis Khan . . . tough little brown men" who offered quixotic smiles and unnerved many British officials with their primitiveness. At other times, the Russians assigned young and attractive female soldiers in immaculate uniforms boasting combat ribbons, which also disconcerted the British, but for different reasons. One British delegate recorded that the sight of the young women nearly caused a large number of minor traffic accidents, although strict rules against fraternization on both sides kept British men and Soviet women from doing anything more than stare.[22]

Still, British delegates found the accommodations at Potsdam a major improvement from the rather simple arrangements at Yalta. All fifty houses assigned to them appeared untouched by the damage of the war, and each had a piano. Churchill occupied a large and handsome red brick mansion that, he later noted, was much better furnished than Truman's. Attlee's house featured what at first glance looked like an impressive library. The bibliophile Attlee examined the books only to find that almost all of them dealt with fascism, including the works of the British fascist Diana Mitford, whom Attlee had known before the war. The American delegation stayed just two blocks away from the British on the Ringstrasse. The physical proximity of the British and American delegations may have given Churchill cause to hope that the close Anglo-American relationship he had built with Roosevelt would revive with Truman at Potsdam after the coldness of Yalta.

The British got a taste of Russian security paranoia when Molotov came on day three for an informal lunch at Eden's house. He brought with him a phalanx of guards and had them stay in the garden with tommy guns while he ate. The whole arrangement seemed so unnecessary, given the security Molotov had passed just to get to Babelsberg, not to mention the presence of British soldiers nearby. "It must be grim to spend a life guarded like that," Eden recalled. "No wonder the man is a most able but ruthless automaton."[23]

HARRY TRUMAN WAS still learning his responsibilities for the upcoming conference when his ship, the USS *Augusta*, secretly left Newport News, Virginia, on the morning of July 7. For Truman—who had always bought his own railroad tickets and carried his own bags, and had never had a bodyguard, even when he was vice president—the pomp and circumstance of a presidential voyage seemed overwhelming. "When a president of the United States leaves Washington, even on a short trip, many special operations and people are set in motion. But when he travels overseas under wartime conditions, it is a vast undertaking," he noted later in his memoirs. "The White House, in a sense, had to be moved to Potsdam for the duration of the conference." The new commander in chief did not seem anxious to make the trip, however, as he confided to his mother and sister in a letter written just before he left: "I am getting ready to go see Stalin and Churchill, and it is a chore. . . . I have a briefcase all filled up with important information on past conferences and suggestions on what I'm to do and say. Wish I didn't have to go, but I do and it can't be stopped now."[24]

As his ship pulled away from the American coastline, the poker-playing Truman knew he had a strong hand. Most importantly, the US Senate was about to vote overwhelmingly in favor of the United Nations Charter. Truman also knew that despite an occasionally intense debate and some serious reservations from important senators, the Bretton Woods agreement would pass by a comfortable margin. On July 19, the Senate indeed passed the

Bretton Woods treaty by a vote of 61 to 19, and at almost the same time passed the United Nations Charter 89 to 2 (both votes had numerous abstentions). Truman thus had at Potsdam what Woodrow Wilson never had at Paris: a public statement of support for his policies from the Senate.[25]

The *Augusta*, a 10,000-ton heavy cruiser that had hosted Roosevelt and Churchill's discussions of the Atlantic Charter in 1941, and served as Omar Bradley's command post for D-Day, left from the same berth Roosevelt had used on his voyage to Yalta. At Truman's request, the crew had rendered no honors, and the new president boarded unceremoniously. The *Augusta* sailed across the North Atlantic under normal peacetime conditions, taking eight days to reach Europe. On board, Truman spent his days in intensive meetings with Byrnes, Leahy, and other close advisers; he passed his nights playing poker with those same advisers or watching movies with the crew. He enjoyed the trip, his first trip to Europe since World War I, and even relished the daily routines of ship life, including the evacuation drills and taking a regular place in the chow line. Those on the *Augusta* with him noticed his genuineness and his ability to relate to the sailors on board. How that personal touch would translate in meetings with world leaders like Joseph Stalin and Winston Churchill, however, remained anyone's guess.[26]

The policy meetings required Truman to pore over stacks of documents on a myriad of topics, and the American positions on many of them remained in flux. Truman's advisers painted for him a stark picture of the future of Europe if the United States failed to do a better job of setting the conditions for peace than Wilson had in 1919. The same menace of Bolshevism that had terrified Americans in 1919 terrified them in 1945 as well, notwithstanding the close alliance of the Americans and the Soviets during the current war. Still, Truman was optimistic. "I'm not afraid of the Russians," he wrote in his diary. "They've always been our friends and I can't see any reason why they shouldn't always be." After all, he was coming to Europe to settle scores with Germany, not Russia. A survey taken of the American people showed that almost three in four hoped for a future of cooperation with the Russians.[27]

Not all of Truman's advisers were so sanguine. On the *Augusta*, Truman heard a briefing that predicted that France, Germany, Italy, and all of the Scandinavian countries would likely become communist in a few years unless the United States acted decisively to prevent it. For his part, Truman reacted philosophically and historically, locating the problem Europe faced in 1945 in its violent but redemptive past: "Since Julius Caesar, such men as Charlemagne, Richelieu, Charles V, Francis I, the great king Henry IV of France, Frederick Barbarossa, to name a few, and Woodrow Wilson, and Franklin D. Roosevelt have had many reminders and still could not solve the problem. . . . Europe has passed out so often in the last 2,000 years and has come back, better or worse than ever, whichever pleases the fancy." This schoolbook history view of Europe—learned, Truman boasted, by reading every book in the library of his hometown of Independence, Missouri—inclined Truman to see the problem of 1945 in the long view. He hoped to base his postwar vision not on specific policy solutions to specific problems, but, as Wilson had, on grand principles. Unlike Wilson, however, Truman planned to bring with him the elements of American power that could see the vision through to reality. He hoped, he confided to his diary, to give Europe ninety years of peace.[28]

Byrnes recalled the transatlantic crossing as a time of intensive study and reflection on American goals for the conference, which he believed represented "the first step down the long road to peace." He remembered poring over documents and listening to briefings in an attempt to set American priorities for the conference. Having attended the failed conference at Paris in 1919, Byrnes hoped that Potsdam would not stand as the end of a process, but as the start of a series of conferences that could move thoughtfully and deliberately through the problems Europe and Asia faced. He must surely have remembered how seemingly inconsequential decisions made in haste in Paris on areas like the Sudetenland, China, and the Middle East later had catastrophic consequences. Now he had to avoid a repeat of those mistakes with a president who was largely uninformed on the details of the crises of the day.[29]

On the *Augusta*, Byrnes pushed Truman to prioritize three main issues. First, the Allies should determine their policies for what Byrnes and others expected would become a joint three- or four-power occupation of the whole of Germany, depending on the future status of France. Second, he hoped the Big Three would decide how to interpret and implement the agreements made at Yalta. Third, he hoped that they might come to agreement on the delicate topic of German war reparations, the same topic that had divided the delegates at the Paris Peace Conference and laid the groundwork for the economic catastrophe of the 1930s. The question of reparations promised to be just as volatile this time around.[30]

Truman's own list of goals for Potsdam was also short. He sought above all to ensure Russian participation in the war against Japan as early as possible. Doing so involved setting the Soviet Union's price for its belligerence. The Russians had agreed at Yalta to confine their contribution to an invasion of Manchuria, and recalling the Allied landing of troops in northern Russia after World War I, they had steadfastly refused American requests for air bases or other support on Soviet soil. They had refused a routine American request for two weather stations on Russia's Pacific coast, although they did offer to share their own weather data. They had also increased their price tag: in return for entering the war, they had demanded more Lend-Lease aid and hinted at wider territorial acquisitions in East Asia. Truman wanted to ensure that the Soviets would honor their commitments—or, perhaps, moderate their terms.[31]

The president also wanted to solidify the Soviet Union's willingness to participate in the United Nations, especially after his rocky encounter with Molotov before the San Francisco conference. Truman knew that without Soviet participation, the new organization did not stand a chance of succeeding. If he could get agreement on those two points, he felt, he could both ensure an earlier end to the Pacific war and fulfill the great dream of both Wilson and Roosevelt of a functional international organization for the peaceful resolution of international disputes. Truman went to Potsdam convinced that he could attain both goals, because he believed the Soviets both wanted America's friendship and needed its support. The Russians would therefore be in a position to deal.[32]

The *Augusta* picked up a convoy of British destroyers at Lyme Bay, sailed past the white cliffs of Dover on July 14, then arrived the next morning in Antwerp, where damage from German V-2 rockets was visible everywhere. Crowds gathered to wave flags and cheer the president's arrival, but the reception featured little of the ecstasy that had greeted Wilson in France when the *George Washington* had made a similar voyage at the end of World War I. Perhaps Europeans did not know what to expect from the new president. Perhaps they had grown more pessimistic and more anxious for the future. The situation in the summer of 1945 struck many Europeans as even worse than in 1919: the war had caused much more damage; Europeans were jaded by the failure of the 1919 peace conference; and Truman lacked the nearly messianic hold that Wilson and Roosevelt had once had over millions of Europeans. The future also remained an open question. While some Europeans in 1919 had hoped to go back to the conditions of 1914, no one in 1945 wanted to turn the clock back to 1939, 1933, or even 1919. As British intellectual Alan Bullock put it, "Europe may rise again, but the old Europe of the years between 1789, the year of the French Revolution, and 1939, the year of Hitler's war, has gone forever." The leaders of the Soviet Union, the United States, and Great Britain would have to forge a whole new world out of the rubble.[33]

From Antwerp, Truman and the official party's forty-car motorcade drove to Brussels, guarded along the way by the men of Truman's World War I unit, the 35th Division. He then flew to Berlin on the presidential airplane, the *Sacred Cow*, getting his first glimpse of a devastated Germany. Walter Brown, on board one of the five planes of the official party, recalled seeing entire towns without a single building left standing. Upon landing in Berlin, they drove to Babelsberg, the home of the American delegation for the duration of the conference. No welcoming crowds greeted them along the German part of the journey, apart from the well-disciplined honor guards of Allied soldiers. The Russian delegation moved into homes about a mile away, closer to the center of Potsdam itself.[34]

President Harry Truman meets with Chaplain L. Curtis Tiernan in Berlin on July 22, 1945. The two men had served together in the 35th Division in World War I. (United States Army Heritage and Education Center, Harry Truman Photographic Collection)

Truman settled into a house that soon became known as the "Little White House," a three-story home on Babelsberg's Kaiserstrasse, later renamed the Karl-Marx-Strasse. Byrnes, Leahy, Bohlen, and a few other close advisers also moved into the house, which would have looked perfectly appropriate in almost any comfortable middle-class American neighborhood. The rest of the American delegation stayed in twenty-five houses and villas nearby. The business of the US government continued apace despite the momentous events at Potsdam, with Truman having to deal with issues as diverse as federal funding for hospitals in North Dakota and Montana, the naming of senators for a trip to Peru, and the selection of the next collector of internal revenue for Arkansas. Truman also approved the low bid ($36,000) for a long-overdue repainting of the interior of the White House.[35]

The Americans had initially planned to bring with them a relatively small delegation of just forty-four people, including seven Secret Service agents and a handful of personal staffers. Eventually, though, diplomats, area experts, and press secretaries found reasons to attend, which in turn led to more staffers. Journalists, too, found their way to Potsdam, which was easily the biggest story in Europe at the time, although the government did not make arrangements for them, and the Russians did not allow them to stay in either Potsdam or Babelsberg.

Unlike the secret Yalta and Tehran conferences, which had focused as much on military strategy as on peacemaking, Potsdam dealt almost exclusively with the postwar world. As a result, military advisers attended only parts of the conference and confined most of their advice to military matters. Thus Chief of Naval Operations Admiral Ernest King, General Dwight Eisenhower, and other military luminaries made only brief appearances at Potsdam, mostly to pay their respects to the new president. Eisenhower, who came to meet Truman in Antwerp and later met with delegates unofficially in Potsdam as well, told Truman that he no longer placed much value on the need to have the Russians join the war against Japan. Even without factoring in the atomic bomb, he thought the Pacific war would soon end, thus rendering Russian support unnecessary. Leahy, King, and the US military's attaché to the Soviet Union, John Deane, all agreed. They argued that the Japanese military would soon collapse under the combined weight of a strangling naval blockade, a devastating air campaign of fire bombing, and the threat of an invasion of the home islands; the Americans therefore no longer needed the Russians. Eisenhower also warned Truman, however, that "no power on earth," not even a demonstration of atomic weaponry, could keep the Soviets out of China. Truman listened carefully and told a surprised Eisenhower that he could count on Truman's support for anything he wanted, including a run at the presidency in 1948.[36]

Other guests came to Potsdam without getting the White House's approval beforehand. Several doyens of Roosevelt's administration showed up unannounced out of concern that Truman and Byrnes could not handle the conference without their experience

President Harry Truman and US Secretary of State James Byrnes meet with General Dwight D. Eisenhower. In 1945, Truman promised Eisenhower his support if Eisenhower decided to run for president in 1948. (United States Army Heritage and Education Center, Harry Truman Photographic Collection)

and knowledge. They included Secretary of the Navy James Forrestal, Secretary of War Henry Stimson, and the US ambassador to the Soviet Union, Averill Harriman, all of whom traveled on their own and came to Potsdam to offer their help. They caused a tremendous headache for the conference protocol officers, unceremoniously throwing more-junior officials out of their assigned quarters and trying with varying degrees of success to get Truman's ear. All three were hardliners on policy toward the Soviets as well as members of the Ivy League clique Truman distrusted. Although he did not order them to go home, he did not let them dominate his advisory group.[37]

STALIN REMAINED EAGER TO meet with his allies, although a mood of pessimism and paranoia inside the Russian camp deeply influenced attitudes and behaviors toward the Potsdam Conference, most notably its security arrangements. Stalin's chief of secret police, the much-feared Lavrenti Beria, tried one last time to convince Stalin to fly to Potsdam, telling him that security arrangements would be far simpler if he took a plane instead of a train. Stalin held firm, causing the Russian security apparatus no end of headaches to arrange an overland journey of almost 1,100 miles for a paranoid dictator. Stalin and others in the Russian high command feared not just loose bands of German soldiers trapped behind the lines, but Ukrainian and Tatar partisans—a reasonable fear given Stalin's astonishingly brutal treatment of those two groups in the 1930s and 1940s.

Beria worked hard on the security details, but he faced constant questions from Stalin on everything from the exact route his train would take to the thickness of the armor on his personal car and the backgrounds of the men traveling on the train with him. To assuage Stalin's fears, Beria developed one of the most elaborate and expensive security arrangements in history. Stalin's personal train car would be preceded by five armored trains and followed by another three; all eight contained mobile security teams able to respond to any crisis with heavy weapons. En route to Yalta, Stalin had had an enormous bodyguard retinue of 620 soldiers, but Potsdam far exceeded even that figure, because his trip involved leaving Soviet territory. More than 17,000 troops from the NKVD (the Communist Party's dreaded People's Commissariat for Internal Affairs) and 1,500 military police patrolled the route. Regular Red Army troops provided security at railway stations and towns. Every kilometer that Stalin traveled inside Russia had six armed guards; inside Poland, the number increased to 10, then to 15 once Stalin's train entered Germany. A full delegation preceded him to Potsdam, including almost 2,000 soldiers for perimeter protection around his villa, two bakeries, Russian chefs and waiters, and seven NKVD regiments to provide additional security. Beria arranged for Russian troops to seize local poultry farms and vegetable gardens so that no German would handle any of the food served to Stalin and the Russian leadership. If Stalin wanted to go for a walk in the woods on the villa's grounds, an entire platoon of machine-gun-wielding soldiers would be ready to accompany him, with NKVD agents and Red Army snipers standing nearby.[38]

The Russian security needs struck most of the westerners as excessive and unnecessary. "There were Russian soldiers everywhere," recalled Lord Moran, Churchill's physician and friend. "Lining the road, behind bushes, knee deep in the corn." Presidential aide George M. Elsey, who had attended many high-level meetings, described the security as "tighter than anything I had seen before, or since for that matter." When General Lucius Clay, head of the American occupation forces in Germany, arrived at Potsdam a week before the conference to discuss security arrangements, the Russians allowed him to see only the parts of Potsdam where the American and British delegations would stay. They prevented him from getting anywhere near the area that housed the Russian delegates. They also warned him and his men against taking any shortcuts or using any roads not specifically authorized for American and British use.[39]

Stalin sought more than security; he wanted to arrive in Potsdam in a manner befitting a conqueror. His personal train comprised four luxury cars that had once been used by Czar Nicholas II and had been taken out of a museum for the occasion; the symbolism would have gratified those Western analysts who saw Stalin's behavior as reflecting that of the old Russian aristocracy, not that of a global revolutionary. Stalin indeed wanted to come to Germany not as the Bolshevik insurrectionary of his youth, but as the leader of a powerful and dominant state with the ability to get what it wanted in the international arena. At Yalta, Stalin had given Roosevelt the best accommodations, Nicholas II's old summer home, the Livadia Palace, an ornate and graceful building that Mark Twain had praised in his 1867 travelogue *Innocents Abroad*. At Potsdam, however, the Russians took the best, for Stalin a fifteen-room villa once owned by one of Germany's best-known World War I generals, Erich Ludendorff.

Stalin arrived a day late, his doctors claiming that he had suffered a mild heart attack. Throughout the conference he would moderate his alcohol intake on doctor's orders, slipping water into his vodka glass and slowly sipping wine at dinner. No one at Potsdam suspected Stalin of a ruse, although they might have speculated a bit more had they realized that the American and British delegations would spend their free day before the Soviet leader's arrival doing a bizarre form of tourism in the wreckage that was Berlin.

$$6$$

"What a Scene of Destruction"

IF INDEED JOSEPH STALIN intentionally delayed his arrival at Potsdam by one day in order to give the British and American delegates at the conference time to see the wreckage of Germany for themselves, his plan worked. Although Stalin may not have known it, Woodrow Wilson had infuriated the French and British in 1919 for spending as little time as diplomatically possible outside Paris. He told his hosts that he did not want the battlefields to turn his heart hard toward the Germans. By contrast, Harry Truman, Winston Churchill, Clement Attlee, and dozens of other influential delegates in 1945 formed themselves into odd bands of tourists for a most unusual sightseeing trip on July 16, the day before the conference officially opened. Seeing Germany, and particularly Berlin, in ruins confirmed in their minds some of the positions they already held. But seeing the Europe that the war had made also caused the leaders of 1945 to ask new questions about where ultimate responsibility for the damage of the war should rest. How much should the suffering German civilians they saw have to pay for the damage that their government had done in their name? Such questions would have been quite familiar to Wilson and the diplomats of 1919.

Few of the delegates who toured Berlin before the opening of the Potsdam Conference remarked then or later on the complete freedom of movement the Russians temporarily allowed them. Although no direct evidence exists to support the supposition, the circumstantial evidence certainly points to the conclusion that the Russians wanted the British and American delegates to see as much of Berlin as they desired. Nor did the Russians try to direct the movements of delegates from the West into some dystopian, anti-Potemkin villages staged for their benefit. The delegates could go anywhere they wanted to go, and for the most part, they all saw the same kinds of ghastly sights no matter what area of the city they visited. Whether Stalin's belated arrival at Potsdam was part of a planned design or not, it offered Western delegates an extra day to see the war's impacts at close hand. Having already prepared their briefs and settled in at their villas, they found themselves with little to do on July 16. They decided to drive to nearby Berlin and see the once formidable capital of the Nazi empire for themselves.

NOTHING COULD HAVE quite prepared them for what they were about to see, hear, and smell on this most unusual of sightseeing expeditions. Only on this one day did the delegates not complain about the intrusive nature of Soviet security. They did not see the absence of road blocks and pass checks, on which the Russians normally insisted, as indicating anything strange, but, then again, the entire day was strange. Instead of the immense security many of them had noted on their arrival in Germany, on July 16 they found the Russians exceedingly polite, unfailingly helpful, and attired in brand-new dress uniforms replete with medals. On this day and this day only, none of those Russian soldiers tried to hamper their movements. Instead, they did all they could to clear passageways through the debris for the delegates in order to make their journeys easier. The only complaint came from the US military's liaison to the Soviet Union, General John Deane, who traveled through the ruins of Berlin with Ambassador Averill Harriman. Deane recorded that he had to return the endless salutes of Russian soldiers, all given with such an impressive "snap and precision" that he felt compelled to return the courtesy again and again. "I envied Harriman his civilian clothes," Deane recalled.[1]

In principle, nothing that the delegates to the Potsdam Conference saw in the Berlin area or in Germany more generally should have surprised them. The military and political leaders of the Grand Alliance had seen almost daily reports on the damage that the war had inflicted. They knew, for example, about the fire bombings of Hamburg and Dresden, which had destroyed those cities with incendiary bombs and killed an estimated 70,000 civilians in the tempest of heat and flames that ensued. Many of the delegates had not only known about these operations, but had approved them or received classified briefings on them. Carrying out and ensuring this destruction had been their duty.

They also knew, at least in broad outline, of one of the human side effects of their policies, the enormous number of refugees then clogging the roads of Europe. They knew, too, of the vast damage to the infrastructure of Europe, much of it caused by the Anglo-American combined bomber offensive that struck not just Germany but also France, Italy, and the Benelux countries, all in an effort to destroy the logistical network on which the German military had depended in the war years. As the delegates surely understood, European economies would need that same transportation network in the months and years to come to be functional in order to feed their populations. Thus did the very tools of victory complicate the process of reconstruction. And by the time they met in Potsdam, Allied leaders had full reports on the death camps, and thus were aware of the mass murder the Nazis had committed on an industrial scale. That information was also by now common knowledge around the world, the first newsreels of the camps having arrived in Britain and the United States in May.

The widespread damage of Europe should therefore have offered little to surprise these men. Still, most of them had learned of the destruction from the safety of their own headquarters, normally quite far from the battlefield, and the destruction of Germany had therefore remained for most of them a distant event. Seeing Berlin for themselves offered a distinctly different and altogether more immediate view of the shattered world they would now have to put back together. As they quickly realized, the challenges of reconstruction might be even more daunting than the challenges of the war itself, especially because no consensus vision for the postwar world yet existed. Their job was to provide that vision and lay the groundwork for transforming it into a reality that could give Europe a chance for a future of peace.

Even for veteran military men like Field Marshal Alan Brooke and General Lucius Clay, the devastation of Germany surpassed anything they had seen before. The destruction of 1945 seemed to those who had also seen World War I's effects as being an altogether different order of magnitude. Although the destruction of 1914–1918 struck Europeans of that era as unprecedented, the very nature of that war had, paradoxically enough, worked to limit its damage, at least in Western Europe. The frustrating stasis of the western front had the one benefit of concentrating the damage to civilian territory to a relatively small stretch of France and a much wider stretch of Belgium, as well as a slice of the frontier between Austria-Hungary and Italy. Most of Western Europe emerged in 1918 relatively unscathed, at least physically.

Most of the damage of 1914–1918, moreover, came in the countryside and small towns. Paris, Berlin, and London, as well as smaller cities like Hamburg, Birmingham, and Rouen, had largely escaped physical damage. Although both sides had used strategic bombardment, and its novelty had deeply shocked contemporaries, the technology and doctrines of air warfare did not yet exist to cause the kinds of damage seen from 1939 to 1945. The damage of 1914–1918, therefore, never posed a threat to the immediate living conditions of the millions of people in the large cities of Europe. Approximately 550 British civilians died from strategic bombardment in World War I, a number that may have augured a harsher world to come, but hardly had the kind of strategic or industrial impact for which its planners had hoped.

World War II, by contrast, with its fluidity, its technological changes, and its more murderous ideology toward civilians, caused far more damage to the infrastructure of Europe than World War I had. In World War II, the British lost more than 60,000 civilians to

German strategic bombing. The Anglo-American combined bomber offensive may have killed more than 500,000 civilians in all, including thousands of forced laborers brought to Germany to work in its factories. The damage was also far more widespread. Virtually every corner of Europe possessing a train station, a bridge, or even a road crossing presented a potential target. In Berlin, more than 75 percent of the dwellings were uninhabitable by war's end, much of that damage having come intentionally from the "dehousing" bombardment strategy designed by British Air Marshal Sir Arthur "Bomber" Harris. Unable even to hit targets as big as factories with any reasonable degree of accuracy in the early stages of the war, Harris had decided to target workers' neighborhoods, on the theory that workers could not be productive if they had no place to live. Some German cities suffered many times more damage from the air than all of Germany had in World War I. The British and American air forces, for example, targeted the city of Cologne 262 separate times.

The Allies could not limit their strategic bombardment to Germany and Austria alone, of course. The war had also destroyed more than 500,000 French buildings as well as innumerable rail yards, bridges, and canals. Allied air raids killed 67,000 Frenchmen and women, despite the moral qualms of Churchill and others about bombing a nation that the Allies were, in fact, trying to liberate. Romania and Italy also suffered widespread damage from air raids, which grew more powerful and more destructive as the war continued. Parts of Europe would require years, perhaps decades, to return to normal levels of agricultural or industrial production, even if the Americans proved willing to invest their money in the future of the continent; to many Europeans and Americans, that proposition remained quite a large "if" indeed. Truman himself said at Potsdam that he was "giving nothing away except to help starving people[,] and even then I hope we can only help them to help themselves." The Marshall Plan still lay years in the future.[2]

Outsiders who saw Europe in 1945 reacted to it with revulsion. American journalist Martha Gellhorn saw the damage firsthand during a flight over Germany in a C-47 cargo plane leaving the city of Regensburg. She noted that her fellow passengers, most of them combat veterans, likened leaving the devastated country to "escaping from a fire." No one on that plane, she said, ever wanted to see Germany again. Others made analogies to Carthage after the Punic Wars, or even to Armageddon and the end of the world. The horrors of the concentration camps only seemed to solidify the impression so common in 1945 that Europe might never emerge from this era of bestiality and inhumanity. Nor was anyone in 1945 willing to conclude that the world was safe from the possibility of another era of war in the near future.[3]

The delegates to the Potsdam Conference knew about this damage on an intellectual level. They had seen the aggregate statistics describing the destruction, the photographs of a devastated Europe, and the reports from men and women on the ground. But seeing it for themselves forced them to confront it on an emotional and personal level. James Byrnes noted, after his bizarre day in Berlin, "We were greatly impressed by the streams of people walking along the road. They were mostly grandparents and children. As a rule they carried their possessions on their backs. We did not know where they were going and it is doubtful that they did. . . . Despite all that we had read of the destruction, the extent of the devastation shocked us. It brought home the suffering that total war now visits upon old folks, women, and children." Like Franklin Roosevelt's tour through the Crimea six long months earlier, the tour of Berlin brought home to the delegates the realities of the problems of the postwar period with a suddenness for which they were emotionally unprepared.[4]

Berlin, with its destruction and destitution, presented an astonishing contrast to Potsdam. Although Potsdam was just fifteen miles from Berlin, it had escaped the war with remarkably little damage. Because it was largely a residential community, with no real places of industrial or military value, Allied aircrews had had no reason to target it. Fifteen miles, moreover, proved far enough away to spare the small town from the collateral damage from bombs that were aimed at Berlin but missed their targets. Potsdam and Babelsberg, with their villas and parks, looked as if the war had passed them by.

Not so Berlin. A primary target of Allied air operations, and the scene of a murderous climactic battle between the Wehrmacht and the Red Army, the city resembled a wasteland. It was so completely destroyed that words seemed unable to do it justice. A Royal Air Force (RAF) flight lieutenant who walked through Berlin before the VIPs arrived noted, of the area near the Brandenburg Gate and the Unter den Linden: "What a scene of destruction. Not a single building in this district remains. [No] shops, flats, [or] hotels. The world famous Adlon Hotel is a complete ruin. . . . The damage has to be seen to be believed, words cannot describe the destruction." These scenes struck the officer as particularly poignant because he believed his own air force had caused them. "The bombs and incendiaries which wrought this terrible havoc," he noted with some sadness, "were carried from England, fully 600 miles away." His reflections were an acknowledgment of the power of modern militaries to deliver death and devastation from a greater distance than ever before. The world would see an even more vivid demonstration of that trend almost as soon as the Potsdam Conference ended. But for the time being, Berlin seemed as devastated as any city in history.[5]

For a neophyte like Byrnes's adviser Walter J. Brown, a man who had seen nothing of the war except Berlin, the city seemed like "the greatest mass wreckage in history. . . . Mile after mile we drove through Berlin, every building shattered beyond imagination." With crashed airplanes and burned-out vehicles lying beside the once beautiful avenues of Berlin, the city took on a sinister feel. "There is a deathly smell in many streets," a British pilot recalled, "and smells of open sewers and stagnant water make one realise, if any reminder is necessary, that Berlin has 'had it.'" A staffer from the British delegation wrote home to her mother: "Everything is very depressing. . . . London has *never* seen anything like the destruction that there is here. It is quite incredible. . . . People are living in cellars, there is nowhere else. Streets are unrecognisable, mountains of rubble, with here and there an old iron smoke stack with smoke coming out of it—which means someone is making some kind of home beneath the debris. The men one sees are very sullen, for there seems no hope for them ever to rebuild Germany from such a tragic rubble heap." One British soldier who had lived in Berlin as a child went to find his family's former apartment building amid the widespread

The ruins of central Berlin at the time of the Potsdam Conference. The remains of the Adlon Hotel sit to the right of the Brandenburg gate. (United States Army Heritage and Education Center, Charles H. Donnelly Collection)

devastation of the city he had once called home. He found the entire block completely gutted and in a total shambles.[6]

Senior leaders at Potsdam saw Berlin in much the same way that their staffers did. General Lionel "Pug" Ismay found his tour of Berlin to be a "depressing experience." He saw "scarcely a home that was habitable. There was a smell of death and decay, and one wondered how many corpses still lay in the ruins." Field Marshal Brooke twice used the phrase "absolute chaos" in his diary to describe Berlin. He wrote, "The more one sees of it [Berlin] the more one realises how completely destroyed it is." Still, a grizzled veteran of the wars of the twentieth century like Brooke could not help but be awed by the sheer spectacle of it all. As he walked through the city, a Russian private came up to him and handed him a German medal taken from the Reich Chancellery building. Recalling all the death and

President Harry Truman, US Secretary of State James Byrnes, and Admiral William Leahy drive through a conquered Berlin on July 16, 1945. (United States Army Heritage and Education Center, Harry Truman Photographic Collection)

destruction of the long years of the war, Brooke wrote that night: "If I had been told a year ago that this would happen to me I should have refused to believe it. In fact, the whole afternoon seemed like a dream, and I find it hard to believe that after all these years of struggles I am driving through Berlin!"[7]

President Truman, too, drove through Berlin, in an open car sporting a large white star, with Leahy and Byrnes along for the ride. The entire US Second Armored Division, 1,100 vehicles strong, lined the road from Potsdam to the capital, both for security and to impress Berliners with a show of American power. The US commander of the Berlin Military District escorted the three VIPs and a handful of generals through the Tiergarten, the Unter den Linden, and the Wilhelmstrasse, the latter the traditional home of the German Foreign Ministry and other government offices. "Well known places

The Interior of the Reich Chancellery building once housed Hitler's Berlin headquarters, but in July 1945 it became Europe's most unusual souvenir shop. (United States Army Heritage and Education Center, Charles H. Donnelly Collection)

just a short while ago," the official report noted, "but today just piles of stone and rubble." The president noted in his own diary that he had never seen such destruction in his life. The seemingly endless streams of refugees struck him the most. He recalled "the long, never-ending procession of old men, women, and children wandering aimlessly along the autobahn and the country roads carrying, pushing, or pulling what was left of their belongings. In that two-hour drive I saw evidence of a great world tragedy, and I was thankful that the United States had been spared the unbelievable destruction of this war." And it's no wonder he felt the need to give such thanks. An estimated 25 million Germans (more than seven times the 1940 population of Truman's home state of Missouri) had no homes in 1945, and the country lacked almost its entire infrastructure.[8]

American diplomat Joseph Davies toured Berlin separately from Truman, Leahy, and Byrnes, venturing off into residential areas as well as the central government district. He saw charred vehicles on almost every street and rode through "miles upon miles of the most handsome streets of Berlin, the entire length of which could not show a single habitable structure on either side of the street." An American general who escorted him explained that the stench he smelled likely came from "human bodies buried in the debris, . . . which had not yet been removed." The destruction of Berlin left Davies despondent. He wrote, "Nothing I have seen created such an impression of the horror and magnitude of the destruction incident to modern war as did the ruins of this once-beautiful city."[9]

The main attraction for most of the visitors, the Reich Chancellery building, contained the bunker where Hitler had spent his final days. Now just a heap of rubble on the surface, it contained within it piles of medals, stacks of documents, and other objects that soon became Europe's oddest souvenir shop. Virtually everyone took something or paid a Russian sentry to escort them through the rubble and into the remains of the bunker's many rooms and corridors. One British delegate took stationery featuring Hitler's name and the address of the Chancellery. Harry Hopkins took books from Hitler's own library, and another senior American official took a chair belonging to Hitler's mistress, Eva Braun. Joseph Davies took chunks of concrete as well as a box of medals given to him by a Russian sentry; the Russians, he wrote that night, "can't do too much for a friend, just as they can't be rude enough to those they consider their enemies." Harry Truman's bodyguard picked up a copy of *Mein Kampf*. Other visitors took Iron Crosses still in their original boxes, never to be awarded to the defenders of Berlin as Hitler had intended. Pens, typewriters, ashtrays, ink stands, books, paper-weights, and even furniture, all bearing swastikas or other symbols of the regime, disappeared into the hands of British, American, and Russian officials. An enormous pile of medals, which would "have brought pride to brave men" under other circumstances, instead seemed, in Ismay's mind in this particular setting, "to be a symbol of utter degradation." For those who missed out on the tour, these and other items soon appeared in Berlin's ubiquitous black market at reasonable prices.[10]

This once-in-a-lifetime opportunity provided delegates the chance to see Berlin at the end of the war, and few could turn down the chance to see the spectacle for themselves. Still, some delegates soon wished that they had stayed at Potsdam. Lord Moran, Chur-chill's physician, could not get the smell of the city out of his mind; he felt nauseous for hours afterward. "It was like the first time that I saw a surgeon open a belly and the intestines gushed out," he later recalled. General Ismay, another man who had seen more than his share of destruction and blood, recalled, "I was sorry that I had gone sightseeing. My first act on returning to Babelsberg was to plunge into a hot bath with a great deal of disinfectant in it; my second was to take a very strong drink to get the taste out of my mouth."[11]

A few British and American officers took a measure of profes-sional pride from the German defeat. One British lieutenant colonel noted with a sense of triumph that "many of the Master Race were pushing and pulling little vehicles along the road," their stations in life having changed quite dramatically in a short time. He also noted that although the Germans would face shortages of food and coal for the coming winter, "they will suffer what their leaders have made other countries suffer over many years." Brooke noted in his diary after the day trip that "in every way throughout this war the

American officials walk amid destruction along the Wilhelmstrasse toward the Unter den Linden. (United States Army Heritage and Education Center, Charles H. Donnelly Collection)

Germans have been made to suffer the same misery as they inflicted on others, but with 100% interest."[12]

It seemed as if the city could never find a way to recover. When Admiral Leahy, riding alongside President Truman, remarked that "this once beautiful city, capital of a proud nation[,] [is] now wrecked beyond repair," he did not intend to be hyperbolic. It truly seemed to him, as to most others, that the city lacked not only buildings and infrastructure, but also that most critical element of all, hope. That a new city could ever rise from those ashes seemed both necessary and at the same time impossible. The same, of course, could easily be said for dozens of major cities across Europe. Seeing Berlin—which stood, in the minds of many, as an example of all the damaged cities of Europe—with their own eyes reminded the delegates of the enormity of the task before them.[13]

Still, for most observers, the physical damage paled in comparison to the psychological damage. Somehow, Germany and Europe would need to find a way to clean up the debris and erect new cities. But the sight of so many refugees and so many people with nowhere to go and nothing to do seemed a far more daunting problem. As one Briton observed, Berlin, once a thriving and cosmopolitan city, now seemed like one giant refugee camp. "Men, women, and children seem to be roaming from place to place carrying on their backs, pulling on improvised trolleys, or pushing crazy hand carts loaded with their few, very few, remaining belongings."[14]

Truman, too, noted the pitiable condition of the refugees. Although he likely did not know it, many of those refugees had come west from East Prussia, Poland, and the Baltic states. Unlike the policies of Woodrow Wilson in 1919, which used the concept of national self-determination to settle the ethnic problems of Eastern Europe, the Russian solution centered on brute force. As the Red Army moved west, it forcibly removed millions of ethnic Germans from Latvia, Lithuania, Estonia, Ukraine, Czechoslovakia, Romania, Poland, and elsewhere. The Red Army made no attempt whatsoever to distinguish between those Germans who had lived in the East for decades and those transplanted by the Nazi regime since the start of the war. In Russian eyes, all Germans represented potential fifth columnists and thus posed too great a risk to remain. Thereafter, all Germans, regardless of their political views or their personal preferences, would live inside a new Germany whose borders the Big Three had yet to determine.

The numbers remain contentious, but they are, at the same time, staggering. By January 1945, an estimated 3.5 million ethnic Germans had fled their homes in the East, often with nothing but the items they carried and the maximum allowable 500 marks in cash. Refugees could not carry any foreign currency with them, thus rendering their bank accounts worthless. En route, Russian soldiers frequently robbed them of money, jewelry, and any other possessions they tried to take with them. Red Army soldiers raped women and young girls, and often shot German men who resisted or who tried to argue. The end result of the process, George Kennan wrote, resembled a mass of forced human migrations "that had no parallel since the days of the Asiatic hordes" of Genghis Khan. Elsewhere, Kennan wrote that the forced movement of peoples on such a scale was a disaster with "no parallel in modern European experience."[15]

In fact, as Kennan must have known, such a parallel did exist, if on a smaller scale. After World War I and the Greco-Turkish War of 1919–1922 that immediately followed it, Greece and Turkey agreed to a massive exchange of populations. The 1923 Treaty of Lausanne forcibly removed 1.5 million ethnic Greeks from Turkey and 500,000 Muslims from Greece. Although forcible repatriation did not exactly follow the ideals of Wilsonian self-determination, it did, at least in Western eyes, produce the desired result of two reasonably homogeneous states.

Western leaders often saw the Greek and Turkish deportations as a positive example for the post-1945 period, rather than as an example of what we might today call ethnic cleansing. Franklin Roosevelt had, in 1943, cited the Greco-Turkish movements as a "harsh procedure [but] . . . the only way to maintain peace" between quarreling ethnicities, as well as a way to avoid the mistakes of 1919. Churchill, too, had praised the idea of forced population transfers, telling Parliament in December 1944 that expelling Germans from the East would provide a "most satisfying and lasting" solution to the problems of 1919. The Versailles Treaty had left 2 million ethnic Germans outside the borders of Germany, setting up the problems of multiethnic regions such as the Sudetenland, Danzig, Memel, and many more. During the war years, in accord with Nazi ideology, the Germans had settled millions more Germans in the land they cleared for *Lebensraum* with their own policies of murder, deportation, and starvation. In 1945, Western leaders showed a willingness to tolerate forcible deportation on a massive scale to try to solve the nationalities problem. They had the support of the Czechs (who expelled the Sudeten Germans as soon as the opportunity presented itself), the Poles, and, of course, the Russians.[16]

Western officials asked the Russians to take greater care in ensuring the safety of the refugees, but they did not object to what they knew was a deliberate Soviet policy of forcibly removing ethnic Germans from the East. By the end of the war, an estimated 5.6 million ethnic Germans had fled from the East, with another 3.3 million fleeing from Czechoslovakia. Modern estimates place the total number of German refugees at 13.5 million people. Almost 1.4 million of them remain unaccounted for; most of them no doubt died on their travels, although the exact number will never be known for sure. One recent estimate put the number of refugees who died while fleeing to the new Germany at 2.25 million.[17]

Not knowing where else to go, hundreds of thousands of ethnically German refugees came to Berlin, creating the kinds of scenes that Truman and others witnessed. Almost 1.5 million German refugees had come to the city in the first half of 1945 alone. By the time the Potsdam Conference opened, the Berlin area had 48 refugee camps, although there is no evidence that the delegates to the conference even knew about these camps, let alone expressed any desire to see them. Berlin also had more than 1 million orphans. To one American aid worker who came to the city to try to help, the refugees "looked like wild creatures" with no hope for the future. To a British major, the generation of young Germans growing up in this environment faced a future of begging, stealing, and borrowing just to get by. "Every child born under the Hitler regime," he lamented, "is a lost child. It is a lost generation."[18]

American and British delegates did not know how to interpret the refugee problem. Some suspected an intentional Soviet policy to rid the East of Germans in order to clear the way for the Russians, or one of their satellite states, to take over. At the time, however, they had no firm evidence that the refugee problem had come from direct Soviet policy. To the extent that they thought about it at all, and most diplomats clearly preferred not to, they saw the refugee crisis as part and parcel of the ravages of war. They relied heavily on the new United Nations Relief and Rehabilitation Administration (UNRRA) to deal with the daily plight of the millions of refugees while they tried to focus on the long-term problems.

UNRRA symbolized the new American approach to Europe's problems. An international organization, it would ease some of the burden on individual countries by establishing a supranational method for providing food and medicine to those in need. In theory, it would reduce inefficiencies and redundancies in the process, while also demonstrating that America would work with Europe, rather than retreating to its own borders as it had in 1919. The Americans, in the same spirit that drove Bretton Woods, would work through international organizations that they led but for which they were not solely responsible.

The West needed an effective UNRRA, because the refugees posed a special problem for the British and the Americans in their zones of occupation. The majority of the refugees wanted desperately to enter the western part of Germany in order to get away from the vengeful Russians or avoid a future under Soviet rule. Most of them must have been eyewitnesses to German brutality in the East from 1939 to 1945, and therefore feared that the Russians would seek to exact revenge on them. Thus the British and the Americans soon found themselves with millions more mouths to feed even as the most fertile agricultural parts of Germany fell into Russian hands. Few westerners wanted to repatriate people into the Soviet zone by force, but no one knew whether the West could provide enough food to keep these people alive.[19]

Nor were the Germans the only problem. Germany also had some 7.8 million displaced persons in the country who were there against their will at the end of the war. They made for an even more pitiable sight and an even larger political problem than the Eastern refugees. The Germans had forced most of them to come to Germany as involuntary laborers; many others had only recently left death camps. Most had no place to go; either their homes no longer existed, or, in the case of many Jews, their native states were not exactly eager for them to return.

The displaced persons crisis completely overwhelmed American administrators. Frankfurt had just 21 aid workers to care for 40,000 displaced persons in that region alone. The US Army eventually reassigned 20,000 soldiers from other duties to help care for the displaced persons. They entered American care hungry, angry, and, not least of all, bitter at having to enter another camp so soon after thinking they would regain their freedom. With borders shifting, the legal status of millions of refugees also came into question. Many of them, most notably the Ukrainians and anticommunist Poles, refused even to consider going to lands now under Soviet control. In some notable cases, displaced persons committed suicide rather than face repatriation to the new Eastern Europe of Soviet rule.[20]

The problem of refugees and displaced persons was not merely a question of providing humanitarian aid to those in need. Failure to deal with the problem, UNRRA officials feared, could lead to an outbreak of epidemics to rival the terrible influenza pandemic of 1918–1919. Such epidemics respected neither ethnic differences nor the borders of refugee camps. Another outbreak of influenza or some other disease in the primitive conditions of Europe in 1945 could add millions more deaths to the toll of the war itself. Thus, deciding the future status of Germany had to take into account desires to mete out punishment as well as humanitarian needs and the interests of the great powers themselves.

As the tour of Berlin demonstrated, in 1945 the war hit Germany in a way it had not in 1918–1919. This time, the Germans felt the full force of the destruction, occupation, and impoverishment that they had inflicted on others. As Rudolf Paul, the minister-president of Thuringia, observed, "the collapse of 9 November 1918 [when he was twenty-five years old] was a tempest in a teacup compared to the typhoon of the year 1945." In Breslau alone, as many as 400 people died of starvation each day, most of them refugees from the East. British and American newspapers began to report on the miserable conditions of the camps and the refugees, eliciting both sympathy from their readers and calls for their leaders to do more to solve the problem.[21]

Although most delegates to the Potsdam Conference expressed sympathy for the elderly and the young, they also believed deeply that the Germans deserved much of the suffering they were now experiencing. They also found the Germans hard to read. Truman's bodyguard, who himself had four grandparents born in Germany and thought he understood German culture, kept a close eye on the German policemen he saw. He noted that they were polite and efficient, but he "was never quite convinced that they had clean re-cords." Indeed, the Allies had no way to determine what, exactly, the Germans with whom they were working had done during the war years. As in so many other countries of Europe, Germany faced the ominous problem of dividing its war criminals from its victims. Not knowing exactly who they were dealing with made many outsiders to the German system understandably suspicious.[22]

The delegates also knew that many of Germany's victims, nota-bly Poland and the Soviet Union, had suffered even more than Ger-many had. John Deane, the American liaison to the Soviet Union, who had spent much of the war among the Soviets, understood the poverty and desperation in Germany, as well as the need for the United States to deal with it in some way, but he had little sympathy for the Germans themselves. "Having just come from the rigors of life in Moscow," he noted just before the Potsdam Conference began, "I think I could appreciate more than most people the stupidity of Hitler and the German people in risking the loss of what must have been such a peaceful and happy existence." Similarly, Walter Brown noted in his diary, "Why Germans could not be satisfied with a coun-try like this is a question that I thought of all during the trip." They, like most Americans and Britons, had a difficult time reconciling their anger at the German people with a natural inclination to take pity on refugees and those rendered homeless by the war.[23]

Anger at the Germans was widespread, even if the American and British delegates rarely took their fury to the level of the Russians. Still, few Britons or Americans in Berlin spent much time convers-ing with the Germans, preferring to explore the city at a safe dis-tance from people who both repulsed them and needed them. Strict non-fraternization policies in place at the time of the conference also limited interactions; one soldier got a $65 fine just for speaking to a German in the street, and another nearly got a fine merely for smiling back at a German child. One American who did interact with Berlin-ers on a regular basis, General Lucius Clay, would soon become the commander of the American occupation zone. Just a few days before the opening of the Potsdam Conference, he recorded his opinion that the attitude of the German people left quite a bit to be desired. He likely had in mind the defiant reaction of the Germans who in 1918 and 1919 had refused to acknowledge their defeat and passed blame onto their fellow Germans. The new occupiers, he pledged, would not tolerate such an attitude this time.[24]

Indeed, there were signs that a repeat of the attitudes of 1918–1919 might occur. Karl Dönitz, the admiral who briefly succeeded Hitler as chancellor, said at the end of the war: "We have nothing to be ashamed of. What the German Wehrmacht achieved in combat and the German people endured during these six years is unparalleled in history and in the world. It is a heroism such as there has never been. We soldiers stand here without blemishes on our honor." Those words sounded too much like those of the German leaders of 1918–1919. Especially given the realities of the concentration camps, German denials of the nation's twentieth-century wartime roles rankled. They also kept Allied leaders on the alert for other signs of German defiance.[25]

Not all Germans carried their defiance as far as Dönitz did. In April 1945, the mayor of the German town of Gotha, located next to the Ohrdruf concentration camp, toured the camp on the orders of Eisenhower himself. After returning home, the mayor and his wife hanged themselves, prompting Eisenhower to remark, "Maybe there is hope after all." Of course, neither Eisenhower nor anyone else could say whether they had hanged themselves out of guilt, fear of punishment, or some other motivation. Nevertheless, Eisenhower, who called the camp one of the most horrible sights he had ever seen, saw in the suicides an almost positive omen for Germany's future.[26]

Many other Germans refused to accept the new reality, let alone take the option that the mayor of Gotha had chosen. Those ejected from the East fully expected to return to their former homes, and some even demanded financial compensation for their losses. And while some Germans recognized the truth about the death camps, others either would not or could not accept the evidence before their own eyes. Anxious to prevent a repeat of the 1919 experience, Allied commanders ordered German civilians to walk through the camps and also to feed, clothe, and house the liberated prisoners at their own expense.

For his part, Clay remained on the lookout for signs of the attitude of the German people at the end of the war. Although he found little evidence of Nazi or communist underground movements among the people he would soon govern, he did not see much remorse, either. In a July 5 memo entitled "Conditions in Germany" that he sent to the Pentagon, Clay wrote that "no general feeling of war guilt or repugnance for Nazi doctrine and regime has yet manifested itself. Germans blame Nazis for losing [the] war, protest ignorance of regime's crimes and shrug off their own support or silence as incidental and unavoidable." Such attitudes tempered the sympathy of British and American officials, who often read defiance in the stares and silences of the Germans with whom they interacted.[27]

The sight of so many desperate people nevertheless had a dramatic impact on those who saw Berlin. "Berlin has to be seen to be believed," one British staffer wrote to her husband. "I thought ahead to the winter. They will have nowhere to live, most of them, no food, no heating, none of the ordinary comforts of life." The only major source of food, she noted, was the massive black market that operated in plain sight right in front of the rubble that had once been the Reichstag. Berlin, she found, was "almost intolerable" for the British, to say nothing of the Germans who would have to live there. One American noted that cigarettes, not money, had become the currency of Berlin; a haircut had cost him just a small handful of cigarettes, which Berliners found useful for curbing their ever-present hunger.[28]

Shockingly, the devastation the delegates saw in Berlin paled in comparison to what the city had looked like just a few weeks earlier. John Deane had entered Berlin on May 9 with the victorious Russians. He then returned on July 13, just four days before Truman, Byrnes, and Leahy toured the city. He was stunned by how much better Berlin already looked. "The streets had been cleared of rubble, broken-down streetcars and motor transport had been removed," he noted with wonder. He credited the Red Army for the cleanup, with Soviet soldiers directing work crews of German prisoners of war or doing the work themselves. The Russians had also put up enormous pictures of Stalin, some of them three times larger than life, "everywhere one looked." The posters covered up some of the

Soviet occupation officials erected large portraits of Joseph Stalin to hide some of the worst damage to Berlin and to remind the conquered Germans who now controlled their fate. (Harry S. Truman Presidential Library, Richard Beckman Collection)

worst damage and, not incidentally, reminded Berliners who now controlled their fates.[29]

Notwithstanding the efforts of the Germans and Russians to start the process of getting Berlin back to normal, the city still looked bad enough to scare and surprise the delegates at Potsdam. The pathetic state of the refugees combined with the delegates' revulsion at the Nazi regime to create both sympathy and anger. Although the delegates understood that the elderly, children, and widows had had little to do with the Nazi policies of war and genocide, they wondered openly how much time, money, and effort their own countries should devote to helping them out of a situation that their own government had created. "One feels sorry for the children and old people," wrote an RAF officer to a friend at home, "but not for the average German. There is little evidence of fraternisation. . . . The British, I am sure, have no desire to mix with people who must have been aware of the horrors which were being perpetuated in the concentration camps and elsewhere." Another Briton wrote home that "the majority of the British soldiers and officers I met were not so keen on fraternisation. Most of them would not speak to the Germans unless it was absolutely necessary."[30]

Others saw in the ruins of Germany a taste of what might have happened to them if the Germans had won. "I felt sorry for them," recalled one staffer from the British delegation, "and then I remembered that it was only what they would have done to us." Such thoughts further undermined whatever sympathies the British and Americans might have felt toward the refugees and toward the Germans more generally. It also made them all too happy to leave Berlin and retreat to the heavily guarded enclave of Potsdam, where they would find unlimited food, comfortable accommodations, flowing champagne, and, perhaps most critically, no Germans. "I am very sure," Truman wrote, "no one wants to go back to that awful city." Thus, even though the conference took place within an easy drive to the capital, the delegates at Potsdam showed no more desire to interact with the German people than the delegates at Paris had a generation earlier. Their day of battlefield tourism over, they returned to the comforts of Potsdam.[31]

Still, the leaders of the British and American delegations knew they somehow not only had to make sense of what they had seen, but also figure out how to move Berlin, Germany, and Europe forward. Few of them found themselves in a forgiving mood, even if the sight of refugees pulled occasionally at the heartstrings. In a letter home to his wife, Truman found himself caught between pity and castigation. "This is a hell of a place," he wrote. "Ruined, dirty, smelly forlorn people, bedraggled, hangdog look about them. You never saw as completely ruined a city. But they did it."[32]

Exactly what "they did" remained a point of some debate. Curiously, few of the leaders of the delegations blamed the Germans they saw for war crimes or the horrors of the camps. Instead, they blamed the Germans for following the Nazi regime. In the span of one diary entry, Leahy referred to the "false philosophy," "false prophets," and (twice) "false leaders" that Germany had produced since the end of World War I. These false leaders had driven the Germans, he concluded, into an unnecessary war with their "racial kinsmen" in America and Britain. The destruction they now faced, he concluded, was the price they had to pay for their mistakes. Now their "ancient and highly cultured country" would have to face occupation, starvation, and poverty. Truman blamed the "gangster government" of the Nazis, suggesting that he understood the need to get the postwar governance of Germany right in a way that his predecessors at Versailles had not.[33]

As Truman recognized, Berlin, and Germany more generally, carried an especially poignant historical warning. Those Europeans and Americans who blamed the Treaty of Versailles for creating debilitating economic conditions in Germany and elsewhere in the 1920s and 1930s feared a repeat of the cycle. In short, if the economy of Germany suffered after 1945 as it had after 1919, then the impoverishment of the German people might lead them to seek another extremist form of government, whether fascist, communist, or something horrible to come. With an estimated 25,000 refugees arriving in Berlin every day, the task of caring for them thus posed an enormous political and economic challenge.

On the other hand, caring for the Germans too well might be politically unacceptable at home and in the states recently liberated from German rule. Even though few people blamed the refugees for the war's devastation, someone in Germany had to have been responsible, and none of the delegates at Potsdam wanted the German people to receive more help than the victims of the war in France, Poland, and elsewhere. The governments of those countries were demanding not aid for Germany but reparations from Germany. The Russians did not want the Germans to receive any aid until Russia's own needs had been met. As in 1919, someone would have to pay.

Either owing to his intentionally late arrival or his disinclination to do so, Stalin did not tour Berlin. He did not need to. He understood the brutality of the German system better than either Truman or Churchill did. And it is difficult to imagine that the sight of so many refugees in so impoverished a condition could have moved Stalin to soften his position on postwar Germany or reduce his demands for reparations that would only further drive Germany into poverty. He ordered Marshal Georgi Zhukov, the highly decorated Soviet commander in Berlin, to receive him in Berlin with little ceremony, and then he went straight to Potsdam to begin the work of settling the future of Europe. In 1919, the Russians had had no voice in the postwar peace conference. In 1945, Stalin came to Germany not as a negotiator, but as a conqueror, confident that this time, Russia would not just have a voice, but that its voice would dominate. He came not to make deals, but to settle scores.[34]

"In Seventeen Days You Can Decide Anything"

A T LONG LAST, THE BIG THREE were ready to start discussing the problems of Europe. They did so in the relatively undamaged picture-postcard towns of Potsdam and Babelsberg, which became oases from the death and widespread destruction the delegates had seen in and around Berlin. The American and British delegates did not know the lengths to which their Russian colleagues had gone to make Potsdam such an inviting a place for a conference, but they did appreciate the end result. A British soldier who had lived in Berlin and visited Potsdam many times before the war saw it even in 1945 as "a series of parks surrounded by ornamental gardens in a huge park-like setting." Potsdam must have seemed all the more idyllic given the absolute devastation surrounding it.[1]

Once a favorite country retreat of the Prussian aristocracy, Potsdam was home to many of the Berlin area's most famous buildings and gardens. They included Frederick the Great's famous eighteenth-century rococo-style summer palace, Sanssouci ("Care Free"), then and now one of the region's most popular tourist attractions. There Frederick had discussed philosophy with Voltaire and also planned many of the military campaigns that made Prussia a continental power. Potsdam also housed Kaiser Wilhelm II's preferred residence, the baroque-style Neues Palais (built between 1763 and 1769), where Wilhelm had signed the orders to mobilize the German Army in 1914. Nearby sat the more modern Charlottenhof palace of Frederick Wilhelm IV (built between 1826 and 1829) and dozens of other stately homes and gardens. Many of the Potsdam villas from the second half of Frederick Wilhelm III's reign (1797–1840) featured Russian designs and architectural styles that were in vogue in the aftermath of the allied defeat of Napoleon. In 1815, no less than in 1945, the power of a Russian Army transformed the destiny of this German center of power.[2]

The palaces and the sense of royalty and history pervading Potsdam had given the town a regal air even in the interwar and Nazi eras. Connected to Berlin by a tram line since the beginning of the twentieth century, Potsdam had grown into an elegant suburb and favorite tourist sight in the years after World War I. In the 1920s and 1930s, Potsdam had emerged as a popular weekend or day-trip getaway for middle-class Germans who wanted to leave behind the hustle and bustle of the capital for the town's parks, castles, quaint streets, and shops. Its trees, parks, and gardens set Potsdam off from the industrial congestion of the capital. Members of the new German elite, many of them businessmen with links to the Nazi regime, had moved there in the years before the war, refurbishing old villas and building exclusive new neighborhoods.

In the interwar years, Potsdam and Babelsberg had developed a new and quite different kind of royal association as the capital of the German film industry and the home of many of its stars and producers. By the time World War II began, most people knew Potsdam more as a German version of Hollywood than as the German version of Versailles that Frederick the Great had envisioned. The name thus carried with it an aura of glamour and ultramodern elegance. The Filmstudio Babelsberg boasted that it was the oldest large-scale movie studio in the world. Conrad Veidt, the popular star of the 1942 American blockbuster *Casablanca* (he played Major Strasser), always claimed to have been from Potsdam, although he was born and raised in Berlin. He left Germany in 1933 with his Jewish wife and became one of the best-paid and most recognized German actors working in Hollywood.

The movie connection gave Potsdam an air of fame and celebrity even amid the devastation of 1945. One British staffer explained in a letter to her mother that she was "living in a film star's colony, rather like Beverly Hills." The major studios became must-see stops for conference attendees and the settings for many of the conference's most memorable social events.

The staffers commented on Potsdam's beautiful lakes and pastoral scenery, which all had seemingly been untouched by the ravages of six years of war. They lent a fairy-tale atmosphere to the town. Western delegates found only small problems to complain about, such as the unreliability of the drinking water and the lack of screens for the windows during the hot, mosquito-filled summer. Potsdam, at least the parts the delegates saw, seemed as charming as it had seemed to visitors for centuries. In fact, parts of the town had suffered some limited wartime damage, requiring the demolition of many unsafe buildings after the war. But the Russians had carefully designed the routes in and out of Potsdam to hide that damage. In direct contrast to Berlin, Potsdam, they believed, should seem as pristine as possible. The parts of it that the delegates saw showed almost no damage from the war and looked on the surface much as they had in 1939.[3]

Only the Germans themselves were missing. The Russians had issued orders calling for the arrest of all Nazi Party officials and anyone identified as a "Nazi supporter" in their zone of occupation. The latter classification might well have accounted for the vast majority of the German population at one point or another in the previous twelve years. In case that provision proved insufficiently elastic, the Russians assumed in the same decree the power to arrest "any other persons dangerous to the occupation or its objectives," a clause that gave Soviet authorities the legal justification to detain or deport anyone, even non-Germans.[4]

The Russians used those powers liberally in clearing Potsdam and Babelsberg of their residents. In the days just prior to the opening of the conference, Potsdam struck the US military liaison to the Soviets, General John Deane, as a "ghost city," because of the complete absence of the local population. The Russians had forced all Germans out of both Potsdam and Babelsberg for the duration of the conference, ostensibly on grounds of security, leaving homes and villas, as well as the shops and restaurants, completely empty. With a combination of amazement and admiration, Joseph Davies remarked on the "thorough job done by the [Russian] military" to ensure that the delegates saw no Germans once the conference officially began.[5]

Few delegates, of course, asked or much cared about the fate of the locals. Most of them believed that the Germans deserved some level of collective punishment; few people outside of Germany—or in Potsdam for the conference—saw the temporary evacuation of German citizens from their homes as in any way harsh. Moreover, in Germany, as in the rest of Europe, separating the guilty from the innocent proved to be a tremendous challenge. Even the categories of guilty and innocent made no sense in the environment of 1945. Simply trying to define the terms of collaboration with the Nazi regime seemed to most statesmen an impossible task. None of the delegates lost any sleep wondering where the owners of the houses they occupied had gone for the duration of the conference.

AS A CONFERENCE LOCALE, Potsdam suited the needs of the Allies perfectly. The Russians had originally eyed Potsdam as a conference site because it lay inside the Soviet zone of control, because it had escaped most of the war's worst damage, and, in all likelihood, because it sat close enough to Berlin to give the British and American delegates the chance to explore the ruins of the German capital for themselves. The conference sessions took place at Potsdam's Cecilienhof Palace, a sprawling structure built in a neo-Tudor style during World War I for the crown prince and his wife, Cecilie. Designed with half-timbers and graceful archways, it resembled an English country house, but on a much larger scale. The palace had six courtyards, more than 170 rooms, 55 fireplaces, and expansive gardens bordering a graceful lake. It thus had plenty of space to host working groups from the three national delegations, each in its own part of

The Cecilienhof Palace, the Potsdam Conference locale, built for Crown Prince Wilhelm during World War I. (United States Army Heritage and Education Center, Harry Truman Photographic Collection)

the palace. Each delegation received its own suite of rooms in which to set up offices as well as smaller meeting rooms for lower-level delegates, plus its own kitchen and communications network.[6]

To most delegates and staffers, the palace, mostly undamaged by the war, seemed an ideal setting. One British staffer, who had attended the meetings at Yalta and Tehran, called Cecilienhof "the most romantic place imaginable. It exudes atmosphere and tradition." With the gardens in full summer bloom and the ornate interiors largely intact, it presented the starkest imaginable contrast to the rubble of nearby Berlin. To the Russians, it must have underscored the tremendous wealth of Germany and the senselessness of its invasion of a much poorer Soviet Union. Not everyone, however, was impressed. A few attendees, especially the upper-class English delegates, disdained the palace as both too middle class and too ostentatious in its design. Even Clement Attlee, in a line worthy of Winston Churchill, dismissed it as "stock exchange gothic."[7]

Russian Marshal Georgi Zhukov had used Cecilienhof a few weeks earlier for conferences with his British and American counterparts about joint occupation policies and found it more than satisfactory. The palace had been employed as a hospital by both the Germans and the Soviets during the war, and the Russians had found some of the palace's rooms in need of furniture, paint, and decorations, but otherwise in the best shape of any of the large Potsdam palaces. Being also the newest of the great palaces, it had modern plumbing, modern kitchens, and electricity in every room. To make sure that it could serve as a conference headquarters, the Russians brought in new furniture, some of it from as far away as Moscow, and cleaned it from top to bottom. They also brought in the experienced manager of Moscow's Metropole Hotel to oversee hospitality arrangements.[8]

The renovated palace met the needs of the conference perfectly, although the Russians decided on a few alterations to prepare it for its role as the conference headquarters. Most obviously, they planted hundreds of geraniums in a twenty-four-foot-wide red star pattern in the central courtyard for all arriving visitors to see as their cars dropped them off at the main entrance. As Truman's bodyguard noted, the flowers "strikingly inform all that the Russians are the conference host," and, by extension, the conquerors of Berlin. Red dominated as the primary color not just of the flowers, but also of the cushions and drapes.[9]

As part of a general policy of de-Germanizing the areas under their control, the Russians had torn down statues in the Potsdam villas that they deemed too Teutonic in design. They painted over frescos and other artistic renderings whose symbolism they disliked, and also removed many of the tapestries with overly Germanic themes. In one case, the Russians painted a red star over a cloud in a fresco at Cecilienhof that had somehow offended an important Russian delegate. They also burned most of the books with pro-fascist themes that they found in the libraries of the homes they occupied. The Russians intended quite literally to put their own stamp on the former home

The Red Star of geraniums that the Soviets planted in the courtyard of the Cecilienhof Palace to demonstrate their power and influence in the new Germany. (United States Army Heritage and Education Center, Harry Truman Photographic Collection)

of the German prince. In the years that followed, Russian occupation troops would continue the denazification process across the Berlin area, tearing down entire buildings that they deemed too celebratory of German militarism.[10]

The conference setting, in the home built for the crown prince, one of the key German militarists of 1914, had a satisfying symbolism. To General Lucius Clay, who was in charge of the American occupation forces in Germany, Potsdam represented "the City of the Kings of Prussia, where German aggression had its origin." If the delegates did their jobs well, it might also become the place where German aggression met its final end. In any case, falling as it did inside the Russian sector, Potsdam would host no more German militarists for the foreseeable future. It would eventually become one of the major training and research centers of the East German military, itself firmly under the control of its Soviet masters.[11]

As with the Reich Chancellery in Berlin, Cecilienhof became a vast souvenir shop, although, once again, no one paid for anything. The Russians took the palace's remaining furniture and the kitchen silver even while the conference was still taking place. By the time the conference had ended, everything from bathroom fixtures to light bulbs had disappeared. "Apparently, Russian ideas of private property in occupied countries is not ours," remarked a British officer, who had himself taken twenty-one medals and a "heavy bronze inkstand out of the rubble of some exalted person's office" at the Reich Chancellery. His selective qualms notwithstanding, a few other Britons and Americans also helped themselves to keepsakes, most often from the library. American delegate George M. Elsey took the crown prince's personal copy of one of his favorite books, British naval theorist Julian Corbett's 1911 classic *Some Principles of Maritime Strategy*. In the environment of 1945, German property counted for little in the eyes of the victorious Allies. Truman's bodyguard wrote to his father asking if their German-speaking neighbor would like a beautiful, leather-bound book he had taken from the crown prince's library. "If he doesn't want it," the letter concluded, "I can toss it in the river."[12]

THE MAIN CONFERENCE ROOM had once served as the palace's reception hall. One British staffer recalled it as "magnificent." "It is about three storeys high," he said, "with deep red carpet and red plush chairs," all recently imported for the occasion. The Russians also brought in red drapes and red bunting for decoration, as well as a table twelve feet in diameter that quickly filled up with papers. Small British, American, and Soviet flags sat in the sconces on the walls and decorated the center of the table. Each nation had five seats at this table, with the chairs for the delegation heads just slightly higher than the others. Each delegation entered from a separate door that led to the suite of rooms that held that delegation's advisers, servants, and staffers, who sat ready at a moment's notice to answer a query, fetch drinks, or clean the ashtrays that Churchill, At-tlee, Stalin, and other smokers constantly filled up. Security guards sat just outside the doors and, just for good measure, the Americans checked their suite every morning for listening devices. They never found any, but they always suspected that the Russians were eaves-dropping on their every word.[13]

The daily routine at Potsdam centered on the nocturnal habits of Churchill and Stalin. Unlike those two, Truman preferred to rise early; but the Russian and British leaders rarely made themselves available for serious discussion until well after lunch. Consequently, the mornings featured meetings for the foreign ministers and the military men, who were much more accustomed to working before lunch. These groups then briefed the heads of delegations in prepa-ration for sessions that began in the late afternoon and ran until din-nertime. Most of the dinners involved huge, hours-long banquets that ran well into the wee hours of the morning. Truman and most of the newly appointed American delegates, unaccustomed to the end-less social engagements of international diplomacy, found the sched-ule demanding and tiring, but they had little say in the matter.

The Russians spared no expense to make the conference a mem-orable one. They assembled what a British general called "the most spectacular collection of wine glasses I have ever seen" for an unfor-gettable banquet held before the arrival of the official delegations. Despite the poverty and misery all around Europe, the banquet, held for the advance parties and their protocol staffs, featured Russian soldier-waitresses who served drinks and food while wearing their dress uniforms, with medals for bravery prominently displayed. The impressive banquet led the general to conclude with evident delight that Russian hospitality "should not lightly be indulged in without considerable previous training."

The banquet lasted three hours and provided a hint of the gener-osity to come for the senior delegates. It featured, in the recollection of one British delegate, "caviar, smoked salmon, sprats from the Bal-tic, and fresh fruit from Georgia." The Russians also provided vodka, brandy, white wine, red wine, and champagne. When the British general began to slow down after numerous toasts, a Russian officer

Senior American, British, and Soviet generals meet for a morning session at the Potsdam Conference. General George Marshall, General Henry "Hap" Arnold, and Chief of Naval Operations Admiral Ernest King are all present. (United States Army Heritage and Education Center, Harry Truman Photographic Collection)

came up to him, proposed yet another toast, and told him to drink up, "as there was plenty more where this came from." With considerable joy, the Briton realized that the conference would lack for nothing. "The display of glasses and the array of bottles on the side table made it painfully clear to me," he noted, "that I was going to be put to the test" for as long as the conference lasted. Staffers bragged about feasting on steak and drinking endless glasses of wine when off duty. The first large state dinner of the conference boasted a menu of pâté de foie gras, caviar on toast, vodka, cream of tomato soup, celery, olives, perch sauté meunière, vintage 1937 wine, filet mignon with mushroom gravy, potatoes, peas, carrots, Bordeaux, cheese, ice cream, champagne, cigars, coffee, port, and cognac.[14]

Helped along by alcohol and fine foods, the atmosphere in the first few days at Potsdam struck many attendees as far more congenial than that of the recent conferences at Tehran and Yalta. At past conferences, the presence of a common enemy had kept the delegates on task; the focus was not just on talking for the purpose of making conversation, but on making decisions. As wartime conferences, they had also involved at almost every step military men who much preferred decisions and direct talk to diplomacy. Although the matters discussed at Potsdam had far-reaching consequences, few of the participants had the sense of immediacy that discussions over military strategy had had at past gatherings. At Potsdam, the three powers had no common enemy. Japan remained undefeated, of course, but the common sense of purpose in the Pacific war paled in comparison to that which had characterized the European war, and Russia still remained technically at peace with the Japanese. Most delegates, moreover, expected that Japan would soon surrender. As a result, Charles Bohlen, a veteran of many such conferences, remarked on the "sense of relaxation" and the "freer exchange of opinions" at Potsdam. One of the Russian delegates agreed, but noted that many of the new American officials brought with them a more difficult and more confrontational attitude toward the Soviet Union than Roosevelt's team had displayed at Yalta.[15]

Their hospitality notwithstanding, the Soviets came to Potsdam eager to decide on practical matters. They showed little patience for lectures about guiding principles. During the Potsdam proceedings, Stalin generally appeared uninterested when Churchill or Truman waxed philosophical, playing with his mustache or doodling on a notepad. He was particularly fond of drawing pictures of wolves or writing the word "REPARATIONS" over and over again. As Truman observed, Stalin "was not given to long speeches." He often sat grinning while his interpreters discussed among themselves how best to translate the essence of the item then under debate. His demeanor led Truman to suspect that Stalin understood much more English than he revealed. Stalin normally spoke in what Truman described as a "quiet, inoffensive way," making his occasional outbursts on matters of special importance to him all that much more effective.[16]

Whether as a function of personality or a prearranged strategem, Stalin played the good cop while Foreign Minister Molotov played the bad cop. Molotov, who was then fifty-five years old and had been a member of the Communist Party Central Committee since 1916, had survived the internecine party struggles of the 1920s and the purges of the 1930s that had resulted in Stalin's ascent to near-total control of the Soviet Union's political machinery. Molotov had become foreign minister in 1939, and in September of that year had signed the Nazi-Soviet Pact, also called the Molotov-Ribbentrop Pact, that split Poland between the Germans and the Soviets. It had also left the Germans free to attack in the West in 1940, thus putting Norway and France in the face of the full power of the German military and, in the eyes of British and American strategists, likely dooming both to defeat and years of brutal occupation. As a result of that treaty and Molotov's general reputation for deceit, Western diplomats despised and deeply mistrusted the Soviet foreign minister.

Molotov was known within the diplomatic corps as "Mr. Nyet," and, in the words of the Soviet ambassador to Sweden, he had a reputation for "greyness, dullness, and servility" to Stalin. Known also as "Stone Ass" for his ability to sit emotionless for as long as necessary in diplomatic discussions, Molotov rarely compromised. He held to the party line and seemed more than happy to take the heat from Western foreign ministers so that Stalin could play the role of the gracious leader offering deals that Molotov would not make.[17]

Eden, Churchill, and others in Britain put Molotov in what they called the "unfriendly group" of Soviet officials. In the best-case scenario, they saw Molotov as the barrier to better relations with Stalin. If they could get past or around the difficult foreign minister, they rather optimistically concluded, they might be able to cut favorable deals with the more amiable Stalin. Byrnes and Davies agreed, with the latter noting that Stalin had given up on the idea that "the world had to be communistic [sic] for Russia to be safe," but Molotov had not. Given how bad British relations with Molotov were, and given

Joseph Stalin and President Harry Truman pose with their senior diplomats at
the Potsdam Conference. US Secretary of State James Byrnes and Soviet Foreign
Minister Vyacheslav Molotov (far right) stand arm in arm. (United States Army
Heritage and Education Center, Charles H. Donnelly Collection)

the disastrous first meeting he had had with Truman, Molotov would
present a challenge. He would require, British statesman Lord Halifax noted, a "united front" of Anglo-American diplomacy if the West
hoped to come away with anything at Potsdam.[18]

Throughout the conference, Molotov spoke in harsh ideological
terms, defending the ideals of the Bolshevik revolution and railing
against the perfidy of the West. Harriman had warned Truman that
Molotov remained "far more suspicious of us and less willing to
view matters in our mutual relations from a broad standpoint than
is Stalin." The tense meeting in Washington could only have exacerbated Molotov's prickliness and suspicion about the Americans.
"Stone Ass," not the tyrant for whom he worked, provided the West
with its toughest negotiating partner.[19]

At several points during the Potsdam meeting, Molotov went a step or two too far for Stalin's liking, leading Stalin to calm his foreign minister down with a few words of Russian spoken softly into his ear. Although Molotov certainly had a reputation for bombast and directness, the act was likely part of a plan to make Stalin appear as the good Russian, yielding on points where Molotov had stood firm. When Stalin did not want to discuss a point any longer, he would ask that the Council of Foreign Ministers, which the great powers created at Potsdam, consider it further. The council intended to bring together the senior diplomats of the great powers on a regular basis, but Stalin knew that Molotov could use council deliberations to delay or even kill any issue he did not want to discuss himself.[20]

THE WAR IN EUROPE WON, a sense of triumph pervaded the conference, at least in its opening days. The positive spirit marked that of the weeks following the German surrender more generally, with the senior leaders of the three armies chatting amiably and expressing their confidence in a future of cooperation, especially over the joint occupation of the unified Germany that they all then envisioned. Even at lower levels, Russian, British, and American soldiers generally got along well, not just in the bubble of Potsdam, but also in the slowly reopening nightclubs of Berlin. "Russian and American soldiers smiling at each other and slapping each other on the back," Walter Brown noted. "Everyone understands a smile." American comedian Bob Hope even showed up in Berlin on the day the conference closed to entertain some of the 31,000 American soldiers then in the Berlin area as well as some British and a few Russian soldiers. A demand by the American occupation authorities for resources to open twenty-two venereal disease centers in their sector of Berlin may indicate that other kinds of entertainment were available, and that not all westerners avoided fraternization with the locals.[21]

With at least one part of the war over, delegates felt more comfortable enjoying lavish banquets, and the staffers could host larger parties. The Red Cross hosted a hugely popular "Terminal Dance" for staffers, and the diary of the head of arrangements for the British delegation is filled with appointments for receptions, dinners, and dances. Another British staffer recalled "parties and dances every night," including one in the former mansion of one of the directors of UFA, a major German movie studio. Another party hosted by British officers in a pub to "entertain all the girls on the Delegation" featured, one staffer recalled, more champagne than she had ever seen in her life. "The evening was literally flowing with it," she wrote to her husband, who may not have been too happy to read about all of the attention paid to his wife and her friends.[22]

The senior delegates at Potsdam shared in the sense of goodwill that immediately followed the successful triumph over Germany. One US general, who had worked with the Soviets on the tense issues surrounding occupation policy, found the Russians "very friendly and cordial," especially at the conference's many social functions. Although everyone understood the differences that separated American, British, and Soviet policy at the end of the war, they also recognized the tremendous achievement that they had shared in winning the war. At least in the conference's opening days, optimism tended to reign, with most delegates still hopeful that the Big Three would find a way to smooth over their differences and work toward a modus operandi for the postwar years. Solving the problems of Germany and Europe together remained the primary task at hand.[23]

As the preconference banquets suggested, the social functions helped to project an air of amity. They were among the most lavish that veteran delegates had ever seen. Truman, as impressed as anyone, described one of the Russian dinners in a letter to his mother as "a wow." It featured caviar, vodka, champagne, two kinds of fish, venison, chicken, and duck. Stalin made no fewer than twenty-five toasts, although Truman noted that the Soviet leader drank small amounts of wine rather than the vodka served to others, an indication of his recent health problems. The Russians had also brought an entire orchestra to entertain the delegates.[24]

The Americans tried to match the Russians in lavish hospitality. They brought in the Filipino mess staff from an American battleship dressed in immaculate livery to serve food and drinks. When Truman decided he wanted better music, he sent for the best piano player in the US Army, the famous concert pianist Eugene List, and had him flown in from Paris, where, as a sergeant, he was leading the Seventh Army Symphony Orchestra. When List requested different sheet music than that available at Potsdam, the Americans sent a plane to Paris to get it. No detail seemed too small for the delegates despite the devastation of Europe all around them.

Potsdam also featured moments of frivolity. Truman particularly enjoyed introducing a bodyguard and special assistant, a friend and former federal marshal from western Missouri, by his American title as "Marshal Fred A. Canfil." The Americans then watched the Russians fall over themselves to try to figure out the correct protocol, since a marshal in their system was equivalent to a five-star general. To the continued amusement of the Americans, senior Russian officers clicked their heels and saluted for the remainder of the conference whenever the "marshal" entered the room.[25]

The conference saw more than its share of pageantry and ceremony. The American delegation brought with it the flag that had flown over the United States Capitol building on the day that the Americans had declared war on Germany. It had also flown over liberated Rome on July 4, 1944. Now, in the presence of President Truman, General Eisenhower, and a galaxy of senior American officials, the flag was raised over the headquarters of the US military occupation authority in Berlin. It would later fly over MacArthur's occupation headquarters in Tokyo as well. The flag-raising ceremony struck Lucius Clay, the American commander of the Berlin occupation forces, as the most poignant moment of the conference and a reminder that "no one who had seen our flag raised by right of victory but dedicated to the preservation of freedom and peace could possibly see it withdrawn until peace and freedom had been established." As the symbolism of the flag ceremony seemed to underscore, the Americans had indeed arrived in Germany to stay, one way or the other. Unlike in 1919, the Americans would not return to their side of the Atlantic and simply leave Europe to its fate.[26]

The glaring spotlight of the international media also gave Potsdam a different feel than the secret meetings at Tehran and Yalta. Stalin had at first insisted that, as in past conferences, the Big Three should ban all reporters from the proceedings. Initially, the British

General Dwight D. Eisenhower, General George S. Patton, President Harry Truman, Secretary of War Henry Stimson, and General Omar N. Bradley salute the American flag in Potsdam. (United States Army Heritage and Education Center, Harry Truman Photographic Collection)

had agreed, with Anthony Eden telling the British media in early June that they could not enter Potsdam itself. The delegations would instead send official daily updates to their press bureaus in Berlin from which the journalists could then write their stories. Eden reiterated the ban on July 13, just days before the departure of the official British delegation for Potsdam. At that point, the British media still did not know exactly where Churchill would stay. Only partially tongue in cheek, they sometimes referred to his residence as "No. 10 Downing Street, Potsdam." The Americans, too, tried to keep reporters away, telling them that if they came to Germany, "all they could do . . . would be to wait in Berlin for official handouts."[27]

Despite these efforts, scores of journalists descended on Potsdam. By the time the conference ended, more than two hundred journalists and forty photographers had made their way to the Berlin area hoping to score a scoop on the biggest story of the day. Unlike the reporters at Yalta or Tehran, reporters at Potsdam knew where and when the meeting was taking place; damage to the city notwithstanding, Berlin still offered sufficient accommodations to house them. Many wondered why they had come at all, once they saw the restrictions and the secrecy. Russian guards kept all reporters out of Potsdam and Babelsberg, and official press officers kept them in the dark about what the delegates had discussed, providing them with daily updates utterly devoid of substance. Reporters from the *Washington Post* and the *Philadelphia Inquirer* lodged formal protests to the State Department, complaining that "it is extremely unsuitable, in a world in which famine is widespread[,] to provide for the correspondents 'piles of trivia' concerning the social aspects of the conference, the menus, and the clothes worn by the participants" in lieu of real news. They also complained about the excessive security, including the barbed wire that separated the press corps from the conference attendees.[28]

Life magazine went even further, taking its complaints with security public. Its reporters wrote in their first story about the conference that the "tight news blackout" prevented them from sharing any more information with their readers than a vague description of the conference room and brief portraits of the famous men inside. The American press office in Berlin, *Life* complained, issued communiqués about irrelevant matters that "read like notes from a society column" rather than providing substantive information about a three-power conference that would determine the future of Europe.[29]

Partly out of frustration and partly to satisfy their editors' demands for copy on the biggest story of the day, journalists in Berlin began to report on what the White House called "all sorts of wild tales" and rumors, much of it inaccurate and almost all of it about the social side of the conference. This included stories on the lavish accommodations and the enormous amounts of food and drink being served while so much of Europe went homeless and hungry.

The reports created a potential public relations nightmare. The White House press secretary wrote in a secret communiqué to Washington: "I should like to give you my opinion of the acts of some of these correspondents, but it would have to be written on asbestos." White House officials remained angry about a press leak involving the time and place of Truman's departure for Europe, and they saw the restrictions on press participation at the conference as justified punishment. The journalists, however, decided to push back. Some reporters, the White House press office complained, had threatened to publish "the sheerest rot" and "some very weird stories" if they did not get more access. The Russians continued to argue for a complete ban on journalists, but the Americans and the British, coming from states with traditions of a free press, knew that they had to do more. Within a few days of the conference opening, public affairs officers saw no choice but to give the reporters more substantive information, although they still banned journalists from Potsdam itself and still refused to allow the journalists to interview any of the delegates.[30]

Had they been permitted to report freely on the conference, journalists would have noted that the Big Three met thirteen separate times. Nine of those thirteen sessions occurred before the announcement of the results of the British general election on July 26. The Council of Foreign Ministers, which everyone hoped might become a permanent body that met several times a year, met twelve times at Potsdam. It would meet in the future with the foreign ministers of France and China included in the deliberations, modeling the arrangements for the United Nations Security Council. At Potsdam, the foreign ministers dealt with some of the thornier and more concrete problems, but rarely came to important decisions.

The Big Three still disagreed about the ultimate purpose of the conference. Stalin called it "a conference to prepare for the future conference," either an indication that he wanted to move slowly, in order to avoid the mistakes of Versailles, or, as the British and Americans suspected, as part of a ploy to buy time. With the Americans and British increasingly becoming weaker on the ground in Europe, the future seemed to offer more opportunities for the Russians.

Several times during the conference, Stalin suggested future Big Three meetings as part of a lengthy peace process, holding out the lure of the next conference taking place in Tokyo. When the Americans suggested that the next conference take place instead in Washington, so Stalin could see the United States for himself at long last, he responded, "God willing."[31]

Truman, by contrast, wanted concrete decisions, preferably recorded and officially sanctioned by the Big Three, at the end of each day. "I was there to get something accomplished, and if we could not do that, I meant to go back home," he later recalled. Unlike Woodrow Wilson, who had spent more than six months in Europe, Truman had decided that he would not stay any longer than three weeks and would return home immediately at the end of the conference, notwithstanding British desires that he come to London for a formal state visit on his way back to the United States. His attitude reflected his view of the conference as a poker game, not a dinner party, as well as his reluctance to risk the conference turning into a forum for debate on dozens of questions affecting people around the world. Unlike Wilson, he had come to Europe to deal, not to make long speeches.[32]

The longer the conference went on, the more frustrated Truman became at its failure to reach firm agreements; Potsdam, after all, was his first major international conference, and his inexperience showed. On just the fourth day, Truman's frustrations led him to write that he "felt like blowing the roof off the palace." A week later, just over halfway through the conference, Truman wrote to his mother and sister that "I'm still in this Godforsaken country. . . . I had hoped to be finished by now." Closer to the end, Truman showed both his frustration and his inexperience when he said to Byrnes, "Jimmy, do you realize we have been here seventeen whole days? Why in seventeen days you can decide anything!" The president had learned at long last that the Russians were not like the men of the Kansas City political machine, and Byrnes had learned that international diplomacy involved more than a trade of post offices.[33]

Potsdam also notably lacked the flair and international feeling that had so characterized the Paris Peace Conference. In Paris, representatives from around the world had come to plead their cases. They included Emir Faisal, dressed in his finest Arab attire and accompanied by the famous T. E. Lawrence (known as Lawrence of Arabia); the young Ho Chi Minh, then known as Nguyen Ai Quoc, who failed to get his desired audience with Woodrow Wilson; and the determined Japanese delegates who failed in their effort to include a racial equality clause in the final Treaty of Versailles. Delegations also came from countries such as Brazil, Cuba, Siam, and Liberia, which had played minor roles at best in the Allied victory, but came to Paris with long lists of desires and demands.

The international dimension of the Paris conference provided an air of romance and exoticism in the French capital, but it also created endless headaches. The conferees could not possibly have hoped to reconcile the desires of such a diverse group of nations; nor did they really care about the interests of the small powers. As the Paris Peace Conference dragged on, moreover, the smaller states and lesser powers appeared increasingly parochial in their demands at a moment when the great powers had taken upon themselves the enormous task of trying to solve global problems. As one American delegate, General Tasker H. Bliss, had noted in Paris, "The 'submerged nations' are coming to the surface and as soon as they appear, they fly at someone's throat. They are like mosquitos—vicious from the moment of their birth."[34]

The Americans, British, and Russians had no intention of repeating that mistake at Potsdam. The only non-white faces at this conference belonged to the Filipino waiters the Americans used and the Central Asian soldiers who patrolled the grounds in the uniforms of the Red Army. It is only a slight exaggeration to say that Potsdam represented the apex of the power of white Americans, Britons, and Russians to rule over others. Soon, and without the great powers discussing it at Potsdam, the powerful winds of anticolonialism began to blow with much greater force.

Not discussing imperialism at Potsdam suited the British, for it meant that India would have no representatives there. For the Paris conference, the British had found sufficiently pliable Indian leaders to represent their interests, but in 1945 no serious discussion of the future of India could have occurred without the inclusion of such people as Mohandas Gandhi, Jawaharlal Nehru, and Mohammad Ali Jinnah, all of whom opposed continued British rule. Nor would China send a representative, although all of the delegates at Potsdam understood that China would play a key role in stabilizing the postwar world if it could emerge from the war intact. At this point, both the Americans and the Soviets expressed their faith that it would, most likely under the hand of the noncommunist Chinese leader Chiang Kai-shek.

France and Italy, important prewar continental powers, posed a different kind of problem. Both states technically belonged to the winning coalition; the Allies recognized Charles de Gaulle's Provisional Government of the French Republic as the legitimate government of France, and Italy had changed sides in 1943. Still, no one at Potsdam took the contributions of either country to the final victory seriously, and they thought of both France and Italy more as conquered nations than as liberated ones. If they talked about the French and Italians at all, they spoke with a thinly veiled contempt for, in the French case, the defeat of 1940, and, in the Italian case, a series of transgressions that dated back to Mussolini's march on Rome in 1922. Italy's sins included the installation of the first fascist government, aggression in Ethiopia, and, especially for the Soviets, the dispatch of Italian forces to the eastern front in support of the German war there. Churchill and the British delegates despised Italy as much as the Russians did; Churchill argued against its inclusion in the United Nations until it could prove it had changed its ways, a condition he only applied to one other state, Germany.[35]

The denial of Italian and French representation at Potsdam demonstrated how little the great powers wanted a return to the prewar world. They treated Italy much as they treated Germany and Austria, with both the Soviets and the British demanding reparations and, if necessary, an Allied occupation. They likely would have insisted on a similar, if slightly less punitive, arrangement for France, had de Gaulle not grabbed the reins of the French government with as much force as he did. The Americans had, in fact, planned for an American occupation government in France. But the ecstatic reaction of the French people to de Gaulle showed the Allies that he had their clear support even in the absence of an election. More importantly, de Gaulle could either bring France in line with British and American goals, or take France in a separate direction. An Anglo-American occupation of France would serve no one's interest, and the Americans quickly dropped the idea.[36]

The British had also begun to see how much they would need Italy and France, especially France, to help them in the postwar world. If the Americans demobilized their forces as both Roosevelt and Truman had suggested, then the French and Italian armies would form the cornerstones of any continental deterrence strategy aimed at either a resurgent Germany or the Soviet Union. But the crimes of fascist Italy, and its intellectual fellow traveler in Vichy France, put the delegates of Potsdam in an unforgiving mood. In both cases, moreover, no democratically elected government existed, however popular de Gaulle seemed in the summer of 1945. The personal dislike that many Americans and Britons had for de Gaulle contributed to the isolation of France as well; Truman suspended American arms supplies to France just before leaving for Potsdam in retaliation for de Gaulle's statement implying that France might oppose American participation in the occupation of Italy. Diplomats in both the United States and Great Britain openly hoped for de Gaulle's fall from power and his replacement by a less nationalist professional politician with whom they could more easily negotiate.[37]

For all these reasons, as well as because of fear of repeating the debacle of the Treaty of Versailles, an air of uncertainty hung over the Potsdam festivities. As the conference prepared to open, Joseph Davies confided to his diary his fear that the delegates, especially the Americans and the British, did not fully understand what they had agreed to less than six months before at Yalta. He therefore worried that each side might reach for scraps of temporary gains at Potsdam based on its own understandings of those agreements. He noted his concern that the conference might turn into a negotiation over minor points rather than becoming the "meeting of the minds" on a wider agreement on the future of Europe that all parties needed. Robert Murphy, an American diplomat, agreed. With so much turnover of expertise, beginning with the 1943 State Department purge that had followed the Sumner Welles scandal, the United States had lost some of its best people. It had, of course, also lost its chief, Franklin Roosevelt. The American delegation thus often felt it was operating without a solid foundation, especially given Truman's own impression that the Yalta agreements offered multiple interpretations.[38]

Harry Hopkins had warned Truman about the problem of multiple interpretations of Yalta before the president left for Germany. He told the president that Roosevelt and Churchill had, for domestic political reasons, presented the transient compromises of Yalta as definitive diplomatic achievements. As a result, he feared, the flawed and tentative agreements of Yalta might make for a poor starting point for Potsdam, even if the three sides could reach consensus on what they had decided in the Crimea. Truman also worried about how the Russians might read the increasingly anti-Soviet statements being offered by American politicians looking to score some points at home, ironically enough, much as he himself had once done.[39]

According to international diplomatic protocol, Truman, the only head of state present, outranked Churchill and Stalin. As a result, and like Woodrow Wilson before him, Truman became the presiding officer of the conference despite being by far the least experienced among them. The privilege gave Truman few real powers, not even the power to hold the meetings before lunch. It did, however, lead him to express his amazement that a country boy from Missouri could find himself in such a position. He had indeed undergone a remarkable transition since arriving in Chicago for the 1944 Democratic National Convention expecting to give his support to James Byrnes. Now he would have to face Winston Churchill and Joseph Stalin on a much bigger stage and in a much different game.[40]

"I Dreamed That My Life Was Over"

JOSEPH STALIN, THE BEST PREPARED of the Big Three at Yalta, repeated that preparation for Potsdam. He spent countless hours strategizing for the upcoming meeting despite the fatigue that had set in after four years of war. He had also ordered the preparation of psychological profiles of Churchill and Truman. At Potsdam Harry Hopkins noted of Stalin that "there was no waste of word, gesture, nor mannerism. It was like talking to a perfectly coordinated machine." Often replying in short, clipped sentences, Stalin rarely revealed more than he had to and seemed to revel in giving ambiguous replies to direct questions. Molotov, for his part, answered in vague, diplomatic Russian when he did not want to answer a question. Together, they formed a formidable duo for their Western counterparts.[1]

All of the members of the Russian delegation projected confidence at the bargaining table, believing that they held in their hands three cards that gave them leverage over the West. First, the Soviet Union had the world's largest army, and Stalin had no intention of demobilizing it on anything like the rapid timetable of the Western democracies. He expected that while the West either demobilized as quickly as it had after World War I or shifted most of its military assets to the Pacific for its ongoing war with Japan, Russia would remain strong on the ground in Germany and in Eastern Europe. Roosevelt had announced at Yalta that he did not expect the American people, or their elected representatives, to support any plan for keeping US troops in Europe for more than two years beyond the end of war with Germany, a statement that terrified Churchill as much as it pleased Stalin. Truman, too, looked forward to demobilizing as much of the US Army as he could once hostilities with Japan had ended. Even if US troops remained in Europe, however, they could not possibly dedicate more than a few divisions to occupation duties. With millions of men under arms, Stalin believed he could both shape the political future of Eastern Europe and ensure that the West abided by Russian interpretations of treaty agreements on borders and zones of occupation.

Second, Stalin knew that the importance of Russian entry into the United Nations had grown since Roosevelt's death. Roosevelt had desperately wanted to revive Woodrow Wilson's dream of the world having an international organization to maintain the hard-won peace. Since Roosevelt's death, the idea had grown into something of a moral crusade in the United States to honor the late president. Harry Truman's first statement to a reporter in his new role as president affirmed that the San Francisco conference to organize the United Nations would take place as scheduled on the watershed date of April 25. Rather than postpone the conference because of Roosevelt's death, Truman said that holding it as scheduled would honor Roosevelt's memory. The conference would advance the project that had been closest to FDR's heart.

But whereas the Americans saw the new United Nations as a way to honor their fallen president and atone for the failures of the League of Nations, the Russians remained wary of it—and all other multilateral institutions that Western nations dominated. The League of Nations had banned the Soviet Union until 1934, and the Russians now looked at the United Nations less as a second try at a fundamentally sound idea than as a vivid reminder of their former isolation, as well as of the unsupportable concept (in Soviet eyes) that small nations had the same rights as large ones. As Ambassador Harriman told Truman in a June 8 cable, Stalin did not subscribe to the notion that "a country is virtuous because it is small." Rather, Stalin told Harriman, small nations like Serbia, Czechoslovakia, and Poland had been the cause of much of the trouble of the twentieth century. Nor did the Russians put much faith in international bodies not backed up by adequate force. As a result, Ambassador Harriman observed, the Soviets found it difficult to "appreciate our faith in [the] abstract principles" that formed the basis of the United Nations. Instead, as Joseph Davies noted, they feared that it would become an American-led "united front" against Soviet interests.

The Russians knew that the United Nations meant more to the Americans than it did to them. They could therefore trade concessions on issues related to the United Nations for something much more important to their core interests, as when they offered at Potsdam to accept Italy in the United Nations in exchange for American concessions on the borders of postwar Poland. Alternatively, they could cause problems in the United Nations to express dissatisfaction with American actions elsewhere, as Molotov had done with the issue of Argentine membership after his volatile meeting with Truman in April. The Security Council arrangement agreed to at Yalta, with Russia having a permanent veto power, ensured that the body could not easily harm Russian interests; the Soviets could therefore use the United Nations strategically, knowing that the Americans valued the organization far more than they did.[2]

Third, Stalin knew that the Americans wanted Russian participation in the war against Japan in order to reduce the number of American casualties required to force Japan's surrender. The Americans had made great progress in their island-hopping and aerial bombardment campaigns, but the majority of the Japanese Army deployed outside the home islands remained in China, where the Americans and the British could not get at them. American attempts to build Chiang Kai-shek's Nationalist Party into an effective fighting force had largely failed, meaning that the Japanese troops in China remained a serious military problem. Only the Russians could solve that problem.

The former Soviet ambassador to Great Britain, Ivan Maisky, argued for not helping the Americans and the British in Asia as payback for their delay in setting up a second front in Europe, but the lure of the East shimmered too brightly for the Soviet leadership to refuse it. Now that the existential war with Germany had ended in triumph, the Russians could break their nonaggression pact with Japan and send troops into Manchuria. Soviet strategists, Stalin included, dreamed of recovering Russia's losses from the humiliating defeat in the 1904–1905 Russo-Japanese War. They had their eyes fixed on Sakhalin Island, the Kurile Islands, the railways of Manchuria, and the port of Dairen. As the Soviet Union shared a long border with China, Stalin also had an interest in the winner of the Chinese Civil War between Chiang Kai-shek's Kuomintang Party and Mao Tse-tung's Communist Party that would almost certainly begin in full once the Japanese left.

Stalin also had up-to-date intelligence that gave him a bargaining advantage with his Western counterparts. In early May, Soviet agents had told Stalin that they had found and positively identified Hitler's remains in the smoldering ruins of the Reich Chancellery building. Stalin kept the information so secret that not even Marshal Georgi Zhukov, who was leading one of the Soviet army groups advancing on Berlin, knew that Hitler had died. Soviet agents buried the Nazi dictator's body in Magdeburg to preserve the secret, taking Hitler's jawbone and part of his skull to Moscow in case Stalin needed further forensic proof; those same agents had matched the jawbone to Hitler's dental records. Stalin seems to have relished his nearly exclusive knowledge about Hitler's death, occasionally prodding Zhukov with messages asking whether he knew anything about Hitler's fate.[3]

Stalin used his knowledge about Hitler's death as a ploy both at Potsdam and in meetings before the conference with Harry Hopkins. Whenever a Western official talked about Germany having been defeated, and therefore no longer posing a threat to Russia, Stalin would respond that he believed the threat still existed and that Hitler probably remained alive, plotting with Joseph Goebbels in Spain or Argentina—not coincidentally, two nations Stalin wanted to see punished for their support of the Nazi regime. Safe in these hideouts, he alleged, Nazi leaders could then rehabilitate the German Army and renew the war. Stalin thus used Hitler's presumed unknown whereabouts to urge stronger punitive measures to prevent Germany from resuming hostilities as Napoleon's France had in 1815.[4]

Stalin also knew that the Americans had made substantial progress toward the development of an atomic bomb. A network of Soviet spies operating in the United States had kept Soviet intelligence well informed of the progress of the Manhattan Project since March 1942. The Russians therefore had a precise understanding of where the project stood and how soon it might produce a usable bomb. Just before the conference began, Stalin and his widely feared chief of secret police, Lavrenti Beria, discussed what they should do with this information. They decided that they would wait to see if Truman informed them of the atomic bomb's progress at Potsdam. If he did not, it would signal America's unwillingness to cooperate on equal terms as well as its desire to, in Stalin's words to one of his interpreters, "blackmail" their erstwhile allies at some future date. If Truman did let the Russians in on the secret, then Stalin would pretend not to understand, thereby not revealing to the Americans how much he already knew.[5]

Finally, Soviet spies had informed Stalin that the British and the Americans had a number of disagreements that Russian diplomacy might exploit. A ring of spies known as the Cambridge Five, led by British intelligence officer Kim Philby, had kept the Russians apprised of detailed conversations between London and Washington. Stalin thus concluded that the chill in Anglo-American relations he had witnessed at Yalta had accelerated. Observers at Yalta had noted the growing separation between Churchill and Roosevelt, resulting from the widening gap in power between the United States and Britain as well as divergences of opinion on colonial and financial issues. The Soviets believed that these divergences would likely continue to grow with Truman in the White House.[6]

COMPARED TO THE RUSSIANS, the British looked out of sorts and disorganized from the start of the Potsdam Conference. Those who had seen Churchill firsthand both at Hendaye and in London did not expect him to perform well in the meetings of the Big Three, and their fears were confirmed in the first few days at Potsdam. On the evening of the opening day of the conference, Eden recorded in his diary that "Winston was very bad. He had read no brief and was confused and woolly and verbose." Alexander Cadogan, Britain's permanent undersecretary for foreign affairs, agreed, saying that even on important matters Churchill "talked irrelevant rubbish." They both agreed that they "had never seen Winston worse." Even the Americans could tell that Churchill was ad-libbing his government's positions due to a lack of preparation, thus making it difficult for British diplomats to adhere to consistent positions. Complicating matters further, Churchill constantly interfered with his advisers, especially Eden, to whom the prime minister looked "unwell and tired" despite the recent vacation. Eden himself was suffering from ulcers so badly that the British staff sent back to Britain for English milk in the hope that it might somehow make him feel better than the German milk that the rest of the delegation drank.[7]

Much as Eden had predicted, Churchill had predicated British strategy on his own personality and his power of persuasion, especially his ability to reason with Stalin. Also much as Eden had predicted, the strategy failed. Eden grew increasingly frustrated with Churchill's unfounded faith in Stalin's basic goodwill. For their part, Stalin and the Russians wanted no part of Churchill or his supposed charm. Beria later wrote that "of all the western leaders, Churchill had the best understanding of Stalin and succeeded in seeing through almost all his maneuvers. But when he is quoted as suggesting that he gained an influence over Stalin I cannot help smiling. It seems amazing that a person of such stature could so delude himself." If Churchill could see through Stalin, it seems clear that Stalin could also see through Churchill, negating most of the prime minister's advantage.[8]

A second key plank of Churchill's strategy, that of cementing the special relationship with the United States, also failed. Churchill had hoped to charm Truman, or at least to make him see that American interests required a continuation of close Anglo-American relations. As Roosevelt had done at Yalta, however, Truman refused to discuss matters of substance with Churchill unless Stalin was also present in order not to present the image that the West was ganging up on Russia. Churchill's attempts to present a united Anglo-American front sometimes bordered on the pathetic. At one photo session, Churchill insisted on sitting to Truman's right rather than in the middle as the photographer had suggested. He then began subtly to move his chair closer to Truman's so that he would appear physically closer in the resulting pictures. Truman saw through Churchill and moved his own chair closer to Stalin's. The Russian dictator just sat smiling through it all.[9]

Truman appeared to tire of Churchill's antics and even decided on a few of his own. On the third night of the conference, the American delegation hosted a dinner that both Churchill and Stalin attended. Truman chose Chopin for the music, which he had heard Stalin liked but Churchill did not. He then took the piano himself, playing a beautiful rendition of Ignacy Jan Paderewski's Minuet in G, which a twelve-year-old Harry Truman had played with Paderewski himself following a performance in Kansas City. Truman surely knew that Churchill hated both the piece and Paderewski, who had served in the interwar years as Poland's prime minister and had clashed with Churchill over Poland's boundaries at the Paris Peace Conference.[10]

During the conference itself, Churchill frequently lectured and rambled in an unfocused manner that discomfited his own advisers. Truman contrasted the vocal Churchill to Stalin, whom he noted "just grunts." Churchill, he observed with evident frustration, "found it necessary . . . to make long statements then agree to what had already been done." When outvoted, Churchill would eventually yield, but, Truman complained, "he had to make a speech about it first." Churchill's own advisers disliked his performance as well, with Cadogan remarking that "every mention of a topic started Winston off on a wild rampage" disconnected from policy papers or serious dialogue. Stalin, too, quickly grew tired of Churchill's speeches. On several occasions, when Churchill began one of his discourses, Stalin interrupted him and told him that he might as well just agree to the point under discussion now, as he would inevitably do so once he finished his speech.[11]

Some topics virtually guaranteed a Churchill outburst. Predictably, any mention of the British Empire elicited a sharp response, as did several of the brief mentions of the future of Italy. Churchill had a particular hatred for Italy, which he viewed as avaricious in attacking southeastern France in 1940, invading Greece in 1941, and launching a major offensive against the British positions in North Africa; all three had led to costly military commitments for Britain. Churchill repeatedly urged a harsh treatment for Italy until it could prove that it was ready for democratic government. Churchill doubtless also recalled that Italian dissatisfaction with the Versailles Treaty had led to the growth of fascism and Mussolini's emergence as the first fascist leader in Europe in 1922. He wanted to do everything in his power to prevent a repetition of Italy once again causing trouble because of its dissatisfaction with the decisions of a postwar conference. He must also have realized that the British might need Italy as part of a future alliance designed to balance a growing Soviet Union. He therefore let his emotions carry him only so far on the subject of Italy, despite his evident hatred for Italian duplicity.[12]

Churchill did not get much support from his advisers. The ailing Anthony Eden had already lost faith in Churchill and disagreed with him on several key issues, especially Poland, where Eden advocated a harsher line than Churchill did. Nor did Eden, whose ulcers clearly impaired his performance at Potsdam, inspire much confidence in senior British strategists. In the middle of the conference, Field Marshal Alan Brooke, the chief of the imperial general staff, recorded in his diary: "Delightful as [Eden] is, in my opinion he always seems to just miss the point."[13]

The blame did not rest solely with Eden. He had recognized that Great Britain lacked the power to determine the course of events at Potsdam. As he told Alexander Cadogan before the conference began, "It is beyond the power of this country to prevent all sorts of things crashing at the present time. The responsibility lies with the United States and my desire is to give them all the support in our power." Recognizing as he did that American and British goals hardly overlapped, he must have known how weak a position his country had, especially given Churchill's lack of preparation.[14]

Eden grew despondent, noting in his diary early in the conference that he no longer had confidence in Churchill. "Depressed and cannot help an unworthy hope that we may lose, or rather have lost, this election," he confided. "If it were not for the immediate European situation I am sure that it would be better thus, but that is a big 'if,' I admit." Although Eden did his best to shake off his gloom, he clearly needed some time away both from his responsibilities in the foreign office and from Winston Churchill. In another diary entry, he wrote, "Am beginning to seriously doubt whether I can take on F.O. [Foreign Office] work again. It is not [the] work itself, which I can handle, but racket with Winston at all hours."[15]

The uncertainty regarding the elections added to the anxiety among the British delegation. They all knew that the British people had voted and that they had already selected a leader, but no one knew the outcome yet. Almost everyone at the conference, including Attlee, expected the Conservatives to win, but the margin of victory and the exact composition of the new government remained unknown. The Soviet delegation could not imagine a scenario under which the British people would vote Churchill out of office, and so they continued to overlook and ignore Attlee, whom some delegates had taken to calling "Churchill's toy." British communist agents had assured Stalin that the Tories would win the election handily, probably with an 80-seat majority.[16]

Ironically, Attlee had defied his own party and supported Churchill's desire to postpone the election until after the defeat of Japan. A postponement would keep the national unity government together through the end of the war and also into the crucial period of setting the foundations of the peace. Several senior members of the Labour Party, however, had grown tired of languishing in Churchill's shadow, and urged immediate elections in order to begin the process of implementing the party's postwar program of domestic reform. Surprisingly, Churchill had agreed, expecting as he did that the elections would produce a broad mandate for him into the postwar period. His decision upset Conservatives who had hoped to keep the stability of the coalition government in place until all of the guns had fallen silent.[17]

On July 25, the conference took a two-day break so that the most senior British officials could return to London for the tabulation of the votes. Stalin went into seclusion, either to rest or to plot strategy for the second half. Truman went to Frankfurt to meet with American military officials and to review a series of parades. While the big cats were away, the mice who stayed behind took the time to play, throwing what one staff veteran of multiple conferences called "the best party *ever* given (at) *any* conference" for the British staffers who remained in Potsdam. It went on until 3 o'clock in the morning while Churchill's staff back in London took down the war maps of Europe in his office at No. 10 Downing Street and replaced them with electoral maps of the major districts.[18]

No one saw the two-day pause in the conference as signifying any great watershed. Virtually everyone anticipated that Churchill and Eden would return with a slightly smaller majority, although Churchill later claimed that he had had his doubts. Churchill recalled after the conference that the night before he left Potsdam he had had a nightmare. "I dreamed that my life was over," he later recalled. "I saw it—it was very vivid—my dead body under a white sheet on a table in an empty room. I recognized my bare feet projecting from under the sheet. It was very life like. . . . Perhaps this is the end." Maybe the dream reflected Churchill's anxiety about his political future but, as with all of Churchill's dramatic recollections, separating fact from his flights of fancy is never easy.[19]

Eden recalled the Soviet and American delegates wishing him well in the election and expressing their certainty in his party's victory. Molotov "expressed his good wishes in the warmest terms, saying they all hoped for my success, and much more besides. I must be a very bad foreign secretary and give way too often that they should want me back." The Americans, he remembered, were "also very warm in their good wishes, to an extent which was almost embarrassing in Attlee's presence."[20]

Eden did not share the confidence of his Tory colleagues. His son, who was then serving in Burma, had written to him that the soldiers in Asia would likely vote overwhelmingly for Labour. "From the contacts I had in the army," Eden wrote, "I shared his opinion." He also knew that Tory Party officials in several contested areas had begun to have grave doubts. Still, he found Churchill confident and unwilling to hear anyone's negative prognostications. Most people in Britain expected a Tory victory; all that seemed in doubt was the size of the majority.[21]

The elections produced a historic surprise, however, a landslide victory for Labour and its leader, Clement Attlee. The Conservative majority in the House of Commons disappeared as the number of Tory seats plummeted from 585 to 213. Labour, with 393 seats, now emerged as the dominant party, meaning that Clement Attlee would return to Potsdam as Britain's prime minister, and that Churchill would at least temporarily leave government. Churchill briefly thought about returning to Potsdam and forcing the new Parliament to vote him out, but he soon bowed to the inevitable and resigned. Attlee offered Churchill and Eden the chance to return to Potsdam with him as advisers, to show the world the continuity of the British system, but both declined. Eden noted sympathetically that the new prime minister seemed relieved not to have either Churchill or Eden returning to Germany. His task was already difficult enough without two such towering figures looking over his shoulder.[22]

Attlee himself could hardly believe that he and his party had won, and by such an enormous margin. When he went to Buckingham Palace to meet the king, George VI told Attlee that he looked quite surprised to have won. "Indeed I certainly was," Attlee replied. No one quite knew what to make of the change; Winston Churchill now had no role in British policy. The news took some time to sink in. In his diary, Admiral Leahy recorded his concern that, Churchill's flaws notwithstanding, Britain simply could not go on without him. Churchill's defeat also struck Leahy as a blow to American interests. The change in government, Leahy wrote, "is in my opinion a world tragedy. I do not know how the Allies can succeed without the spark of genius in his qualities of leadership." Now, instead of Roosevelt and Churchill at Potsdam, the Allies had Truman and Attlee, both of whom seemed to Leahy to be grossly inadequate substitutes for their illustrious predecessors.[23]

The news stunned members of all three delegations at Potsdam. Molotov could hardly understand it. "I still cannot comprehend how this could happen that he lost the election," he bemoaned. "Apparently one needs to understand the English way of life better." Molotov wandered around the Russian delegation area of Potsdam asking how Churchill could not have known the election results in advance. Stalin struck those close to him as genuinely worried. He blamed the nature of "rotten democracies" for throwing out a man of such stature. He and Molotov had just assumed that, if necessary, Churchill would have found a way to rig the results.[24]

Stalin neither liked Attlee nor trusted the British Labour Party. However much Churchill had tried to paint the "Labourites" as pro-Soviet, neither Attlee nor Stalin saw their respective parties as fellow travelers in any sense at all. Even though Labour and the Soviets had been on the same side in the civil war in Spain, as well in advocating anti-appeasement policies in the 1930s, they each had done so for their own reasons. To the Labour Party, moreover, Soviet-style economic models were anathema, whereas to the Soviets, the Labour Party seemed no less capitalist or imperialist than the Tories. Far better, therefore, in Stalin's mind, to deal with the Churchill devil he knew rather than the Attlee devil he most certainly did not.

Attlee fully understood the mutual antipathy between British Labour and Soviet communism. "I knew from experience," he wrote, "that the communists had always fought us more vigorously than the Tories because they thought we offered a viable alternative to communism. They regarded the Tories as advocates of a dying cause while they thought we were a rival" for the support of the working classes of Europe. Attlee therefore did not expect Stalin and the Soviet delegates to give him a warm reception upon his return to Potsdam.[25]

British delegates were no less surprised and no less puzzled by the democratic process than their Soviet counterparts. Cadogan called Churchill's defeat "a display of base ingratitude" on the part of the British people and "rather humiliating for our country." Field Marshal Alan Brooke saw the timing of the election itself as another in a long line of Churchill's mistakes in domestic politics, but one with potentially catastrophic repercussions. "What a ghastly mistake to start elections at this point of the world's history!" he wrote in his diary that night, "May God forgive England for it." Brooke blamed Churchill personally, saying, "If only Winston had followed any advice, he would have been in at any rate till the end of the year!" Instead, Brooke noted, Churchill had counted on his personality to carry the election, just as he had counted on his personality to win over Truman and Stalin. Tragically, he had failed at both.[26]

In the dissections and postmortems that followed the massive Conservative defeat, several explanations for the surprising outcome emerged. Some Tories blamed Churchill's June speech that had likened Labour to the Gestapo, believing that it had frightened the British people and made Churchill seem ill-suited to lead Britain in the peacetime years to come. Clementine Churchill berated her husband for his past opposition to women's suffrage, which she supposed had cost him the female vote. Others tried to tell Churchill that the British people had not rejected him, but the Conservative Party in general. The data, however, tell a different story. The Tories actually performed worse in districts where Churchill himself had campaigned. Clearly, he had lost the faith of the British people even if he could not quite figure out why. "It may well be a blessing in disguise," Clementine told him. "At the moment," he replied, "it seems quite effectively disguised."[27]

Attlee thought that the reasons for Labour's victory had less to do with Churchill or the war than with trends dating back to the 1930s. Labour did particularly well in cities and large towns, which Attlee attributed to the failed economic policies of the Tories in the 1930s. He also believed that the British electorate blamed the Tories, although certainly not Churchill personally, for the disastrous policy of appeasement under Neville Chamberlain. Now Attlee faced the challenge of delivering to the British working classes a peace that would not require any future rounds of appeasement or, worse still, another continental war.[28]

Churchill returned to No. 10 Downing Street for one last meeting as prime minister. He told Eden, whom he had selected during the war as his successor should anything befall him, that he expected his own political career to be at an end, but that Eden would himself one day return to Downing Street as prime minister. Churchill appeared to Eden as "pretty wretched, poor old boy." Losing the election, Churchill told Eden, was "like a wound which becomes more painful after the first shock." The British government had even taken away his bodyguards, leading the American delegate Walter Brown to observe that "the Empire he had saved did not think enough of him to keep a guard for a single night after he had been defeated." Churchill drove down to Chequers for a final weekend at the country home of the prime minister, writing his name and "FINIS" in the guest book as his tenure as Britain's wartime leader came to an end.[29]

The end was both swift and complete: no one even asked Churchill to deliver an address to the nation when the Japanese surrendered in August. Churchill told Lord Moran that "it would have been better to have been killed in an aeroplane or to have died like Roosevelt." When the king announced he was awarding the Order of the Garter to Eden, Eden replied that he could not accept it, given that the British people had just given him the Order of the Boot. Churchill and Eden may also have worried about the strategic situation they had bequeathed to their successors. When Ernest Bevin told Eden that he would seek to become the Chancellor of the Exchequer in the new government, Eden shot back, "Whatever for? There will be nothing to do there except account for the money we have not got." He then advised Bevin to seek the Foreign Office as, in Eden's judgment, Bevin was the only Labour politician qualified for the job.[30]

ATTLEE, BEVIN, AND THE LABOUR ministers now found themselves in the unexpected position of not only having won a substantial majority, but of having to govern as well. Bevin, who would soon take Eden's advice and become foreign minister, told a friend, a lieutenant general from the Ministry of Defence, that he had not even expected to return to Potsdam. Like Attlee, he had already put a deposit down on a cottage for the rest of the summer "in the practical certainty that he would not be in office." Now Labour had just forty-eight hours to get affairs in order before returning to Potsdam. Attlee had time to make just six political appointments.[31]

Several members of the outgoing government shared Churchill's derisive view of the new prime minister. Cadogan remarked that with Attlee representing Britain, the Big Three would become the Big Two and a Half. He had also described Attlee's villa in Babelsberg as a "drab and dreary little building. . . . very suitable—it's just like Attlee himself." To help him along and help him deal with the transition, every member of the British delegation except Churchill and Eden returned to Potsdam with Attlee, further underscoring the continuity in policy despite the changes at the top.[32]

Attlee found himself, like Truman, cast suddenly in a role that he had not expected to perform. Truman must have had some sympathy for Attlee, although his reactions to the new prime minister varied. On the one hand, he thought that Attlee and Bevin looked like a pair of "sourpusses." On the other, he found them a great improvement in some ways over Churchill and Eden. Eden, especially, he characterized as upper-class and pompous, a "perfect striped pants boy"; he must have reminded Truman of the Ivy Leaguers who had surrounded Roosevelt. Bevin, by contrast, reminded him of the American labor leader John L. Lewis, which gave him great comfort because he recognized Bevin's blunt, direct style. As he wrote to his daughter, Bevin "doesn't know of course that your dad has been dealing with that sort all his life, from building trades to coal mines, so he won't be new."[33]

The new prime minister struck Truman and Byrnes as having the same upper-class mannerisms as Eden, but, mercifully, Attlee was far less prone to making long speeches than Churchill. With Attlee now representing Britain, they would not have to endure Churchill's habit of talking for thirty minutes to end up delivering "one gem of a sentence and two thoughts maybe which could have been expressed in four minutes." The less talkative Attlee might let the Big Three get down to business and get much more accomplished in far less time. In all, Truman and Byrnes saw Churchill's defeat as a setback for the conference, but not a fatal one.

Attlee and his team—like Truman—largely continued the policies of their predecessors. British policies on critical topics, such as
Poland, Greece, and reparations for Germany, did not change. As
one general who stayed at the Potsdam Conference for the duration,
and thus served under both Churchill and Attlee, wrote to his friend
General Ismay: "The King's Government must be carried on. In any
case, I had a considerable regard and admiration for both of them
[Attlee and Bevin]. They both love our country as much as you and
I do, though they may express it rather differently. As it turned out,
they were both excellent at the council table—knew their parts and
spoke their minds." Truman also came to think highly of Attlee's
performance at Potsdam, admiring his "deep understanding of the
world's problems." Truman and Attlee seemed to get along on a personal level, on one occasion sitting together at a piano to sing bawdy
soldier songs that they remembered from their time as junior officers
in World War I.[34]

Attlee shared one mannerism with Churchill: both smoked constantly. Otherwise they seemed as different as two Englishmen at
the upper reaches of their society could be. Nevertheless, if the style
changed without the dynamic Churchill in the room, the substance
of the British position did not. The election did nothing to change
the geostrategic position of Britain in the world; nor, of course, did
it solve any of Britain's financial problems. The fundamental worldview and positions of Attlee and Bevin differed little on matters of
foreign policy from those of Churchill and Eden. Truman, shocked
at Churchill's defeat, nevertheless "knew there would be no inter-
ruption in our common effort," because British policies would not
change. The American commander of the occupation of Germany,
Lucius Clay, noted that "only the diction" changed when Attlee took
over, not the substance of the debate.[35]

A *Life* magazine portrait of the new British prime minister
described him as resembling a "harassed shopkeeper or an ab-
sent-minded professor." It reported that even many in his own party
had little faith in him or in Bevin, the new foreign minister, whom
Life called "bulldogish, blustering, often boastful and egotistical."
Upon Attlee's return to Potsdam, Stalin told Truman that "judging

The Big Two and a Half, as some derisively called the group after Clement Attlee (left) replaced Winston Churchill, at the Potsdam Conference. (Library of Congress)

from the expression on Mr. Attlee's face," he didn't seem too happy to be taking over the British government.[36]

The Americans hardly knew Attlee at all. Walter Brown and others consistently misspelled his name in their journals and diaries. Brown recalled him before the election as "a small meek-mouse man," someone the photographers did not even bother to photograph during the conference's first days. The American photographers had no idea who he was, and the British assumed he would not remain at Potsdam for long. After the election, Brown noted, the photographers of both countries "kicked themselves for not taking his picture, because they found that they had no good shots of Atlee [sic] while at Potsdam."[37]

Short, bald, and unprepossessing, Attlee was nine years younger than Churchill but projected little of Churchill's legendary energy and drive. Attlee, who had attended exclusive British boarding schools and was a graduate of Oxford, belonged to the British elite, but he had expressed a deep concern for the welfare of the British working class, first making his name as a social worker in London's East End. He may have looked sheepish and ordinary, but he could also boast of an impressive military record. Commissioned into the South Lancashire Regiment, he had served in the ill-starred Gallipoli debacle of 1915 that Churchill had masterminded. When that operation fell to pieces and the British had to conduct a difficult retreat off the beaches, Attlee was the second-to-last man to leave. Although Churchill may have derided Attlee, Attlee respected Churchill, even to the point of being in the minority of British officials who believed that the failure of the Gallipoli operation resulted from poor implementation of a sound plan rather than from Churchill's inept strategy.

In the interwar years, Attlee had led the Labour Party's 1937 decision to oppose the appeasement policy of Neville Chamberlain. He had also given so much support to the antifascist Republicans in Spain that one of the International Brigades fighting Francisco Franco's regime named itself after him. Attlee had opposed the Munich agreement of 1938, warning that although it provided temporary peace to Britain, it made Germany too strong. He joined Churchill's wartime coalition government in 1940 and was the only minister to remain with Churchill for the entire duration of the war, providing the government with the support of the Labour Party for its military policies.

Thus there was much more to Clement Attlee than met the eye, even if on the surface he seemed a pale shadow of his predecessor. He struck James Byrnes as the polar opposite of Churchill in appearance, as well as being "exceedingly modest" and having "nothing of the actor in him," a clear backhanded swipe at Churchill. Attlee seemed even smaller when standing next to the massive Bevin, who weighed 250 pounds and seemed to dwarf almost everyone around him. Byrnes nevertheless agreed that the change from Churchill and Eden to Attlee and Bevin made little difference to either British positions on the key issues or the substance of the negotiations at Potsdam.[38]

Unlike Truman, Attlee had been involved in many major decisions since joining the British cabinet in 1940. He had met and discussed strategy with many of the senior American leaders, including Roosevelt and Marshall. Churchill nevertheless expected that as long as the Tories maintained their majority in the House of Commons, it would be Eden, not Attlee, who would succeed him. Thus he relied more on Eden than on Attlee to play the role of a deputy prime minister, even though it was Attlee who formally had that title. At Roosevelt's death, Churchill had not asked Attlee to travel to the United States for the funeral, but Eden.[39]

In any case, the British delegation soldiered on under its new leadership with little real change. Eden noted the continuity in his memoirs, writing of the transition from Churchill to Attlee: "Much has been written of the influence of personalities in the course of their countries' foreign policies, but this can be exaggerated. . . . [Personalities] do not influence policy." At least in the case of Potsdam, even the disappearance of one of the world's most legendary individuals proved Eden right.[40]

9

"Dismemberment as a Permanent Fate"? Solving the Problem of Germany

POTSDAM WAS THE second time in as many generations that the leaders of a victorious coalition faced the problem of what to do with a defeated Germany. The men of 1945 knew perfectly well how poorly the previous generation had handled this same problem. Moreover, the same basic political, military, and economic dilemmas that had confronted the leaders of 1919 existed in 1945 as well, further underscoring both the failures of the past and the need to do better this time. Like their predecessors in Paris in 1919, the leaders in 1945 at Potsdam did not agree on either the core problem or the appropriate solution. They did agree, however, that if they failed again, they might once more lay the seeds of a global calamity.

In both cases, hardliners among the senior leaders sought to dismantle Germany and demolish its infrastructure in order that it might never again pose a threat to European peace and stability. Reparations, territorial losses, and the destruction of German industry, they argued, would serve as just punishment to the people of a guilty nation and provide Germany's victims with equally just compensation for their suffering. They saw the essential problem as the excess power of the German state in the center of Europe. Forcing Germany to become far less powerful than it had been in the past, they argued, offered the best chance of a future of peace.

Moderates believed that without a strong Germany at the heart of Europe, the continent would never recover and rebuild. A harsh punishment, made even harsher by irrational financial penalties, might sow the seeds of future economic instability, just as it had after 1919. A devastated Germany might also lead the German people to answer the siren call of extremist politics once again. Regardless of the guilt or innocence of the German people and their government, therefore, the victors had to ensure that Germany once again became strong. At the same time, however, they had to do a much better job than their predecessors had done in 1919 of ensuring that that German strength did not threaten the wider peace.

Both sets of arguments began from the common assumption that the diplomats of 1919 had failed miserably. Thus the Treaty of Versailles and its consequences in the interwar years cast their long shadows once again over Potsdam. For the Americans, the answer to the problem seemed to lie in a complete rejection of the economic model of Versailles. According to this version of history, America's underwriting of German reparations, and its insistence on the full repayment of all loans and credits by its British and French allies, had had disastrous economic consequences. Reparations, American politicians and economists argued, had been just high enough to destabilize the German—and by extension the European—economies without being high enough to serve as an effective deterrent to future aggressive behavior on the part of the German government. Reparations had thus been debilitating without being effective, just as John Maynard Keynes had predicted in 1920.

Reparations, moreover, were both expensive to the US Treasury and unpopular with the American taxpayers who paid the bill. In the end, the Germans had paid $4.5 billion, a hefty raw sum but a fraction of the $33 billion in reparations agreed to in Paris. Rampant inflation, caused in no small part by the instability the reparations caused in Germany, further undermined the total value of German payments. In 1924, when the German mark had lost so much value that no one outside Germany would accept it, the Americans stepped in and introduced the Dawes Plan, which renegotiated German debt but did not call for American forgiveness of the British and French debts to the United States that made German reparations necessary. Thus, although it solved the temporary crisis and won Charles Dawes a share of the Nobel Peace Prize, it did little to solve the underlying problem caused by a carousel of unsustainable international debts. It also led to the Americans essentially paying Germany's reparations to the benefit of London and Paris far more than of New York or Washington.[1]

Consequently, in American eyes, the reparations that had followed World War I had served to anger the Germans. They had given extremists like the Nazis a weapon to use in their quest for power, but they had not acted as a brake on remilitarization; nor had they provided sufficient assistance to the British or the French. In effect, they had made Germany relatively stronger, not weaker. Americans in 1945 feared a re-creation of the system whereby reparations would again bankrupt Germany and leave the United States to clean up the financial mess. As Truman argued early in the conference, he would not agree to any policy on reparations that paid the bill "from the U.S. Treasury as we had done after World War I." As in 1919, the Americans would insist that its allies repay American private and public loans in full; steep reparations for Germany, they feared, would make it more difficult for America to recoup its money.[2]

British diplomats knew that any post–World War II conference would once again raise knotty problems with reparations, and not just at Potsdam, but at home as well. Reparations had emerged as a dominant domestic political issue in the elections of both 1919 and 1945. In both cases, nationalists called for reparations much heavier than the Germans could possibly pay. Recalling David Lloyd George's experience at Paris, Winston Churchill argued in 1945 against heavy reparations with an unusually laconic "once bit, twice shy." He argued that the more money the Allies took out of Germany, the more the cash-strapped British government would eventually have to put back in, unless the British were willing to see the German people starve to death. The Allies instead had to find a way to give the German people enough resources to fend for themselves without Germany growing too powerful as a result.

The Russians, by contrast, had concluded from the Versailles example that the taking of reparations should occur before any economic rehabilitation of Germany in order to guarantee that the Germans could not resume hostilities in the future. The Americans and the British tended to argue instead that Germany had to have something in order to give something. Thus economic rehabilitation had to happen at the same time as, or even prior to, the taking of reparations. At Yalta, the marked differences in philosophy between the West and the East on reparations had emerged in two exchanges between Churchill and Stalin. Churchill argued for leniency by saying, "If you want a horse to pull your wagon, you must give him some hay," to which Stalin had replied that "care should be taken to see that the horse did not turn around and kick you." The discussion, although oddly folksy, revealed the stark contrast between self-interested leniency and vengeance. At another point, Churchill warned that the Allies did not want to "be confronted by a mass of starving people," to which Stalin icily replied, "There will be none."[3]

The 1945 debate over reparations echoed the fundamental question of whether the Versailles Treaty had been too harsh in its demands on Germany, thereby fanning the flames of the next war, or too lenient, thereby leaving the Germans with sufficient resources to rearm. It also raised the complicated problem of how exactly to enforce any reparations figure agreed to at Potsdam. French efforts in the 1920s to force German miners in the Saar region to mine coal destined for France as part of the reparations deal had led to strikes and the eventual fall of a French government, indicating the difficulties of enforcement. Instead of hard-to-monitor long-term reparations schemes based on cash, some economists argued in 1945, the Allies should take their reparations in kind and all at once. For starters, Stalin had in mind the factories of the industrial heartland of Germany and the remaining German merchant fleet. As the British and Americans soon learned, he and the Russians were ready to cast their nets even more widely.

The economic parallel to 1919 mirrored a strategic one. Those who saw Germany as the main threat to European peace favored its demilitarization. To them, the limits to the German armed forces imposed as part of the Treaty of Versailles would have served as a sufficient check on German militarism if only the Allies had been willing to enforce them. Capping the German army at 100,000 men, eliminating its general staff, and banning it from having an air force had been fundamentally sound decisions even if the treaty had unwisely failed to provide for an effective means of enforcement. The Nazi renunciation of those limits in the 1930s, they argued, started Germany and Europe on the road to war, especially when supporters of appeasement did little to stop German aggression. In this analysis, the answer in 1945 was to once again limit the military means at Germany's disposal. This time, however, a full occupation of Germany would ensure Germany's demilitarization.

Opponents of this line of argument, in both 1919 and 1945, argued that a weak Germany disrupted the European strategic picture too much. They tended to see the problem of European security in terms of imbalances of power. Westerners especially worried, both in 1919 and 1945, that a weak Germany might mean a stronger Russian presence in Central Europe. They therefore argued against hobbling Germany for fear of creating more, not less, instability in the heart of the continent. The American chargé d'affaires in Moscow, George Kennan, emerged as the most forceful, if not always the most influential, voice on this question. In a May 1945 memorandum he wrote for Harry Hopkins, Kennan argued that despite its enormous wartime suffering, Russia stood in as powerful a position in 1945 as in 1940, because of the collapse of Germany as a counterweight to its West. Any reparations given to Russia would make it stronger still and "enable the Soviet government to make good the economic damages caused by its costly and uncompromising political program" of collectivization and forced industrialization in the 1930s.[4]

Especially given the weakness of other traditional European powers, such as France and Italy, many British leaders shared Kennan's thinking and looked to a rehabilitated Germany as the answer to continental stability. The extension of Russian control to Germany and Poland meant that, as Churchill liked to remind his fellow Western leaders, the Russians in 1945 were as far west as they had ever been except for the occupation of Paris after the fall of Napoleon. In order to restore the balance of power on the continent, the British might need to rebuild both Germany and France in order, ironically enough, to counter a Soviet Union that still technically counted as one of Britain's two major allies.

These debates, resumed once again in 1945, would have looked entirely familiar to the delegates at Paris twenty-six years earlier. The fundamental terms of the debate had not changed. Nor had the most basic question: What had caused the outbreak of the two world wars? Woodrow Wilson had argued in Paris that the problem was not Germany, or the German people, but the country's undemocratic government and its outdated aristocratic system. Thus had Wilson stated in his declaration of war speech to the US Congress that "we have no quarrel with the German people. We have no feeling toward them but one of sympathy and friendship. It was not upon their impulse that the government acted in entering this war. It was not with their previous knowledge or approval." Wilson advocated what a later generation of politicians would call regime change; a democratic Germany using its economic power to pursue civilian goals, he argued, would no longer pose a threat to anyone.[5]

The same arguments reemerged in 1945. No one articulated them better than American Secretary of War Henry Stimson when he said that current harsh proposals for the postwar period "provided for keeping Germany near the margin of hunger as a means of punishment for past misdeeds. I have felt that this was a grave mistake. Punish her war criminals in full measure. Deprive her permanently of her weapons, her General Staff and perhaps even her entire army. Guard her governmental actions until the Nazi-educated generation has passed from the stage—admittedly a long job—but do not deprive her of the means of building up ultimately a contented Germany interested in following non-militaristic methods of civilization."

Truman agreed, telling Stimson, no doubt with Versailles in mind, that too many of history's peace treaties had unwisely been based on vengeance. Or, as one American delegate at Potsdam noted, "it is impossible to maintain democracy by bayonets." By this logic, if Germany were to develop as a peaceful nation, the German people would need a fair start unencumbered by heavy reparations, war guilt, or territorial dismemberment. In a memorandum from Stimson that awaited Truman on his arrival at Potsdam, the secretary of war wrote: "On the one hand, it is clear that Germany has created, and twice used, a swollen war industry. On the other hand, from the point of view of general European recovery, it seems even more important that the area again be made useful and productive. . . . The commerce of Europe [prior to 1939] was very largely predicated upon her industry. It is my view that it would be foolish, dangerous, and provocative of future wars to adopt a program calling for the major destruction of Germany's industry and resources."[6]

The French in 1919 and the Russians in 1945 saw matters quite differently from Stimson. Like Georges Clemenceau in 1919, the Soviets in 1945 insisted that the Germans should at the very least not live any better than the people they had victimized; they might well remain exactly at the margin of hunger that Stimson had decried. A Soviet diplomatic paper at Potsdam called only for the German people to have enough food to "subsist without external assistance." Domestic consumption and exports, the paper argued, should be "proportionally reduced" in order to prioritize the payment of reparations. Having suffered so much at German hands, the Russians, as the French had before them, saw the problem of Germany as running more deeply than its leadership. Some saw it as coming from structural disparities, with the Germans being more populous and having more industry than their neighbors, thus causing a fundamental imbalance of power that the great powers could correct through heavy reparations and territorial adjustments. Others saw the problem as the Germans themselves; having never gone through a true period of democracy and having given the military too dominant a role in society for centuries, the Germans lacked the kinds of institutional controls found elsewhere in Europe.[7]

Consequently, although the Nazi period clearly represented something different in German history, it did not really change the

basic question of how to integrate Germany into Europe more generally. The same divisions of opinions from the end of World War I
remained at the end of World War II. The discussions at Potsdam on
Germany's future could have been lifted straight out of the discussions in Paris's Hôtel Crillon between Georges Clemenceau, David
Lloyd George, and Woodrow Wilson.

Still, the Germany of 1945 did not entirely resemble the Germany of 1919. First, and most obviously, in 1945 Germans had little
choice but to recognize the totality of their defeat. Unlike in 1919, the
postwar period in 1945 would undoubtedly involve occupation and
a loss of political control to outsiders for the foreseeable future. No
1945 equivalent to the right-wing paramilitary units known as the
Freikorps developed; nor did the German people continue the war
with guerrilla methods. Germany at least seemed to have accepted
its defeat in a way that it had not in 1919, although the Germans also
seemed not to show nearly as much remorse as its occupiers had
hoped to see.[8]

Second, the crimes of the Nazis exceeded those of the World War
I period by several orders of magnitude. As brutal as the German
occupations of foreign lands had been in World War I, the Germans
of that period had not come anywhere close to the committing the
genocide and widespread mass murder of civilians that characterized the atrocities of World War II. As more knowledge came to light
about Nazi crimes, the mood at Potsdam turned decidedly harsher.
Someone would have to pay for the crimes of the most murderous
regime in history.

Those crimes left most of the senior leaders at Potsdam in a distinctly unforgiving state of mind. Lucius Clay, the US general in
charge of occupation policy, noted in June that the winter to come
would likely involve much "cold and hunger" for the German people. Although he hoped to avoid widespread starvation among the
Germans, he also thought that some suffering would serve the positive goal of making "the German people realize the consequence of
a war they started." British Foreign Minister Ernest Bevin was more
blunt, saying, "I try to be fair to them, but I hate them, really."[9]

Third, the damage to Germany was far greater in 1945 than anything that any country had experienced in 1919. As a result, rebuilding Germany would require a far greater investment of resources than anyone had contemplated in 1919. Yet at the same time, feelings toward Germany were, if anything, even harsher. Thus the Allies would have to make decisions that balanced the humanitarian need to feed starving people against desires for revenge and justice. Truman's Soviet adviser Charles Bohlen observed the tensions inherent in the Allied position. He saw that "the spirit of mercy was not throbbing in the breast of any Allied official at Potsdam; there was no disposition to be lenient with the Germans." Yet, he noted, the Western delegates understood as well that "punishment by itself was useless in international affairs." Clay, Bevin, and Attlee all thought that harsh punishment for Germany was warranted, but they nevertheless wanted to help rebuild Germany as quickly as possible, even if their reasons were as much based in self-interest as humanitarianism.[10]

General Floyd Parks, one of the senior American officials overseeing the occupation of Germany, articulated this paradox in a radio interview he gave on July 22, in the middle of the Potsdam Conference, on the conditions of Berlin: "Many of the electric power stations, water stations, and sewage plants are unable to operate. Schools, courthouses, bakeries, banks, theaters—even little commonplace things like drug stores do not exist. Can you imagine a city the size of, say, Pittsburg [sic] without these things? If so you know what we face here."

Still, Parks sought to reassure his American listeners that the US government would not forget the cause of all of this devastation; nor would it ask the American people to pay for Germany's reconstruction without getting something in return. "Make no mistake," he said, "we are not molly-coddling or kowtowing to these Berliners. You and I, and all of us, will never forget that here was brewed the poison of two world wars. It will not happen again, if we can prevent it." He concluded his remarks by saying, "Swift justice, tempered by the laws of human decency, is the theme of our Military

Government in Berlin." The tension between justice and common humanity proved as much of a challenge in 1945 as it had in 1919.[11]

The issue of war criminals provided one of the most important tests of those principles at the Potsdam Conference. Punishing too many Germans threatened to make the occupation unpopular in German eyes and also to remove many people of talent from Germany at a time when the Allies needed their expertise. But to put too few people on trial meant allowing many people with blood on their hands to walk free. The British favored the lenient approach, both to minimize the risks of the occupation and to lay a foundation for the future of Anglo-German cooperation. Foreign Minister Anthony Eden drafted a note for Churchill on day one of the conference that contained only ten names for prosecution: Luftwaffe commander Hermann Goering; Foreign Minister Joachim von Ribbentrop; former deputy führer Rudolf Hess, who had been in British custody since his flight to the United Kingdom in May 1941; Robert Ley, who headed the Nazi labor organization Deutsche Arbeitsfront; Wilhelm Frick, the chief author of the Nuremberg Laws; Wilhelm Keitel, Hitler's senior military adviser; Nazi ideologue Alfred Rosenberg; SS leader Ernst Kaltenbrunner; propagandist Julius Streicher; and Hans Frank, the Nazi governor of Poland. The notion that just ten men, plus the dead Adolf Hitler and Joseph Goebbels, had caused so much death and destruction made no sense, but it served a political imperative.[12]

The Soviets thought the list far too small and demanded a much more thorough purging of the Nazi system. At Potsdam, the Russians argued that the British had violated the spirit of agreements already in place that called for much wider punishments for Nazi officials. In October 1943, Stalin, Churchill, and Roosevelt had all agreed to the Moscow Declaration, which pledged that the Allies would punish and hold accountable those responsible for wartime atrocities. The agreement, like so many of its kind, said nothing about the final numbers of war criminals to be prosecuted, or about legal procedure, but the Russians clearly thought in terms of a much broader system of war crimes trials.

Rudolf Hess presented a critical litmus test. In May 1941, he had flown from Germany to Scotland, apparently without permission from Hitler, as part of an effort to foster peace between the Germans and the British. He hoped to enlist British help in the coming German war with Russia. The British judged him to be of questionable sanity and placed him under psychiatric observation. For having proposed a joint Anglo-German war against the Soviets, Stalin wanted the British to transfer Hess to Russian custody. At Potsdam, Stalin repeated the demand, even offering to pay Hess's British hotel bills in order to speed up his transfer; the comment was a swipe at what Stalin viewed as Britain's inexcusably lenient treatment of Hess.

At Potsdam, the British won their argument for holding the war crimes trials in Nuremberg, home to the notorious Nazi rallies from 1923 to 1938. Trials in Nuremberg, they argued, would better symbolize the denazified condition of the new Germany than trials in Berlin. The British also won their argument for keeping the number of trials small. At Potsdam, the Allies set the ground rules for future war crimes trials, which they put in writing in the London Declaration of August 8. All of those on Eden's list went on trial at Nuremberg between November 1945 and October 1946, in addition to twelve other senior Nazi officials. Of the ten the British had listed, all but three were found guilty and hanged. Goering and Ley avoided that fate only by committing suicide. Hess received a life sentence, which he served in solitary confinement in Spandau Prison. Although the British, French, and Americans approved Hess's release in the 1970s, the Soviets refused to agree to the decision, which required a unanimous vote. Hess died in Spandau in 1987.

THE JOINT POLICY ON WAR criminals was part of a larger plan for cooperation and coordination among the victorious allies in postwar Germany. Even before the conference began, the senior military leaders of the three powers had worked out an arrangement for a joint occupation of a unified Germany. At American and British request, the French joined as a fourth power in order to share the obligations of occupation, but at Soviet insistence the French zone was formed from the British and American zones. The Soviets also opposed French participation on the reparations committee unless Poland also had a vote, but they later yielded on that point. All four powers would have an equal voice, and all decisions on occupation policy would require a unanimous vote. Supreme command over the occupation would rotate among the four powers every fifteen days. A CBS News broadcast presciently called the system "an experiment and a challenge to see whether the good sentiments we express about each other really work in practice."[13]

All four powers had pledged to begin food shipments into Berlin starting on July 15, just two days before the conference began. The Americans began their full allotted shipments on schedule, but complained that the Russians had only shipped two-thirds of what they had promised. For the most part, however, the system of joint occupation seemed to function smoothly, with the four powers developing joint policies toward the reestablishment of German media, the reopening of civic institutions such as schools, courts, and theaters, and efforts to control the ubiquitous black market, where cigarettes were selling for as much as $100 per carton and even large items like US Army jeeps had begun to appear. German civilians fueled the market by selling most of their possessions in a desperate effort to obtain hard currency in order to deal with the rising inflation in food and fuel prices. Better, most Germans concluded, to sell their items for what they could, than to risk the Russians just taking them.[14]

The Allies intended the four-power joint occupation of Germany to serve as a model of cooperation going forward and a statement of how far they had come since the debates on the future of Germany held earlier in the year. At Yalta, Soviet diplomat Ivan Maisky had proposed the division of Germany into three countries: a Protestant north, a Catholic south, and the industrial Rhineland. Roosevelt had proposed five states, and Stalin had once argued for as many as seven. Churchill, who did not want to see a power vacuum in Central Europe, expressed his preference for two, along the traditional religious divisions of north and south. The French, as in 1919, called for the detachment of the Rhineland and maybe the Saar and Ruhr industrial regions from Germany. Stalin agreed, arguing also for an international trusteeship over the Ruhr and Westphalia.[15]

The dismemberment of Germany had for a time become Allied policy. Developed during the height of the war, and championed by Henry Morgenthau, the American treasury secretary and a friend of Franklin Roosevelt, the plan called for the postwar creation of two German states, a largely Protestant one in the north and a largely Catholic one in the south. The industrial areas of the Saar, the Ruhr, and Upper Silesia would either go to Germany's neighbors or into the international trusteeship Stalin supported. The remaining German states would then lose all of their industrial assets, with most of them being sent to Russia in lieu of long-term cash reparations. The German people would receive no international assistance for several years in order to drive home to the Germans their guilt for the war. Thereafter, the German states would be pastoralized and denied permission to reindustrialize. They would also lose all representation in international organizations, but they would not face a military occupation or the kind of long-term reparations Germany had faced after World War I. Morgenthau put it bluntly when he said, "We either have to castrate the German people or you have got to treat them in such [a] manner so they can't just go on reproducing people who want to continue the way they have in the past."[16]

The harshness of the plan and the publicity that Nazi propagandists gave to it led many Western military leaders to worry that it would cause the Germans to fight to the bitter end. Secretary of War Henry Stimson, in an unvarnished shot at Morgenthau's Judaism, called it "Semitism gone wild for vengeance," predicting that such a plan would "lay the seeds for another war in the next generation." Roosevelt underplayed the plan in public, fearful that the Republicans might make an issue of it in the 1944 election. They did so anyway, with Republican nominee Thomas Dewey saying that the harshness of the plan would extend the war unnecessarily and was as good as giving ten new divisions to the German Army.[17]

Almost from the inception of the Morgenthau plan, however, key leaders in both countries began to raise objections on moral, economic, and political grounds. Anthony Eden argued that an impoverished Germany could not purchase British exports. Stimson continued to lead the charge from Washington, calling the plan "mass vengeance . . . in the shape of clumsy economic action," and claiming that it would "produce a very dangerous reaction in Germany and probably a new war." Veteran American statesman Cordell Hull agreed, adding the chilling estimate that, if enacted, the plan could lead to the starvation of 40 percent of the German population. Stalin, too, objected, telling Harry Hopkins in May 1945 that he wanted to threaten Germany with dismemberment as punishment for "bad behavior," but did not support dismemberment as postwar policy. He preferred a joint occupation of a single Germany instead.[18]

Truman objected to the Morgenthau plan as well, but in May 1945 he signed JCS Directive 1067, which banned the US government from funding any measures designed to rehabilitate the German economy. This measure was a seeming victory for Morgenthau and the ideas behind the plan that carried his name. By the time of Potsdam, however, the Allies, especially Truman, had moved completely away from the Morgenthau plan. Truman saw it as bad public policy, and his intense personal dislike of Morgenthau could only have strengthened his views.

Here again, the ghosts of 1919 haunted the delegates at Potsdam. The American delegation, James Byrnes noted, determined that it would be "guided by our experience in World War I" to ensure that the United States would not repeat what its leaders saw as the two great mistakes of that year. First, the delegates argued that the United States had, through the international system of loans and credits, essentially paid for Germany's reparations after World War I. Byrnes was especially adamant that the United States would not do so again. Second, the delegates said, the United States had not effectively tied the issue of World War I reparations to larger questions of political reform and economic recovery. In other words, the United States had paid for Germany's reparations, and thus indirectly for British and French recovery, without getting anything in return. Truman agreed wholeheartedly, sliding a note across the red table at Cecilienhof to Joseph Davies that read, "Joe, I want continually to let them understand that we want to do our share, but we are *not* going to support Europe nor pay the reparations as we did before." For both men, the events of 1919 remained vivid as an example of how not to handle the sticky issue of war reparations.[19]

The World War I case also found an echo in the 1945 debate over how much money the Allies should extract from Germany. That issue, among the most intensely debated in 1919, had led British economist John Maynard Keynes to write his stinging critique of what he saw as the incompetence and greed of the victorious powers. Having taken too much money from the Germans, he argued, the Allies had set the conditions for the depression that hit Europe in the early 1920s, and then the much larger one that devastated the global economy in the 1930s. In effect, he argued, the Allies had demanded far more of Germany than it could ever hope to pay, setting up the cycle not just of payments from the United States, but also of long-term German anger at the terms of the Treaty of Versailles. Destroying Germany's economy had also impeded the overall recovery of Europe by encouraging states to nationalize their economies.

Thus, echoing his position in Paris in 1919, Keynes found the Morgenthau and similar plans "mad." Destroying the German economy, he argued, only served to cut off Europe's nose to spite its face. With his characteristic acerbity, in a 1944 meeting with Morgenthau he laid out his vision of how the American's plan would play out. "So whilst the hills are being turned into sheep runs, the valleys will be filled with a closely packed bread line," he wrote. "How I am to keep a straight face I cannot imagine." Keynes saw the fiasco of post-1919 Europe repeating itself in the desires of Germany's former enemies to remove its ability to fend for itself. Such a plan struck him as dangerous for the economic recovery of the rest of Europe; it would also force the burden of feeding the German people on an already pressed British treasury that could not possibly meet the challenge.[20]

THE AMERICANS, as in 1919, sought to reduce the total amount of reparations in the interests of rehabilitating Germany. In a secret memorandum to Byrnes written on July 6, US Ambassador to the Soviet Union Averill Harriman argued that the Allies should use reparations to target only "the war making power of Germany by eliminating that part of Germany's industrial capacity which contributes war potential." Harriman specifically contrasted his plan with that of 1919, arguing that any reparations taken out of Germany should be in kind, not in cash; as Roosevelt had argued at Yalta, he suggested that these reparations should go directly to help the devastated victims of Germany rebuild, rather than to the bankers and government treasuries that had made loans to the Allies during the war. Reparations should keep Germans at a living standard equivalent to that in Europe more generally, but should not be so harsh as to force any other state to pay to feed them. Truman approved the memorandum, and it formed the core of his thinking at Potsdam.[21]

The American Joint Chiefs of Staff added their voices as well, arguing in a memorandum to Truman for keeping Germany as one state. They argued that dismembering Germany would not break down "the aggressive nationalism which has characterized the German people during the past century." Instead, it might fuel the same nationalist flames the Allies sought to quench. They opposed international trusteeships over the German industrial regions for the same reason. Only if Germany worked as one unit, governed jointly by its conquerors, could it both feed itself and move toward a more pacific role in the postwar world. Such a policy would also reduce the amount of money and manpower the Americans would themselves have to dedicate to an expensive occupation of Germany.[22]

America's self-interested leniency notwithstanding, history seemed to be repeating itself when the Soviets demanded at Potsdam half of $20 billion in total reparations, a figure sure to cripple the German economy for years to come, although only a fraction of the $128 billion that the Soviets claimed in total wartime damages. Most of the industrial wealth that could have paid the reparations, moreover, sat in the western zone, most notably in the Ruhr Valley. If the Allies held to the high Soviet demands, and if they continued a shared occupation policy, then the German economy would surely face devastation. As Clement Attlee noted, the Russians seemed not to care. "As far as [Stalin] was concerned," he later wrote, "they could all starve." Britain wanted a much more lenient approach, in no small part because the British economy would need German customers and suppliers after the war.[23]

The issue of reparations thus was as complex in 1945 as in 1919, when the US Treasury Department's chief banker had said that the subject "caused more trouble, contention, and hard feeling, and delay" than any other topic debated at Paris. At Potsdam, the subject remained contentious, and the lines of debate had hardly changed, with the Soviets now playing the role of the French. Seeing themselves as the nation most devastated, and believing themselves to have made the greatest contribution to the victory, the Soviets, as had the French under Georges Clemenceau, wanted the Germans to pay. In words that could have come from the mouth of the French prime minister of 1919, Molotov told Byrnes at Potsdam that a large swath of his country "had been occupied and the plants and towns had been laid waste by the Germans." Any reparations taken from Germany would be "small compensation for the damage done by the German soldiers who . . . had not been on United States or British territory."[24]

To solve these problems, Byrnes championed the idea that each side should take reparations from its own zone of occupation. The plan first gained currency at Potsdam in a July 23 meeting of the Council of Foreign Ministers. Molotov demanded to know if the Yalta decision to seek $20 billion in total reparations from Germany, with half to go to the Soviet Union, remained in place. Byrnes argued that it could not, because, since Yalta, more than 4 million Germans had fled to the West (almost 800,000 of them to the Western-controlled zones of Berlin), increasing the immediate costs of the occupation to the Americans alone by $1.5 billion. He could not, he told Molotov, support any reparations plan harsh enough to force onto American taxpayers the burden of feeding so many Germans.

Four days later, America's representative to the Reparations Committee, Edwin Pauley, warned Molotov once again that the system of sharing reparations would place the burden of paying for feeding and housing German refugees on the United States. At the same time, the Russians were increasing their resources by looting Germany. The net result, Pauley warned, was a repetition of the

World War I scheme Americans so desperately wanted to avoid, with the United States putting money into Germany as someone else took money out. He articulated the dilemma in direct and perfectly clear terms in a July 27 memorandum for the Soviet foreign minister: "Thus we would repeat one of the worst mistakes made after the first World War [sic]. The United States has therefore been placed in the position where it must deal with reparations along the same lines as have, in fact, been initiated by the Soviet Government. It was for this reason that we have submitted (two days ago) a further proposal which formally recognizes that removals will be conducted on a zonal basis. This we regard as regrettable, but inescapable, in view of the unilateral actions taken by the Soviet Government."

Pauley recognized that the World War I experience, as much as, if not more than, the emerging mistrust of the Soviet Union, led to the American abandonment of the idea of Germany as a single economic, and later political, unit.[25]

By dividing the reparations into zones, each side could pursue its own policies while simultaneously avoiding the frightening historical example of 1919. The Americans and the British could reduce or even waive reparations payments, thus relieving the United States of some of the burden of paying to feed Germany by keeping German resources in Germany. By acquiescing in the Soviet plunder of eastern Germany, moreover, they could protect against Soviet claims for shares of the valuable western factories and mines upon which Germany would base its economic recovery, given that 81 percent of German coal and 86 percent of German steel production sat in the western zones. According to American intelligence agents in the Soviet-controlled section of Germany, the locals were reporting that "everything is being taken. We don't know where it is going." The Soviet "trophy brigades," they learned, were categorizing everything they saw as war booty, including items with no military utility at all, and taking it all back to Russia. "The work is highly organized," the American agents reported, and the Russians "seem to enjoy their work." A zonal reparations plan might doom the east, but it would at least protect the western sections from what Pauley called Russia's policy of "organized vandalism."[26]

The collection of reparations by zone clearly violated the spirit of the joint Allied occupation of Germany, but Byrnes saw it as a way to protect the vital German industrial assets in the Ruhr from being dismantled and taken wholesale to the Soviet Union. He rejected on principle the idea that the Russians deserved a larger share of the reparations of Germany because of the "greatness of their suffering" or their larger contribution to victory. He knew that regardless of what they decided at Potsdam, the Russians and the Poles had already begun to strip eastern Germany bare, meaning that most of the agricultural assets of the east would likely end up being taken from Germany, and thus would be exempt in practice from the joint occupation in any case. Truman himself claimed to have seen factories in Berlin stripped bare and packed off to Russia, although it is unclear when he could have done so. Dividing the spoils by zones thus protected the German assets in the west from Russian greed while recognizing how little the British, French, and Americans would reap from the east. As an American report of July 30 argued, "our imports [to Germany] are what permit Russia to get reparations out of Germany, which is another way of saying we are paying [Russia] for the reparations." Given the World War I experience, no one in the American or British delegations wanted to see a repeat of such a scheme.[27]

The Americans and the British knew full well that the Russians, "natural looters," as Truman called them, had already begun taking German assets back to Russia. They also knew that the Russians had removed German-owned property in Poland, Hungary, and Romania. They knew, too, that the Russians had plans to pressure the Spanish and Swedish governments to hand over German property in those countries as well. A July 18 report Byrnes received at Potsdam informed him that the Soviets had taken over formerly German oil leases in Romania for themselves; other reports from Washington to the Potsdam delegates showed that the Soviets had also seized Romanian money stored in banks formerly owned by Germans. The Americans also knew that the Russians had seized scientific data relating to the V-1 and V-2 rocket programs, all scientific material from German military laboratories, and what remained of the scientific research plants of the Berlin area's universities and institutes. On hearing of these reports, Truman noted that the Russians had mastered the art of stealing the coffin and disposing of the body. Stimson crassly blamed the Russian character, calling the Soviet policy of looting a part of their "oriental" nature.[28]

Russian intentions to drain Eastern Europe as well as Germany thus seemed clear. At one point in the Potsdam proceedings, Byrnes asked Molotov directly if the Russians had removed "war booty" from the lands it occupied, and if so, how much that booty was worth. Molotov admitted that they had effected "miscellaneous removals" worth $300 million, a number he proposed to remove from the original Soviet demand of $10 billion. Later in that same meeting he offered to reduce Soviet demands by an entire $1 billion to "dispose of the question," a subtle admission of the extent of Soviet removals even without a three-power agreement in place. His offer also acknowledged that removals and reparations by zone already existed de facto.[29]

Nevertheless, no one, certainly not Byrnes, saw the taking of spoils from individual sectors as anything more than a temporary arrangement to handle the tricky issue of reparations. Even Pauley's tough July 27 memorandum to Molotov explicitly stated that "our proposal need not interfere" with the concept of a unified Germany. Most delegates hoped for some version of the joint occupation plan that Hopkins and Stalin had discussed in Moscow in May. Here again, the ghosts of 1919 reemerged. Hopkins noted in his report to Truman following his mission to the Kremlin that month that the Allies could not repeat the mistake of hanging on any new German government the responsibility of a humiliating defeat and heavy reparations. Thinking of Morgenthau's plans to dismember Germany, and noting that "it is impossible to maintain the political vacuum created by defeat," Hopkins wrote that "any political groups which attempt to carry out the heavy demands now contemplated will inevitably be quislings and Vichyites [referring to the Norwegian and French collaborators] in German eyes." Although he argued forcefully for the need to "convince the German people that they have suffered a total military defeat and that they cannot escape responsibility for what they have brought upon themselves," he still wanted to find a way to avoid the mistakes of 1919. Dismembering Germany could create a situation similar to the many irredentist controversies of the interwar period, such as those concerning the Sudetenland and the Polish Corridor. Above all, he wrote, "it is imperative, for long-range considerations, that the Weimar experience be avoided."

In other words, he argued, neither the United States nor the Soviet Union should support any plan that would once again burden a fragile state with the albatross of having to sign an unpopular treaty that required the dismemberment of its own territory. "The German people," Hopkins argued, "will not willingly accept dismemberment as a permanent fate." No significant group, he wrote, "has questioned the verdict of 1871," or sought to undo the unification of Germany accomplished in that year. The Russians, he thought, agreed for both political and economic reasons. Allied policy should therefore emphasize uniformity of policy in all zones of occupied Germany, and should also look for ways to decentralize political power in the country based on the preexisting German federal system. Such a system would reduce the military power of Germany without debilitating its economic or political structures. In the final analysis, he argued for creating a single demilitarized and denazified Germany mostly governed by the states rather than a central government based in Berlin. He also argued for a relatively lenient policy on reparations and a total renunciation of the political and economic dimensions of the Morgenthau plan.[30]

The *western* borders of Germany would thus see no changes from the prewar period. The great powers rejected a proposal to transfer Schleswig and Holstein, along with the strategic Kiel Canal, to Denmark. They also rejected trusteeships for German industrial areas and the detachment of the Rhineland from the rest of Germany, as they had in 1919 when French nationalists had demanded it. David Lloyd George had then called removing the Rhineland from Germany "an Alsace-Lorraine in reverse." In 1945, the delegates made the same argument in much the same language. A July 17 memorandum on the subject noted, in terms that Lloyd George would well have understood, that the British and Americans could not commit indefinitely to an occupation of any part of Germany, and that a detachment of the Rhineland would surely require just such an occupation. Thus the Allies could not risk any territorial changes to the western border of Germany. Once again, the major changes would come in the east.[31]

10

"The Bastard of Versailles"

THE MEETING AT POTSDAM forced the Allies to confront yet again one of the most vexing problems of 1919, the fate of Poland. At the end of World War I, the great powers had re-created an independent Polish state, putting it back on the map of Europe for the first time since the so-called Third Partition of Poland in 1795. Finding borders for the new Poland that would satisfy the Wilsonian principle of self-determination, while also guaranteeing an economically and militarily viable state, proved an immense challenge. The Big Three finally based the Ukraine-Poland border on the Bug River, roughly where it sits today. This line, known since 1919 as the Curzon Line, after the British diplomat credited with its creation, resulted from a compromise that pleased no one. Poland was thus carved out of the former German, Austro-Hungarian, and Russian empires, and its mere existence angered the new Weimar Republic in Germany as well as the Soviet Union. Both of them coveted its territory and disputed the borders that the great powers had made for it without their consultation. The new Polish government, furious that the Curzon Line left millions of Poles outside Poland's borders, rejected it on both strategic and ethnic grounds.

The new Poland had indefensible borders, enemies on all sides, and an ethnic border that did not match the political border that the British, Americans, and French had determined for it on its behalf.

These problems notwithstanding, the West had initially placed great hopes in Poland as a potential counterweight to both Germany and Russia. The French and the British saw Poland as a way to compensate for the loss of their Russian ally from the prewar years, but both states, strapped for defense funding, faced limits to the support that they could provide. Nor did geography do the Poles many favors. As the Poles discovered in 1939, their British and French allies were far away from the viper's nest of Eastern Europe when crises occurred.

Most of Poland's neighbors had opposed its creation and sought its destruction, either for strategic reasons or because of the competition for resource-rich regions. A senior Soviet diplomat called Poland "the bastard of Versailles," and that moniker reflected most German and Russian attitudes toward it. The Soviets, who had had no representatives at the Paris Peace Conference, and therefore played no role in creating the new Poland, sought to ensure that the bastard, if it survived its infancy at all, would have an extremely difficult childhood. War between the revolutionary Soviet state and the new Poland broke out in February 1919, even as the Paris Peace Conference was getting under way. Both sides sought to overturn the borders of the new Eastern Europe that the Big Three had drawn in faraway Paris.[1]

The Russo-Polish War threatened the peace of Europe so recently obtained at such great cost. For a time, Poland became the West's great cause célèbre, a fledgling democracy fighting at long odds against the Bolshevist menace from the East. The Allies, especially France, sent equipment and advisers to the Poles to help them keep communism as far to the east as possible. Contemporaries spoke of Poland's great victory over the Soviet Union at the Battle of Warsaw in 1920 as akin to the 732 Battle of Tours that had stopped the Moorish invasion of France. In this case, the Russians played the role of the Muslims, invading Europe from the periphery and threatening to destroy European civilization.

The Russians, of course, saw the battle quite differently. Defeat at the gates of Warsaw forced the Soviet Union to accept as its border with Poland the so-called Riga Line, named for the treaty signed in that city in March 1921. The new Russo-Polish border added 70,000

The Big Three at the Potsdam Conference (Joseph Stalin, second from left; Harry Truman, center; Winston Churchill, right). Admiral William Leahy is fourth from left, looking to his left. Clement Attlee, who would become the next British prime minister before the end of the conference, is in the background between Churchill and Truman. (United States Army Heritage and Education Center, Harry Truman Photographic Collection)

square miles to the Poland that the Big Three had created in Paris, an area roughly the size of Missouri. The Riga Line gave Poland the cities of Wilno (Vilnius) and Lwów (Lviv), both of which the Poles saw as critical to their past and future, although they both contained large non-Polish populations. The addition of Lwów, which became the third-largest city in the newly enlarged Poland, particularly rankled the Ukrainians, whose leaders wanted it as the capital of their new state.

The failure to take Lwów also rankled the Soviet Union's political commissar in that city during the Battle of Warsaw, Joseph Stalin. The forces under Stalin's command in Lwów never did appear at the battle, and some in the Soviet system, most notably Leon Trotsky, blamed Stalin's inaction and incompetence for the defeat that cost the USSR the war. Stalin's exact culpability for the defeat remains an issue of historical debate, but his personal sense of anger and humiliation does not. Like the vast majority of Soviet leaders, Stalin saw Poland's existence as a threat to Soviet security and a symbol of past defeat. Throughout the interwar period, Soviet officials commonly referred to Poland as "western Belarus" or "western Ukraine," thereby denying it even a nominal place in Europe.[2]

Poland's taking of Lwów and its hinterland, which had valuable economic assets but a multiethnic population, angered Western leaders, who soon became disenchanted with promoting the cause of the same small nations they had just created. David Lloyd George reacted to Poland's annexation of East Galicia by remarking, "It fills me with despair the way in which I have seen small nations, before they have hardly leaped into the light of freedom, beginning to oppress other races than their own." Western governments, although enamored of Poland for a brief period in the 1920s, soon grew disillusioned with the political infighting of the various Polish factions and their demands for even more territory. The 1925 Locarno Pact that normalized French and British relations with Germany and admitted Germany into the League of Nations required the Germans to recognize the inviolability of the borders of Western Europe, but not those of Eastern Europe. Locarno was hailed as a great triumph in the West (the French and German diplomats who negotiated it shared the 1926 Nobel Peace Prize), but Polish leaders could not miss the ominous signal that Locarno sent to their country: Poland could not depend on the Western democracies to look after its interests.

Poland's occupation of the multiethnic region of Zaolzie in Czechoslovakia during the 1938 Munich crisis confirmed Western leaders' negative views of the Poles as acquisitive opportunists interested in ethnic self-determination only when it suited their interests. At the same time, the crisis reinforced in Polish minds the lesson of Locarno, that the West did not really care about the fate of Central European states. Nevertheless, the British and the French made the security guarantee to Poland in 1939 that led them into a world war once more. From Poland's perspective, however, the Western Allies did nothing of substance to support them when Germany invaded later that year. Nor did they act when the Soviets followed suit, restoring the Curzon Line and ending Poland's brief period of independence.

During World War II, Polish troops fought on many fronts for the Allies, but frequently they watched in frustration and anger as the British and the Americans sacrificed Poland's interests in order to maintain their alliance with Poland's great enemy, the Soviet Union. The Poles, for example, had to swallow their allies' acceptance of the Soviet version of the massacre of thousands of Polish officers in the Katyń Forest in 1940. The Poles knew that the Russians had done the killing, but in order to keep the Soviets happy, the British and the Americans acquiesced in the lie that the Germans had perpetrated the massacre. More gallingly, they pressured the Polish government-in-exile to remain silent on the issue.[3]

To Americans and Britons, Poland elicited both sympathy and bewilderment. Just before Potsdam, diplomat Joseph Davies forwarded to President Truman an editorial from the *Baltimore Sun* stressing American sympathy for Poland, which it called "strong and valiant." At the same time, however, it described the Polish leadership as driven by "fanatic folly rather than a well of statesmanship." Above all, the editorial noted, the problems of Poland presented a level of complexity that few Americans could hope to master. "Half a dozen historians could spend their lives in study," the *Sun* noted about the Polish problem, "and still not be sure of the exact truth."[4]

Perhaps because of the complexity of Poland's situation, by the middle of World War II American and British leaders had grown impatient with Polish politicians, who sought a postwar Poland based on both the Riga Line and substantial territorial gains at Germany's expense to the west and north. They demanded all of East Prussia, Silesia, and Pomerania as well as reparations from the Germans. Churchill and Roosevelt did not tell the leaders of the Polish government-in-exile in London that at the Tehran Conference they had agreed to give Stalin the Curzon Line as the postwar Russo-Polish border. Polish leaders first learned of that agreement during

Churchill's speech to the House of Commons in January 1944. Language mattered as well. Even though the Curzon Line represented virtually the same border as the Molotov-Ribbentrop Line, the Big Three used the former term to avoid the ugly anti-Russian connotation of the Nazi-Soviet Pact of 1939 implicit in the latter.[5]

Polish leaders had hoped that President Roosevelt, whose electorate contained a large number of Polish Americans in key swing states, might prove more willing to plead their case than Churchill. Roosevelt was certainly aware of the political realities, but just before the 1944 election he rhetorically asked the Polish ambassador, "Do you expect us and Great Britain to declare war on Joe Stalin if they cross your previous [Riga Line] frontier?" Ever the politician, Roosevelt nevertheless conducted the meeting in front of a giant map of Poland that showed the Riga Line as its eastern border, and photographs of the meeting with the map prominently displayed appeared in newspapers nationwide. In interviews, Roosevelt suggested that he might support a border between the Riga and Curzon lines that would at least give Lwów to Poland. When British Foreign Minister Anthony Eden learned of Roosevelt's remarks, he said, "The Poles are sadly deluding themselves if they place any faith in these vague and generous promises." He knew that Churchill, under urging from Stalin, had already told the Polish government-in-exile that the city would go to Soviet Ukraine.[6]

The Russian position on the borders of Eastern Europe elicited a great deal of sympathy in the West in 1945. Churchill said in the House of Commons in February of that year that Russia had a right to the Curzon Line "not [because of] Russian military force, but the force of the truth in their argument" that the line best represented the ethnic borders of the region. Roosevelt agreed, making the blatantly false statement in March that few Poles lived east of the line. Many people in the West also sympathized with what they saw as Russia's legitimate strategic needs. Having been invaded from the west three times in a century and a half, they believed, Russia had a right to guarantees for its own security. One British newspaper argued in July 1945 that the Russians also had a right to economic compensation from Eastern Europe, given all that its people had sacrificed to defeat Germany: "The Russians have lived on [occupied] countries and stripped them of their machinery. The blunt truth is that Western Russia is a waste as a result of German devastation, and the Soviet government is using this method as an emergency to get its own country going. It may be hard on the countries so affected—it is hard, but it is understandable from the Russian view."[7]

Russia's failure to come to the aid of the Poles who fought in the Warsaw Rising of 1944 had shown beyond the shadow of a doubt that the Soviets intended to let the Nazis destroy Poland and its leaders. As in 1920, Stalin halted his armies before Warsaw, this time allowing the Germans to fight against Polish insurgents in a murderous battle for the city that destroyed half of Warsaw and killed as many as 150,000 Poles. Stalin called the uprising a "foolish adventure" and the Polish resistance itself "a handful of criminals." He even refused to allow the Allies to use Soviet airfields to supply the insurgents. In the West, however, the uprising came to symbolize, along with the liberation of Paris at almost the same time, the beginning of the end of Nazi subjugation of the people of Europe. Stalin's refusal to do anything to help the rising led George Kennan to call Soviet policy "a gauntlet thrown down with malicious glee." Poland, Stalin appeared to be telling the West, belonged to Russia, and Russia alone would determine its fate.[8]

Soviet refusal to help the Poles led to a wave of criticism in the West, but Western leaders had determined that they would not allow a dispute over Poland to become the cause of a third world war. Whereas the British had been willing to make Poland a casus belli in 1939, they were no longer willing to do so in 1945. On April 2, US Secretary of War Henry Stimson noted in his diary, after a discussion with General George Marshall, that the West would have to swallow the Soviet Union's intransigent attitude on Poland. Marshall agreed that Soviet behavior there "would be pretty bad and irritating, but [he] thought that we must put up with them." Stimson himself had come to the conclusion that "we simply cannot allow a rift to come between the two nations [over Poland] without endangering the entire peace of the world." The Joint Chiefs of Staff later warned Truman that "from the military point of view, it would

appear impracticable to offer serious objections" to Russian territo-
rial demands in Germany and Poland "if the USSR insists upon it."
In other words, if the West had to sacrifice Poland to achieve peace in
Europe, it would have no choice but to do so.[9]

In February at Yalta, the Big Three had not even invited the Poles
to the conference that might decide their future. As expected, Stalin
demanded a border on the Curzon Line, which would make permanent the Soviet gains from the 1939 Molotov-Ribbentrop Pact. Giving
the Russians the Curzon Line would validate Russia's 1939 aggression against Poland and would leave Lwów outside Poland, an
eventuality that everyone at Yalta knew the Poles would not easily
accept. For his part, Churchill took the long view, stating that Soviet
demands were nothing more than an attempt to overturn the verdict
of World War I. "The current war," he had told Polish exile leaders in
London in 1942, "is a continuation of the first. Russia demands only
the return of that territory with which she entered the war in 1914."
The Polish leaders with whom he spoke concluded that Churchill
sympathized with the Soviet desire for the Curzon Line, which, after
all, had originally been a British idea.[10]

Churchill understood the central problem, although the Russians' obduracy on Poland made it hard for Western leaders to
empathize with their position. Whether because of his failures in
1920 or his recognition of the need to secure his Western border
(or both), Stalin grew uncharacteristically emotional about Poland
during the proceedings at Yalta. "Did your army liberate Poland,
Mr. Churchill?" Stalin demanded. "Did your army liberate Poland,
Mr. President?" Although the Poles certainly did not see Soviet
forces on their soil as liberators, neither the United States nor Great
Britain stood in a position to force Stalin to accept an outcome he
saw as inimical to Soviet interests. Harry Hopkins told President
Roosevelt that to Stalin and the Russians, Poland represented a
"fundamental, even visceral" issue on which they would not easily
compromise. At one point Churchill challenged Stalin, saying that
Britain had a right to a say in Poland's future based on the £120 million it had spent for Poland. Stalin sharply retorted that any "foreign rulers" who had shown the British the base ingratitude that

the Polish government-in-exile in London had shown toward such generous benefactors ought to be deprived of any voice in their own future. For one of the few moments at Potsdam, Churchill had no response.[11]

However much Western leaders may have wanted to help, the issue of Poland remained far less important to them than it was to Stalin. Roosevelt called Poland "a headache to the world for five centuries," and Churchill had grown so tired of the inflexible opposition of the London-based Polish government-in-exile to the Curzon Line that he warned its leaders to "concentrate on what could still be saved rather than mourn over what they had lost." In October 1944, Churchill angrily told the popular Polish exile leader Stanisław Mikołajczyk,

> I wash my hands [of Poland]; as far as I am concerned we shall give the business up. Because of quarrels between Poles we are not going to wreck the peace of Europe. In your obstinacy you do not see what is at stake. It is not in friendship that we shall part. We shall tell the world how unreasonable you are. You will start another war in which 25,000,000 lives will be lost but you don't care. . . . Unless you accept the [Curzon Line] frontier you are out of business forever. The Russians will sweep through your country and your people will be liquidated. You are on the verge of annihilation.

Mikołajczyk refused at that meeting to consent to the Curzon Line, leading Churchill to dismiss him with a curt, "You are a callous people who want to wreck Europe. I shall leave you to your fate." Seeing the realities in front of him, Mikołajczyk yielded the following day and reluctantly accepted the Curzon Line "for the sake of peace," but he left Eden's office furious.[12]

As they departed for the Yalta Conference, Western leaders understood that they could do little for Poland. Some of Churchill's anger at Polish leaders may well have sprung from his sense of guilt at his own powerlessness. "There is nothing I can do for poor Poland," he told his private secretary. Roosevelt saw the situation in much the same way, telling a group of senators that the United States could only hope to ameliorate the worst aspects of Russian control over Poland.[13]

The Yalta agreements settled the postwar border between the Soviet Union and Poland on the Curzon Line as Stalin demanded and Churchill recognized as inevitable. The Western Allies also agreed that the German port of Königsberg (in Russian, Kaliningrad) on the Baltic Sea would go to Russia even though it sat in ethnically Polish and Lithuanian territory. The Big Three agreed in principle that they might compensate Poland for its eastern losses by giving it some still-undefined German territory on its western border. Poland might therefore "slide to the west," a possibility Churchill had illustrated at Tehran by rolling matchsticks across a table. At Yalta, the Big Three had discussed the Oder and Neisse rivers as possible Polish-German borders, but they made no decisions, leaving it to the delegates at Potsdam to finalize.[14]

The Yalta agreement thus signaled that Poland would lose Wilno, Lwów, the Silesian coalfields, and 70,000 square miles of agricultural lands between the Curzon and Riga lines. More importantly, as in 1919, the Poles had had no say in the decisions, leaving open the possibility that they might oppose the new border by force as they had done after World War I. Mikołajczyk surprised the British by resigning in protest as leader of the Polish government-in-exile and publicly blasting the Yalta agreement as a fourth partition of Poland, done this time with the full complicity of Poland's supposed allies. His successor took an even more strident anti-Soviet position, leading the Russians to shut out the exiled government in London even more. When the Polish general Władysław Anders, then leading Polish troops fighting under Allied command in Italy, heard about the decision at Yalta, he called it "a death sentence" for Poland and openly discussed training his men for a future war against the Soviet Union.[15]

The Big Three at Potsdam thus needed to find a solution to the Polish problem as quickly as possible, in part to prevent the issue from starting another round of conflict. Repatriating hundreds of thousands of so-called displaced persons from all across Eastern Europe to a new Poland posed the most immediate challenge. Refugee camps that at the time of Potsdam were supposed to hold 2,000 people instead held ten times that number with more people arriving every day. One American aid worker likened the largest of the refugee camps to the Sistine Chapel's *Descent into Hell*, except that "Christ was absent." Some Poles refused to go back until they knew who would control the Polish government; Jewish survivors of the death camps often wanted to go to Palestine or America rather than return to an uncertain future in Poland. Many of them wanted to enact a measure of revenge on the Germans before going home. All of the refugees lived on charity provided by the new United Nations Relief and Rehabilitation Administration, which suffered from disorganization, political dysfunction, and a dearth of funds. It could not feed and house hundreds of thousands of refugees indefinitely, and it relied on American largesse for two-thirds of its money. "Almost everything depends on the solution of the Polish problem," said a British general in charge of refugees in the British zone of occupation who came to despise both Jewish and Catholic Poles. If the Poles did not go back to Poland and accept their fate, he feared, the peace of Europe itself might hang in the balance. Setting Poland's borders and getting the Poles to accept them therefore became a high priority.[16]

Giving the Soviets the Curzon Line as their border with Poland solved half of that problem, at least on paper, but it sat uneasily in the minds of some Americans. Arthur Bliss Lane, the American ambassador to Poland, called it "a policy of appeasement," with all of the unpleasant historical associations contained within that remark. Americans like Lane and James Byrnes also worried about the extremely vague language in the Yalta agreements about Soviet obligations to keep the West informed regarding developments in Poland and to ensure that country a government based on free elections. George Kennan complained about the "casualness and frivolity" with which the Americans and British gave Russia Köningsberg and the Curzon Line without getting anything firm in exchange on the future makeup of a Polish government. Admiral Leahy told Roosevelt, "Mr. President, this [Yalta agreement] is so elastic that the Russians can stretch it all the way from Yalta to Washington without ever technically breaking it." Roosevelt turned to his chief of staff and replied,

"I know it. But it's the best that I can do for Poland at this time." For Roosevelt, of course, there would be no next time. Whether Harry Truman would or could do any more for Poland remained an open question.[17]

BETWEEN THE TIME of the Yalta Conference in February and the Potsdam Conference in July, the Soviets tightened their control over Poland. They recognized the pro-Soviet Lublin Committee as the legitimate government of Poland. They also demanded that the Polish exiles in London join the Lublin government, recognize it as the basis of the new Polish state, and turn over all of their financial and military assets to it. The London Poles wanted a brand new government based on general elections and with no privileging of the Lublin Committee, but the ambiguity in the Yalta accords that Leahy decried gave the Soviets sufficient justification to base the government on the Lublin Committee. The dispute kept Poland from having a representative at the first United Nations conference in San Francisco in June. At the same time, the Russians had begun to take important steps to increase their control, such as issuing new Polish currency under the authority of the Lublin Committee and enacting Soviet-style agrarian reform.[18]

The Soviets had begun to change the character of Eastern Europe by force. In September 1944 (that is, several months before Yalta), the Soviet Union and a pliant Lublin Committee signed an agreement to move all ethnic Poles to lands west of the Curzon Line; Nikita Khrushchev signed for the Soviets. In 1944, the Soviets moved 117,212 Poles west, and in 1945 they moved 742,631 more. More than 640,000 Poles followed in 1946. Hundreds of thousands of Germans, many of whom had arrived in Poland since 1939, also went west to avoid the fury of the Red Army; an estimated 85 percent of the German population of Silesia fled. An officer from the Polish Second Army, then serving with the Soviets, said:

> We are transferring the Germans out of Polish territory and we are acting in accordance with directives from Moscow. We are behaving with the Germans as they behaved with us. . . . One must perform

one's tasks in such a harsh and decisive manner that the Germanic vermin do not hide in their houses but rather will flee from us of their own volition and then [once] in their own lands will thank God that they were lucky enough to save their heads. We do not forget that Germans will always be Germans.

This policy of ethnic cleansing forcibly lined up the political and ethnic maps of postwar Europe and made the situation on the ground far less favorable to any reconsideration of the Curzon Line at Potsdam. Some American diplomats, such as George Kennan, saw Russia's heavy hand and worried about it; Kennan had even warned Washington that he had seen photographic evidence of the Polish takeover of formerly German lands. During the Potsdam Conference on July 25, Byrnes received a report stating that the "Polish people enjoy practically no civil liberties, that Soviet officials are behind each local government and that secret service under Soviet direction is making many arrests." But Byrnes and others saw little that the United States could do to correct these problems without risking a major confrontation with the Soviets.[19]

Events just before the Potsdam Conference opened increased the already substantial tensions over Poland. In May, sixteen members of the wartime Polish underground that the West had identified as possible leaders in a postwar Polish government went missing during an official visit to the Soviet Union. It took two weeks to confirm that the Soviets had arrested them. The charges involved "transmitting information about Soviet armed forces collected by espionage to the Polish government in London" and spreading "provocative distortions about the behavior of Soviet troops on Polish territory liberated from the invaders." The latter referred to Polish insistence on Russian guilt in the massacre in the Katyń Forest. The arrests made headlines and angered American and British officials, but they represented just a small fraction of the estimated 100,000 Soviet arrests and deportations of noncommunist Poles. Although the arrests and the sham trial that followed should have shown how little good faith the Russians would show on Poland, the West did little more than issue diplomatic protests.[20]

During his visit to Moscow in June 1945, presidential envoy Harry Hopkins pressed Stalin on the issue of the sixteen arrested Polish leaders. He reminded Stalin that the Russians had arrested them despite issuing them a written guarantee of safety. Hopkins gently advised Stalin that the "atmosphere of the forthcoming consultations [at Potsdam] would be seriously hampered" by the arrests, and he urged the Russian leader to "find in his own way a solution of this question." Stalin smiled at Hopkins and told him that there would need to be a trial, but that he could guarantee lenient sentences. If Hopkins expressed surprise about the assumption of guilt behind Stalin's promise, he made no mention of it.[21]

The arrests did not stop the Western governments from recognizing the pro-Soviet Lublin Committee as the basis of the new Polish government on July 5, just weeks before the Potsdam Conference opened. Harry Hopkins told Truman that it would be a "mistake" to make the release of the Poles "a condition to agreement" on Polish issues more generally, most importantly the question of the new government's structure and leadership. Clement Attlee observed of the Lublin Poles, "I never saw such a collection of shifty-looking individuals in my life," but the West gave them control of Poland nevertheless. Seventeen of the twenty-one cabinet positions in the provisional government went to communists linked to the Lublin Committee, confirming, in Charles Bohlen's mind, the nature of the Lublin government as nothing more than a Soviet puppet. Leahy decried what he called Russian dishonesty and heavy-handedness, but, just as he had earlier warned Roosevelt, he told Truman that the Yalta accords allowed for multiple interpretations. More importantly, they did not leave the US government with much room to challenge agreements that it had itself signed. Joseph Davies agreed, saying that in his reading of the Yalta agreements, "the merits of the dispute are clearly on the side of the Soviet Union."[22]

Having had no role at Yalta, Truman struggled to make sense of the diplomatic wording in the documents of the conference, and complained that he saw something new in them every time he read them. Truman confessed to British ambassador, Lord Halifax, that "between you, me, and the gate post, I do not think we shall get a solution" to the Polish problem. He knew from Harry Hopkins's reports of the May 1945 Kremlin meetings that Stalin considered the Polish question not open for debate; the Russians would hold firmly to Soviet interpretations of the Yalta accords. Stalin told Hopkins that the United States and Great Britain could not possibly understand Russia's position on Poland, because those two countries had never faced invasion, "the results of which are not easily forgotten." At another meeting, Stalin sounded more like the conqueror demanding his spoils, telling Hopkins that if not for the Red Army's "great loss of life" in liberating Poland, "nobody would be talking about a new Poland," in 1945 or ever. Hopkins saw the significance of Stalin's deep intransigence over the question of the sixteen arrested Poles, and advised Truman that if the Big Three did not settle the major questions about Poland at Potsdam, they would not solve them at all. The Soviets, from Stalin on down, saw Poland as nonnegotiable and would not reopen questions at Potsdam that they believed the Big Three had already settled at Yalta. Secretary of War Henry Stimson, with his characteristic bluntness, argued that the Americans should not make an issue of Poland, because "the Russians, with their possession, have 99 and 44/100 percent of the law."[23]

The briefing books Truman read on his transatlantic voyage showed the difficulty of the issue. They argued that Germany should lose Upper Silesia, East Prussia, and Pomerania, despite the "almost exclusively" German populations of the regions. The area between the Oder and Neisse rivers should, however, remain with Germany. "There is no historic or ethnic justification for the cession of this area [to Poland]," Truman's advisers argued. Taking the region away from Germany would cripple the German economy and could "arouse an intense spirit of irredentism. Maintenance of the Oder-Neisse frontier might well become the most critical security problem in Europe during the coming years." Still, the briefings warned Truman that "if the Polish and Soviet governments press insistently . . . we shall have no recourse but to agree to the cession of the area east of the Oder." The United States had also committed to the Curzon Line at Yalta, and the briefings recommended holding to that promise at Potsdam.[24]

Accordingly, both Truman and Churchill displayed an unwillingness to make Poland a major issue at Potsdam. Truman gave the
London-based Poles just twenty-five minutes of his time at Potsdam,
most of it dedicated to introductions and protocol. Churchill refused
to meet with them at all. "I am sick of the bloody Poles," the prime
minister thundered. "I don't want to see them." Of the senior Western diplomats, only Anthony Eden seemed eager to push the issue.
He opposed Churchill's indifference on the Polish question, which
he later called "the most tough and disagreeable" of the discussions
he had with his Soviet counterparts at Potsdam. Eden understood
that American leaders who "knew little of Europe" would not put
much of their political capital into Poland. But England, he argued,
should. "We were of it [Europe]," he argued, "and would be watched
on this." Being "of it," however, did not stop several senior British
leaders from misunderstanding the difference between the eastern
and western branches of the Neisse River. The area between the two
branches, approximately the size of Massachusetts, and containing
2.7 million ethnic Germans, went to the Poles almost as much out
of confusion as design. That confusion echoed the confusion in 1919
over the "A" and "B" variants of the Curzon Line that had caused
some of the conflict between Poland, Ukraine, and the Soviet Union.
In both cases, British and American misunderstanding of the geo-
graphic, historical, and cultural contexts of Eastern Europe impacted
the lives of millions of people.[25]

By the time of Potsdam, Eden saw the risk that the Russians
could grow too powerful if they controlled Poland, but he worried
far more about what Polish absorption of so many Germans would
do to Poland itself. If the new Poland contained too many Germans,
Eden argued, the country would "lay up troubles for themselves in
the future." Here Eden reflected Churchill's classic remark at Yalta
that "it would be a great pity to stuff the Polish goose so full of
German food that it died of indigestion." These remarks show that
Western leaders in 1945 still thought about the problem of Poland in
terms of the irredentism and ethnic troubles of the 1919–1939 years
rather than as a pawn in a rivalry with Russia that did not yet seem
inevitable. Eden, Churchill, and others also had little to no idea of

how hard the Soviets had already worked to make the area between the Oder and Bug rivers Polish. Leahy, however, must have. At one point in the proceedings at Potsdam, Stalin told Truman not to worry about postwar Poland being multiethnic in character, because no Germans remained in the region between the Curzon Line and the Oder-Neisse River Line. "Of course not," Leahy whispered to Truman. "The Bolshies have killed all of them."[26]

Churchill made a symbolic effort at Potsdam to stand up for the Poles, arguing against the Oder River as Poland's Western border on both economic and ethnic lines. Neither Stettin nor Breslau, he argued, were Polish in character, and thus neither one could become part of Poland. Even though he had advocated it at Yalta, he now argued that shifting Poland to the west would mean that "the Poles and the Russians had the food and the fuel, while we had the mouths [to feed] and the hearths [to warm]." He and Truman both argued that Polish demands for the Oder-Neisse Line went too far, especially because any ethnic Germans displaced would come west to the jointly administered Germany, where the burden for feeding them would fall to the British and the Americans. Western leaders were deaf to the demands of Polish representatives that the new borders in the west would serve as "an expression of historical justice" for a tortured Poland. "We don't want to pay for Polish revenge," Truman responded.[27]

None of the West's arguments mattered much in the end. By the time of Potsdam, the Russians had transferred control of all the territory between the Curzon Line and the Oder-Neisse River Line to the new Polish government. With blazing speed, German-language newspapers disappeared, Polish flags flew over public buildings, signs changed from German to Polish place names (Stettin to Szczecin, and Breslau to Wrocław, for example), and Poles took possession of formerly German homes. The Russians then announced that because this territory now fell under Polish control, it was exempt from any reparations the Allies might demand of Germany. The wealth of Silesia's coalfields would therefore go into the coffers of the new Polish government, or through them to the Soviet Union, instead of indirectly to the British or the Americans via reparations.[28]

American leaders recognized their powerlessness to stop this Russian fait accompli. Averill Harriman, the US ambassador to the Soviet Union, observed that in regards to Poland, it didn't matter that Truman, and not Roosevelt, represented the United States. No matter who was president, he said, "the Russians are not going to give in." His observant and perceptive daughter Kathleen Harriman Mortimer understood the reality of the situation as well. "The Soviet Army was there and there wasn't anything we could do about it," she recalled. Charles Bohlen, one of the State Department's senior Soviet experts and Truman's interpreter at Potsdam, agreed, noting in his memoir that "even if Roosevelt had lived out his fourth term, the map of Europe would look about the same. If there was one lesson that emerged from the wartime conferences and our postwar dealings with the Soviet Union, it was that the Soviets were going to hold any territory they occupied . . . regardless of who was President of the United States."[29]

Bohlen, who at the time of Potsdam believed that the United States had more to fear from a resurgent Germany than a postwar rivalry with the Soviet Union, reflected the consensus of American views. According to this view, the enlargement of Poland, while not ideal, would serve to weaken Germany, not least by giving to the Poles much of what had been the German heartland of East Prussia. The most influential dissenting view came from Bohlen's friend George Kennan. He agreed that the Soviets had already achieved their desired mastery over Poland, but he saw no reason for the United States to become complicit in it. Kennan argued for recognizing the de facto division of Europe into spheres of influence, but refusing to sign any agreement that gave American consent to Russian dominance over Eastern Europe. Like Roosevelt and Churchill, however, Kennan saw no point in risking war with the Russians over Poland, and he knew that Poland meant far more to the Soviet Union than it did to the West.[30]

The fate of the Oder River port city of Stettin shows just how completely the Soviets had tilted the tables in their favor on the issue of Poland. At Yalta, Molotov had pressed for Stettin's inclusion in the new Poland, but Western diplomats had disagreed, and the issue remained theoretically open for discussion at Potsdam. Leahy noted in his diary on July 31, near the end of the Potsdam Conference, that he understood Soviet control of Stettin to represent nothing more than an "interim administration," and that the city's ultimate fate still lay open for debate. By that point, however, and mostly unbeknownst to Leahy, the Russians had forced all but 20,000 of the city's 275,000 ethnic Germans to leave. Two weeks before Leahy wrote his diary entry, the Soviets had held a ceremony officially transferring the city to Polish control, and the Poles had converted all of the city's Protestant churches to Catholic churches. At the beginning of 1945, the city had had just 3,500 Polish residents; one year later, it had more than 100,000. Thus, while Leahy could still believe that Stettin's future remained in doubt, the Russians and the Poles had effectively eliminated the German city of Stettin and replaced it with the Polish city of Szczecin.[31]

The new Poland, "slid to the west," emerged as a potentially powerful state in the heart of Europe. It would control a long coastline as well as a sizable number of natural resources and include the formerly German areas of Silesia, Pomerania, and East Prussia. If given free elections, Western leaders hoped, it might still emerge as a powerful buffer to the Germans and the Soviets. Despite the Soviet Union's military sway over Poland, the West might still be able to influence events there through loans, financial credits, and trade.

With the issue of borders essentially decided before the conference even began, Western diplomats turned at Potsdam to the composition of the final Polish government. Part of the rationale for recognizing the Lublin Committee as the basis of the new Polish government centered on Soviet willingness to allow the London-based Mikołajczyk to serve as one of two deputy prime ministers in the interim government, but the strained relations between him and the British made him a less than reliable partner for the West. By the time of Potsdam, moreover, he had largely lost faith in the possibility of a democratic future for his country. So, too, had many Americans. Admiral Leahy, although adamant in public that the United States should press for a democratic government in Poland, believed in late

April 1945 that the Americans could really only hope to create "an external appearance of [Polish] independence."[32]

Again, the debate centered on the exact wording of the Yalta accords, specifically, the interpretation of the phrase calling for the London Poles to "consult in the first instance" with the Lublin Committee on the formation of the postwar government. Western leaders focused on the word "consult," which they interpreted to mean that the London and Lublin-based Poles would share equally in the joint task of forming a government. Thus in April did Truman tell Molotov that the Yalta agreement called for the London Poles to have a determining voice in structuring the new government. With the terms agreed at Yalta, Truman noted, "it only remained for Marshal Stalin to carry it out in accordance with his word."[33]

The Soviets, by contrast, focused on the phrase "first instance," which they said suggested that the West had agreed that the Lublin Committee already formed the basis of the new Polish government; the London Poles could "consult," as the Yalta agreement stated, but they would do so on terms determined by the Lublin Committee. Thus did Stalin reply to Truman's note by remarking that the president's "understanding of the position of the Polish Government and such an attitude towards it is very difficult to reconcile with the decisions of the Crimea conference." Just for good measure, Stalin added that Russia needed a friendly Poland and had earned it "by the blood of the Soviet people abundantly shed on the field of Poland in the name of the liberation of Poland." Stalin also demanded to know why the Americans insisted upon a fully democratic government for Poland, when they had not insisted on one for Greece. Russian diplomats noted that the West had recognized Charles de Gaulle as head of a provisional government for France without elections or the participation of a broad spectrum of French political parties. To Russian eyes, therefore, Western insistence on democracy seemed less about a principle of governance than a selective policy designed to put a capitalist and potentially hostile Poland on the Soviet Union's western border.[34]

For their part, the Poles hardly had more voice in determining their own fate in 1945 than they had had in 1919. Few London Poles celebrated the end of the war, because they knew that they faced an uncertain future under Soviet domination. British recognition of the Lublin Committee as the core of the Polish government meant that £20 million in Polish financial assets in London went back to Poland as well. In the eyes of the noncommunist Poles, the British were thereby subsidizing the very process that would kill democracy in their country. The London Poles also dreaded returning to Poland for fear of being shot by the Soviets or deported to gulags, as indeed unknown thousands were. Eventually, the British agreed to allow Poles who had fought for the British Army to remain in Britain or resettle in the British Empire.

The Big Three did allow the Lublin Poles to make their case in person to the foreign ministers at Potsdam, but their views hardly mattered. British diplomat Alexander Cadogan described the Poles who came to the conference as a "dreadful lot, all of them." Polish communists, led by the widely loathed Bolesław Bierut, addressed the conference on July 24. Predictably, Bierut expressed satisfaction with the Curzon Line as Poland's border with the Soviet Union. The Polish communists also demanded, again predictably, that the great powers give the new Poland enough German land to accommodate the estimated 4 million Poles living east of the Curzon Line who would resettle inside the country's new boundaries. Bierut also demanded a large share of German reparations. Churchill, who particularly despised Bierut, objected that Polish demands would take away as much as one-quarter of Germany's arable land at a time when as many as 9 million ethnic Germans would resettle in the new Germany.[35]

Some hardliners, such as Eden, Leahy, and Kennan, argued that the United States and Britain should take a firm stand with the Soviets over Poland. In April, Truman had agreed, and in his meetings with Molotov in Washington he had insisted that the Soviets follow the Yalta accords as the Americans understood them. But as Truman came to realize, Stimson had been right all along: the Soviets had possession of Poland, and the United States could only change the reality on the ground at very high cost and at the risk of future conflict with the Soviet Union. Even before Potsdam, Truman had begun to back away from his hardline position of April. He learned, too, that his hard line did not have the support of the British, who put less and less of their own political capital into the issue of Poland. Churchill wrote to Truman in late April to say that, in his reading, the Yalta agreements implied a new government, but one in which the Polish communists would emerge "prominent," presumably regardless of what any future elections might reveal about what the Polish people actually wanted.[36]

More significantly, although the result of the debates on Poland at Yalta and Potsdam left the Russians in a dominant position, the conferences did solve the Poland problem as the Big Three understood it in 1945. More than any other issue discussed at Potsdam, Poland added to the mistrust building between the West and the Soviet Union. But, however it had happened, the agreements finalized at Potsdam solved the dilemmas created by the Treaty of Versailles. Most importantly, Poland's political and ethnic borders at last lined up reasonably well, and its government would not be in a position to disturb the peace of Europe as it had in 1919. In his speech on the Potsdam Conference to the American people, Truman admitted that "in all candor I did not like this provision of the Berlin agreement." But, he argued, the Big Three had solved the problem of Poland once and for all. There would at long last be "a short and more easily defensible frontier between Poland and Germany. Settled by Poles, it will provide a more homogenous nation with fewer national minorities." Thus, in Truman's eyes, the conference had solved the Polish problem as he, and Woodrow Wilson before him, had understood it.[37]

That the great powers were perfectly willing to achieve these aims by denying Poland its freedom struck many as tragic, but, given Poland's history, the result should not have been terribly surprising. As the Polish writer and Auschwitz survivor Tadeusz Borowski ruefully (and perhaps somewhat romantically) noted, before the war the ideal of a Polish homeland stood for "a peaceful corner and a log in the fire." By 1945, he wrote, it stood for "a burned house and an NKVD summons."[38]

Dr. Groves's Son and the Fate of East Asia

THE BIG THREE HAD MOSTLY concerned themselves with settling the affairs of Europe at the Paris Peace Conference of 1919, but their decisions changed the history of Asia as well. The most difficult and controversial Asian topic discussed in Paris involved the future of Shandong Province in northeastern China. Shandong had formed the core of the German trade concession zone in China since 1898, and in 1919 the Chinese government desperately wanted it returned to Chinese control. The province had an indisputably Chinese population that made it an almost perfect test case of Woodrow Wilson's principle of self-determination. The birthplace of Confucius, and home to valuable deposits of oil, gold, diamonds, and sapphires, it held great meaning for Chinese diplomats and to the Chinese people more generally. Although China had not fought Germany on the battlefield, it had sent 140,000 laborers to the western front to help the Allies solve their logistical problems and free up more men for the front lines. Most importantly, China believed that it clearly had the merits of the Shandong case on its side and looked at the return of the province as a step toward the end of its quasi-colonial humiliations. By all logic and justice, the Big Three should have had little trouble giving Shandong to its rightful owner, China.[1]

Before the Paris Peace Conference opened, the return of Shandong had seemed to Chinese leaders almost a foregone conclusion. China's Western-educated and well-respected minister in Washington, Wellington Koo, had spoken to Woodrow Wilson just before the president left for Paris. Koo came away assured that Wilson fully intended to apply self-determination to Shandong and grant it to China. Secretary of State Robert Lansing also confirmed to Koo that America wanted to see Shandong returned to full Chinese control. Koo's close reading of the American leadership and the tenor of American public opinion also led him to believe that China had both firmly on its side.

But Japan's military forces actually held Shandong, and Japan's leaders intended to keep it. Control of the province made up the first part of Japan's so-called Twenty-One Demands on China in January 1915. Japan assumed that it could count on the support of at least one of the great powers, because as part of its alliance with Great Britain, the Japanese had declared war on Germany, and Japan's forces, not China's, had taken Shandong from German control. Britain, the Japanese presumed, would honor its promises to allow Japan to keep any German territory it captured as compensation for Japanese help in the war. Thus, Japan also thought that it had the merits of the case on its side. Moreover, the United States, France, and Great Britain needed Japanese support for their plans to pressure the Bolsheviks in Russia; part of those plans involved a Japanese intervention in Siberia that began in August 1918. Although the Americans soon grew suspicious of Japanese aims, they did not want to see the Japanese withdraw their forces.

Japan also argued that it had signed agreements with China in 1915 and again in 1918 that promised at least Japanese influence over, if not outright control of, Shandong. Lastly, the Big Three knew that they had already angered their Japanese allies by rejecting their request for a racial-equality clause in the final peace treaty. If the Japanese came away completely dissatisfied, they might well refuse to sign the treaty or join the League of Nations, a nightmarish scenario for Wilson and his hopes for internationalism.

In late April 1919, the Big Three violated both the letter and the spirit of Wilsonianism by awarding control of Shandong Province to Japan. Although Wilson claimed that the Sino-Japanese agreements of 1915 tied his hands, he knew that Japan had forced the Chinese to sign a document that represented little more than naked aggression in a time of war. When General Tasker Bliss, then serving as Wilson's chief military adviser, heard about the Shandong decision, he considered resigning in order that his name not be associated with a treaty containing so odious a clause. Some junior members of the American delegation did resign. Bliss, Lansing, and a few other senior American advisers tried to change Wilson's mind, but, despite the president's own unease over the issue, they failed to do so.[2]

The decision set off a series of anti-Western and anti-Japanese riots in Chinese cities that are known today as the May Fourth Patriotic Movement. Thousands of students took to the streets of Beijing; most protested peacefully, but in at least one case, they burned down the home of a Chinese diplomat with pro-Japanese views who had signed the Twenty-One Demands. The protesters advocated a boycott of Western and Japanese goods and pressured the Chinese government to reject the Treaty of Versailles. Soon, students and workers from Shanghai and other Chinese cities joined the protests, which dragged on into June, threatening not only Sino-Japanese relations but also the survival of an increasingly unpopular Chinese government itself.

Chinese nationals living in France surrounded the Chinese delegation's Paris hotel to prevent the diplomats from signing any peace treaty that sacrificed Shandong and humiliated China. In the absence of direct orders from their government to sign the final treaty, the diplomats decided in the end not to do so. Their refusal sent a stinging message of rebuttal to Wilson and to the West more generally. The May Fourth Patriotic Movement, commemorated today by a monument in Tiananmen Square, symbolized the turn of many of China's intellectuals and government officials away from the West and toward various versions of Chinese nationalism. It especially helped to inspire Chinese communists, who officially formed the

Chinese Communist Party one year to the day after the signing of the Treaty of Versailles; the timing was hardly coincidental.[3]

Despite getting Western blessing for its control of Shandong, the Japanese government also emerged from the Treaty of Versailles unhappy. The lack of a racial-equality clause stung Japanese pride, and both the British and the American governments soon grew worried about what they saw as Japanese avarice. The British even considered abrogating their 1902 treaty with Japan, the first ever signed on equal terms between a European and an Asian power. In the 1920s, aware that Western attitudes toward them had grown negative, the Japanese returned nominal political rule of Shandong to China, but kept effective control of the key economic assets in the region, including the railways. The question of Shandong, and the many historical issues it symbolized, added greatly to the tensions in East Asia in the years between the wars.

Just as the Big Three had in Paris, so, too, did the Big Three at Potsdam have Asia on their minds. China again formed an important topic of conversation. Now the victim of Japanese invasion and teetering on the brink of a civil war that would likely begin in full as soon as the Japanese left, China sat in an even more delicate position in 1945 than it had in 1919. World War II killed as many as 20 million Chinese and left 90 million more homeless, staggering figures even by the standards of this most terrible of all wars. The Nationalists under Chiang Kai-shek and the Communists under Mao Tse-tung had managed to cobble together a loose alliance against their common Japanese enemy, but it did not always hold, and they loathed each other at least as much as they hated Japan.

China's future, therefore, remained uncertain; the decisions reached about Japan at Potsdam would likely have a critical impact on its fate. On his way to Potsdam aboard the *Queen Elizabeth*, Truman's adviser Joseph Davies ran into Wellington Koo, on his way to Europe on the same ship. Since 1919, Koo had become one of the most experienced diplomats in the world. He had served as a founding diplomat of the League of Nations; had been acting premier, interim president, and foreign minister of the Chinese government;

had represented China as its first delegate to the United Nations; and had served as Chinese ambassador to both Great Britain and France.

The chance meeting on the *Queen Elizabeth* gave Davies and Koo an opportunity to exchange their ideas on the future of China. Both men knew that despite the Marxist lineage Stalin and Mao shared, Stalin did not see Mao as an ally. Their ideologies, one based on an industrial proletariat, the other on a nation of peasants, sprang from the same root, but then diverged in important ways. More significantly, Davies thought, Stalin had a vested interest in a secure and stable China to Russia's south, and Russia, he knew, would always "do what was in its interests," regardless of ideology. Therefore, Davies concluded, the Soviets would likely support the Nationalist government under Chiang Kai-shek that Koo served rather than Mao's communist insurgency. Koo had come to a similar conclusion, but he did not see Stalin's support in the same positive light as Davies. "Yes," he told Davies when asked if Nationalist China would welcome Soviet support in a war against Mao. "But will their price be too high?"[4]

Unbeknownst to Davies and Koo, Stalin had already expressed his support for Chiang Kai-shek to Harry Hopkins in Moscow in late May. The Russian dictator said that he preferred a unified China under Chiang, whom he described as "the best of the lot" and "the one to undertake the unification of China." For these same reasons, he had supported Chiang from 1936 to 1939 and had dispatched Soviet advisers to help the Nationalist Army in its war against the Japanese. In 1941, he had resumed aid to Chiang and had at the same time urged Mao to stop fighting the Nationalists and concentrate instead on Japan. In all, the Soviets trained 90,000 Chinese officers and gave the Nationalists planes, tanks, rifles, and artillery pieces worth hundreds of millions of dollars.[5]

In 1945, Stalin sought a strong, stable Chinese government with which he could negotiate. Chiang, not Mao, offered Russia its best chance at stability on its southern border. Little had changed since 1941, when Stalin had said that "logically, the Chinese Communist Party should be closer to us than Chiang Kai-Shek," but that only the latter could possibly hope to hold China together. Stalin did not even mention Mao by name during his meetings with Hopkins. He did, however, note that the United States would have to take the lead in providing China with economic assistance, and he added the ominous statement that his support for Chiang depended on China making some unspecified "reforms." Hopkins similarly told Truman that Stalin's support for Chiang depended on the latter's "willingness to grant concessions." Koo's suspicions about Russia's price were well-founded.[6]

American officials tried to play the role of middle man. Averill Harriman reported to Truman in early July that Chiang would reluctantly accede to Russian demands for control of Outer Mongolia as well as long-term leases for civilian use of certain airfields, ports, and railways in Manchuria in exchange for an alliance and help in the looming civil war against Mao's Communists. Harriman called these demands "excessive" but consistent with the Yalta agreements, and consistent as well with core American interests, as long as the Soviets did not interfere with America's Open Door policy of free trade in China. The Americans knew that they still needed Stalin's help in stabilizing Asia after the war, and they also knew that Chiang's government sat on an unstable foundation. A Sino-Soviet alliance could steady Nationalist China and provide the region with a badly needed sense of stability. The price of Soviet concessions seemed a fair one to pay to grant that stability. Chiang and Koo showed a willingness to deal on the issues raised by the Russians, but Harriman noted Chiang's unwillingness to concede more; Chiang told him that the concessions already made went "against the traditional convictions of our people." Chiang and Koo had in mind the historical example of China's loss of Shandong after World War I. They were on their guard in 1945 against a repeat performance that might cost them control over Mongolia or even Manchuria.[7]

As on the issue of Poland, the Soviets held most of the cards. By the time of Potsdam, the leaders of the United States and Great Britain needed, or thought they needed, help from the Soviet Union to finish the Pacific war. Militarily, Japan posed at least two major strategic problems. First, Allied strategists had estimated that an invasion of the home islands would likely cause tremendous, perhaps unprecedented, casualties. Truman had given his final approval to the plan to invade Kyushu just two weeks before leaving for Potsdam. A Russian invasion of Manchuria and Korea figured prominently in the grand strategy that underlay that plan. Second, even an invasion of the home islands did little to solve the problem of the estimated 1.8 million Japanese soldiers in mainland China. Henry Stimson noted in his diary that "we must be careful not to get involved in the task of trying to beat the Japanese armies in China. That would be a terrific task and I doubt very much if our country would stand for it." The Soviet Union had the manpower to help solve both problems, especially the latter, but it had a nonaggression pact with the Japanese that had served the Soviet Union well from 1941 to 1945.[8]

Harry Truman had set as a primary goal of the Potsdam Conference getting the Russians to agree to end that pact, as they had promised to do at Yalta, and then to declare war on Japan as quickly as possible. He knew that Japanese diplomats had reached out to the Russians, hoping either to get the Americans to moderate their terms or, perhaps, to negotiate a deal whereby the Japanese might surrender to the Soviets in exchange for keeping some of their conquests in China. In one exchange, the Japanese offered to give the Russians southern Sakhalin Island, Port Arthur, and half of Manchuria in exchange for help in keeping the rest of Japan's conquests in Asia. American code breakers listened in to all of the diplomatic traffic between Tokyo and Moscow and, while the Russians honestly reported the discussions to their American allies and rebuffed the Japanese at every turn, American officials became concerned that the Russians might decide to deal with the Japanese, writing the Americans out in the process.[9]

Truman thus had every reason to try to entice the Russians into joining the Pacific war. He wanted to leave no option unexplored in his efforts to end the war with Japan in 1945, even if most serious strategists saw that goal as unreasonable. At Potsdam, the Combined Chiefs of Staff set November 15, 1946, as their estimated end date for the Pacific war. Most strategists thus expected months of further bloodshed. One of the more optimistic of these strategists, the British

General "Pug" Ismay, bet his friend, a US Air Force general, Henry "Hap" Arnold, two dollars that Japan would surrender before 1945 ended. Arnold, among those who expected the war to go on well into 1946 or even 1947, lost the bet. He sent Ismay a paperweight with two silver dollars in it and a note saying, "Thank God I can pay this now." At the time of the Potsdam Conference, few people, of course, knew about the secret that would result in Arnold being two dollars poorer by the end of the year.[10]

The American people supported Truman's efforts to get the Russians to join the war against Japan, according to a press summary the State Department sent to James Byrnes at Potsdam on July 21. It showed that the consensus of American press opinion agreed with the president's desire to ask the Soviets to assume part of the burden for the defeat of Japan, even if, in return, the Soviets demanded a restoration of some of what they had lost to Japan in 1905. The report also indicated that Russian entry into the war stood out as the most important topic on the Potsdam agenda to the average American, because it alone involved issues of life or death for Americans then still fighting. A separate poll presented to Truman during his transatlantic voyage showed 71.9 percent of Americans in favor of Russia joining the war against Japan. The president's correspondence also included dozens of letters supporting any action that would end the war as quickly as possible. One from an Alabama congressman who had just finished a twelve-state tour told Truman that the unanimous opinion of the Americans with whom he spoke was "to get this terrible war finished and save every one of our boys we can." Truman thus had the full backing of the American media and the American public to try to convince Stalin to enter the war against Japan as soon as possible after concluding the murderous one with Germany.[11]

Truman need not have worried about Russian desires to join the war against Japan. Stalin wanted Russia involved in the war as much as Truman did. As Davies and Koo had discussed on the *Queen Elizabeth*, for the Russians, war against Japan offered an opportunity to regain some of the lands lost by the czar in the 1904–1905 Russo-Japanese War, including the southern half of Sakhalin Island, the Kurile Islands, and the ports of Dairen and Port Arthur (today called

Lüshunkou)—exactly those territories the Japanese held out as a lure to Soviet cooperation. Stimson thought the Russians might also ask for control of Korea, but Truman thought any Russian demands beyond what they had controlled in 1904 would be "bluff."[12]

Truman appears to have guessed correctly on Korea, at least in the context of 1945, but Stalin certainly had his eyes set firmly on the East. On June 28, 1945, even before he set out for Potsdam, Stalin told his commanders to begin preparations for a war with Japan "in the greatest secrecy." As later reported, "army commanders [were] to be given their orders in person and orally and without any written directives." Stalin would give Truman what he wanted at Potsdam, but he needed Truman to think that he was doing so as part of a broader set of negotiations, not solely out of Russia's own interests.[13]

Not all Western leaders at Potsdam thought the United States and Britain needed Russian help. General John Deane, the American military liaison to the Soviet Union, thought Potsdam offered a "comforting" chance to turn the tables. For the first time, the United States could actually turn down Russian offers of assistance, in stark contrast to the immense efforts it had made since 1941 to keep the Red Army alive and fighting. Having seen the devastation of the Soviet Union with his own eyes, Deane assumed that in the postwar world the Russians would need the Americans, not vice versa, because of the immense Russian need for funds for recovery. Deane also worried about the willingness of the Soviet people to fight another war after having lost so much in the war against Germany; the Russian people, he observed, had no hatred for Japan. Other Americans began to worry about Russia growing too strong as a result of its Eastern gains. Secretary of the Navy James Forrestal noted that a July 6 meeting of the State, War, and Navy departments marked the first time discussion began to shift from how to get the Russians into the Pacific war to how to keep them out of it.[14]

By then it was already too late. Almost without debate, Stalin told Truman early on at Potsdam that Russian forces would invade Manchuria no later than mid-August. In return, they wanted an immediate share of the German merchant fleet in order to move military assets from Europe to Asia. The Americans quickly agreed.

Against British advice, Truman pledged on July 19 that Russia would get an equal share of Germany's merchant ships as soon as Stalin declared war on Japan. Truman also agreed to transfer as many as twenty bomber squadrons to Asia immediately and to continue to provide military assistance to China. The Americans promised not to conduct military operations in Korea or the Kurile Islands, a tacit recognition that they fell into the Soviet area of influence. In return, the Russians pledged that while they sought favorable trade terms in Manchuria, they had no intention of occupying any part of Chinese territory and no desire to interfere with American Open Door rights in China. Ambassador Harriman had his doubts about the latter, but Admiral Leahy and President Truman both described the mood over these discussions as "friendly." Truman, elated to have the Russian help he came to get, wrote home to his wife, Bess, "Some things we won't and can't agree on—but I already have what I came for."[15]

How to end the war with Japan remained a question of intense debate. The Allies had insisted on unconditional surrender for Germany, but several strategists argued that the same insistence for Japan might well prove counterproductive. The geography of Japan complicated any attempts at invasion and military dominance. Culturally, the Japanese people had an attachment to the emperor that argued against an insistence on his removal. If the Americans, whose forces would have to bear the brunt of an invasion of the home islands, insisted on dethroning the quasi-divine emperor, it might force the Japanese to fight on for an abstract goal that had little real strategic or political importance. The Americans should, Secretary of War Henry Stimson and others argued, allow Japan to keep its emperor in exchange for ending the war. Most senior US military officials agreed, noting that only the emperor could sign or endorse a capitulation that the Japanese people would respect. Removing him by force might create anarchy and an untenable situation for occupying forces. British Foreign Minister Ernest Bevin drew a direct lesson from World War I, arguing that "it might have been better for all of us not to have destroyed the institution of the Kaiser after the last war; we might not have had this one if we hadn't done so." Thus, he argued, the Allies should remain flexible about the emperor's future.[16]

Other officials recalled with bitterness Pearl Harbor, Bataan, Hong Kong, and Singapore, and insisted that Japan must surrender unconditionally. The still-influential former secretary of state Cordell Hull publicly blasted any concessions to the Japanese as "appeasement." His word choice mattered deeply, as it carried the historical implication of both American weakness and the beginning of another round of conflict. He, Byrnes, and most State Department officials opposed allowing the emperor to remain under any circumstances. They were willing to risk further casualties in order to destroy the Japanese political system and open the way for a full American occupation of Japan after the war.[17]

The diplomats nevertheless realized that they needed to show some flexibility. The State Department argued in a July 21 memorandum sent from Washington to Babelsberg that the "Japs must bow to our terms" and must at least appear to accept unconditional surrender. The memo also noted, however, that unconditional surrender offered multiple interpretations. Looking historically, it argued that Ulysses S. Grant had forced Robert E. Lee into accepting unconditional surrender in 1865, but had still made symbolic concessions and had negotiated the final terms rather than impose them. Above all, the State Department advised, the United States should not "quibble over words," but get peace with the "bewildered, fanatic Japanese people" as quickly as the Americans could arrange it on terms favorable to themselves. Forrestal agreed, arguing that the Americans should do with the emperor whatever saved the most American lives. Truman's own briefing book argued for stripping the emperor of his powers, but not for abolishing the institution, removing the emperor from Japan, or placing him on trial for war crimes. The Japanese people, the briefers argued, would never accept abolition of the institution of the emperor by a foreign power. Better, it argued, to try to use the emperor in helping Japan make the transition from war to peace.[18]

Stalin, too, favored unconditional surrender with some room for flexibility, as he told Hopkins in Moscow in May. An unconditional surrender offered the way to "destroy Japanese military might and [the] forces of Japan once and for all." Stalin recognized, however, that Japan would likely fight harder, as the Germans had, if the Allies remained inflexible on peace terms. Hopkins told Truman that in Stalin's view, "if we stick to unconditional surrender, the Japs will not give up and we will have to destroy them as we destroyed Germany." Stalin floated the idea of making modifications to the policy that would still allow for an Allied occupation of Japan after the surrender. The Allies "can give them the works once we get into Japan," he said. Hopkins got the distinct impression that Stalin had not yet ruled out having Russian troops as part of the postwar occupation force.[19]

By the time of Potsdam, Truman's senior advisers had begun to back off the idea of unconditional surrender. At a critical meeting of the State, War, and Navy departments in late April, the secretaries of those departments noted that they did not want to destroy Japan's economic potential. In Forrestal's revealing words, they did not want to "Morgenthau those islands." A few weeks later he wrote that among the senior leaders of the US military and diplomatic corps, "no one desired the permanent subjugation of Japan, the enslavement of its people, or any attempt to dictate what kind of government the country should have." The question of defining what exactly the Americans meant by "unconditional surrender," Forrestal concluded, represented "one of the most serious questions before the country." He urged Truman to use the upcoming Potsdam Conference to clarify the meaning of unconditional surrender and its practical implications for ending the war.[20]

Letters sent to Truman at Babelsberg urged him, in the words of one writer, to "state the meaning of unconditional surrender." The writer, a minister from Tennessee, called on Truman to announce that it "does not mean the extermination and enslavement of the Japanese people." A *New York Times* editorial on May 11 called unconditional surrender "a senseless policy" that would cause the Japanese people to fight harder and cost lives unnecessarily. "Many say we have won the war," stated another letter to Truman, "and ask 'What are we fighting for?'" Clearly, the United States needed to define more precisely what it meant by unconditional surrender. It also needed to offer the Japanese some way to surrender before they faced complete annihilation.[21]

THE DEBATE ON SURRENDER changed in an instant as a result of an explosion thousands of miles away from both Japan and Germany. On July 18 at 7:30 a.m., Truman received a message at Potsdam marked "TOP SECRET URGENT." It read: "Operated this morning. Diagnosis not yet complete but results seem satisfactory and already exceed expectations. . . . Dr. Groves pleased." The next day another message arrived that read, "Doctor Groves has just returned most enthusiastic and confident that the little boy is as husky as his big brother. The light in his eyes discernable from here to Highhold and I could hear his screams from here to my farm." The "doctor," Lieutenant General Leslie Groves, headed the Manhattan Project. The rather transparently worded memos that Secretary of War Henry Stimson handed to the president confirmed that the expensive gamble Truman had uncovered as a senator had now paid off. The prearranged code indicated that the blast could be seen 250 miles away from Alamogordo, roughly the distance from Washington to Highhold, Stimson's Long Island estate. Its "screams" could be heard 50 miles away. The United States and, through the United States, Great Britain had mastered atomic energy and now possessed the most fearsome weapon in all of human history.[22]

Western leaders initially reacted with relief and elation. The more than $2 billion they had committed to the project had not, in the end, been wasted. Truman, Henry Stimson noted, was "immensely pepped up" by the news and infused with "an entirely new confidence." And well he should have been, for it seemed that Groves had just given him a large and unbeatable stack of chips for the next round of the poker game. Following the poker metaphor, Stimson told Truman that the United States had a "royal flush, and we mustn't be a fool about the way we play it." Churchill reached out to the atomic bomb almost as if it were a deus ex machina, a wonder weapon descended from the gods to solve all of Britain's strategic problems. He walked around Potsdam that day, one diplomat recorded, like a little boy who had hidden something precious under his coat. Churchill hoped that the bomb might compensate Britain for its debts and its massive global obligations. It might also rescue Britain from its decline from great-power status.[23]

Truman and Churchill met on July 24 at Potsdam with their military advisers, and Truman probably decided at that meeting to use the bomb as soon as practicable. It offered a way to get an unconditional surrender from the Japanese without an invasion of the home islands that might cost hundreds of thousands of American and Japanese lives. It also offered a way to end the air raids over Japanese cities that had already killed hundreds of thousands of Japanese civilians, most of them in firestorms caused by the incendiary bombs of the US Air Force. A sense of vengeance clearly played a role as well. Walter Brown overheard Churchill tell Truman that the United States should use the weapon without prior warning because the Japanese "did not give any warning when they bombed Pearl Harbor and killed and mangled your boys."[24]

Beyond its immediate military utility, however, the bomb presented as many problems as it did solutions. Byrnes recognized that the United States could not possibly hope to maintain an atomic monopoly; he quite presciently guessed that the Russians would have their own atomic bombs within five years. The Americans therefore had a responsibility to use the new weapon wisely. A week after getting the first of the Groves messages, the magnitude of it all seemed to have hit Truman. On July 25, he confided to his diary, "We have discovered the most terrible bomb in the history of the world. It may be the fire destruction prophesied in the Euphrates Valley Era, after Noah and his fabulous Ark. . . . It is certainly a good thing for the world that Hitler's crowd or Stalin's did not discover this atomic bomb. It seems to be the most terrible thing ever discovered, but it can be made the most useful."[25]

As most of the military men understood, the bomb did not come close to solving all the problems the Americans and British faced. Serious strategists did not share Churchill's faith in the atomic bomb as a master weapon that would give America and Britain newfound strategic power. After a meeting with Churchill on July 23, Field

Marshal Alan Brooke wrote that he felt "completely shattered by the P.M.'s outlook" that the atomic bomb gave the West new leverage over Russia. Churchill had announced at the meeting that "we now had something in our hands that could redress the balance with the Russians" and "completely alter the diplomatic equilibrium to Britain's favor." Churchill raved: 'Now we can say if you insist on doing this or that we can just blot out Moscow, then Stalingrad, then Kiev, then Kuibyshev, Kharkov, Sebastopol, etc. etc. And now where are the Russians!!!' I tried to curb his over optimism. . . . I was trying to dispel his dreams and, as usual, he did not like it. But I *shudder* to feel that he is allowing the half-baked results of one experiment to warp the whole of his diplomatic perspective."

Brooke knew from the moment he heard of the Manhattan Project that it would change the nature of military strategy forever. A state simply could not use atomic weapons in the manner it used conventional weapons. Once the Russians inevitably built their own nuclear weapons, moreover, they could respond in kind. He saw more quickly than most that after the war with Japan, atomic weapons could only serve as weapons of deterrence. They would not solve any of Britain's long-term strategic problems.[26]

Henry Stimson saw the same problem that Brooke saw. If the Allies used the bomb as Churchill briefly envisioned, they would be committing mass murder on an unprecedented scale. Stimson told Truman that he did not want to see the United States "outdoing Hitler in atrocities," although he did support using the weapon to end the war with Japan. Clement Attlee largely agreed. Although not enthusiastic about the bomb, Attlee understood that with Japanese forces deployed all across Asia, the Allies had to find a military approach that would compel the government in Tokyo to order them all to surrender. Only the atomic bomb held out that possibility. Otherwise, he said, "we might have to winkle them out over half [of] Asia," a prospect that no one found appealing.[27]

Others brought in on the secret at Potsdam immediately grasped the gravity of the new weapon; some recoiled at the thought of its use. Lord Moran, Churchill's private physician, wrote in his diary that he was "deeply shocked" by the news and opposed the Allies using it: "It was all to no purpose. There had been no moment in the whole war when things looked to me so black and desperate, and the future so hopeless. I knew enough of science to grasp that this was only the beginning, like the little bomb which fell outside my hut in the woods near Poperinghe [Belgium] in 1915."

Admiral Leahy, who had doubted the bomb's utility all along, agreed, and worried that once the United States used atomic weapons, it would adopt "an ethical standard common to the barbarians of the Dark Ages." General Ismay, too, expressed his apprehension, writing that he "had always had a sneaking hope that the scientists would be unable to find a key to this particular chamber of horrors." Notwithstanding the end of the war that the world would soon celebrate, that same world had become an infinitely more terrifying place in just thirty years. With the threat of nuclear weapons, even the very concept of peace seemed to be in jeopardy.[28]

These reservations notwithstanding, the bomb did offer a tantalizing, almost irresistible opportunity to end the war with Japan, and before the Russians could demand part of the occupation of the home islands. As Byrnes told Forrestal, it might also end the war before the Russians reached the port of Dairen and dug in their heels in Manchuria. "Once in there," Byrnes noted, "it would not be easy to get them out." But, as Brooke and US Army Chief of Staff General George Marshall both understood, the bomb could play no role in getting them out. It might, however, be possible to keep them from going there in the first place. Still, Truman did not see the bomb as an anti-Soviet measure at this point. As Averill Harriman later recalled, "that wasn't the president's mood at all. The mood was to treat Stalin as an ally—a difficult ally admittedly—in the hope that he would behave like one."[29]

Truman knew he had no choice but to tell Stalin about the bomb before its use. Anthony Eden agreed, even if it meant sharing some of the weapon's technical secrets with the Soviets. Henry Stimson actively supported sharing some of the bomb's secrets, but only in exchange for Soviet cooperation on other matters. Either way, telling the Russians came with some risks. Both Truman and Churchill worried that if Stalin grasped the meaning of the bomb, he might order his forces to push faster and further into Manchuria in order to control as much Chinese territory as he could before Japan surrendered. They also worried about how they would respond if the Japanese chose to surrender to the Soviet Union rather than to the United States and Great Britain.[30]

Once again, Truman need not have bothered worrying. Stalin had known about the Manhattan Project since March 1942, thanks to the reports of his secret police chief, Lavrenti Beria. Russian spies working on the project had kept Beria well informed; Beria may well have known more about the bomb than Truman and Byrnes did. By the time of Potsdam, Beria and Stalin had already discussed how best to respond if Truman mentioned the bomb. They decided to feign ignorance on the matter in order to guard the secret of Soviet espionage. Both Beria and Stalin knew enough to wonder why Truman had not mentioned the atomic bomb in their first meeting together over lunch at Truman's house in Babelsberg on July 17.[31]

Truman finally decided to tell Stalin about this momentous and historic news in as casual a manner as possible. At the end of the evening session on July 24, he approached Stalin as the latter prepared to leave the conference room. Churchill watched from a distance while Stalin's interpreter rushed to his boss's side to translate. "The USA," Truman said, "has tested a new bomb of extraordinary destructive power." By a prior agreement with Churchill, Truman had avoided using the word "atomic." Stalin's interpreter looked carefully at the Russian leader: the moment had come at last. "No muscle moved in his face," the interpreter recalled. Stalin then calmly responded, "A new bomb! Of extraordinary power! Probably decisive on the Japanese! What a bit of luck." The interpreter watched Stalin glance at Churchill long enough to see that Churchill was smiling, then turn and walk away.[32]

Stalin's ruse worked. Truman later said, "I am sure that he did not understand its significance." Churchill had the same response, remarking with almost identical language, "I was sure that he had no idea of the significance of what he was being told." Leahy, who also watched carefully for Stalin's reaction, thought the Russian dictator "did not seem to have any conception of what Truman was talking about. It was simply another weapon." They could not have been more wrong. That night Stalin ordered the Soviet atomic energy department to increase the speed of its work. The Red Army also increased its efforts to move forces to the Manchurian border. They would continue to conduct operations there for two weeks after the bombing of Hiroshima on August 6.[33]

Part of Stalin's reaction may have had to do with the timing of Truman's announcement. Although there is no evidence that he intended to do so or had directly connected the two events in his own mind, Truman told Stalin about the bomb shortly after a particularly intense session about Poland. Two Soviet advisers thought that Stalin saw no coincidence in the timing. Instead, Stalin told one of them, the timing showed "a rather unfriendly attitude towards us and towards our security interests." One of the advisers went as far as to call the announcement, which Truman intended to be as low-key as possible, "atomic blackmail" to get the Russians to change their position on Poland. "They're raising their price," Molotov remarked. Joseph Davies had predicted such a reaction from the Russians, warning that they would "naturally see it as deliberately throwing them out on the junk heap after they had been 'used' to defeat Hitler."[34]

The atomic bomb thus made the issue of ending the war with Japan even more complicated. Both in private and in public, officials wondered when the Big Three would release a statement on Japan and what it might contain. Intensive debate had already begun about that statement, and dozens of proposals and drafts had already circulated among senior leaders in Great Britain and America. Press reports had misrepresented some of those discussions; one report indicated that the Big Three might promise not to invade the Japanese home islands, and another made a premature announcement about American intentions to leave the emperor on his throne.

On July 19, the State Department in Washington told Byrnes in a secret cable that the time had come to "quiet these rumors" coming from the American press and make an announcement of Allied intentions. Truman wanted the Soviet Union informed about any statement the Americans and the British issued, but he knew that the Soviets could not sign it because they were not yet at war with Japan. He also wanted Chiang Kai-shek to approve the document, but getting it to Chiang's field headquarters in a remote outpost near Chongking, then having it decoded and translated, proved quite a challenge. In the end, Chiang did approve it, although the effort to involve him delayed the announcement by almost a week.[35]

The Potsdam Declaration regarding Japan was issued on July 26, in time for Churchill to play a leading role in it before his departure for England to follow the election results. Few people at Potsdam could then have imagined that it would be one of his last wartime contributions. The final text offered Japan "an opportunity to end this war" before the "prodigious land, sea and air forces of the United States, the British Empire and of China, many times reinforced by their armies and air fleets from the west, are poised to strike the final blows upon Japan . . . until she ceases to resist." It also advised the Japanese of what befell the Germans when they fought to the end, and warned that "the might that now converges on Japan is immeasurably greater than that which, when applied to the resisting Nazis, necessarily laid waste to the lands, the industry and the method of life of the whole German people."

But for all its harshness, the declaration followed the advice of the moderates. It did not mention the emperor, either by name or by reference to the institution he represented. It pledged that Japan would retain sovereignty over the home islands of Honshu, Hokkaido, Kyushu, and Shikoku. It further promised the Japanese people "the opportunity to lead peaceful and productive lives" and explicitly stated, "We do not intend that the Japanese shall be enslaved as a race or destroyed as a nation," although Japanese militarists and war criminals would surely face prosecution. Thus the Potsdam Declaration, while threatening the "prompt and utter destruction" of Japan if it did not surrender, offered something to the Japanese if they did surrender. It even indirectly left open the possibility of the emperor staying on the throne. The declaration was a political document, aimed at domestic audiences demanding harsh terms, but at the same time giving the Japanese a reason to surrender rather than fight on.[36]

The Japanese, not knowing about the atomic bombs and seeing the declaration as a political ultimatum, rejected it. The prime minister, whose diplomats had still been talking to their Soviet counterparts in the hopes of using them to get better terms, said, "There is no recourse but to ignore [the declaration] entirely." The Allies expected nothing less, but they could now argue that they had given the Japanese a way out. Having refused it, the Japanese would have to face the full power of Dr. Groves's two babies. Truman then authorized the bomb's use, but not until he had departed Potsdam and his ship had sailed for the United States. Truman wanted to be literally at sea, and thus unavailable to the Russians, when the bomb did its work and a new era in human history opened.[37]

The atomic bomb was the only item of debate at Potsdam that the delegates at the Paris Peace Conference in 1919 would have found unfamiliar. On the last day at Potsdam, the Big Three continued to make decisions that the delegates in Paris would have understood. Almost as an afterthought, they decided that they would divide the French colony of Indochina at the 16th parallel for the purpose of facilitating the Japanese surrender. China would accept the surrender north of that line, and Britain would accept it to the south. Then, if the Americans got their way, Indochina would not return to French control, but would instead enter an international trusteeship. A world away in an office in the Pentagon, a colonel named Dean Rusk made a similar decision for Korea. He chose the 38th parallel as a temporary dividing line in advance of the formation of an international trusteeship for a unified Korea. The Soviet Union had already agreed to that trusteeship at Yalta and confirmed its commitment to Harry Hopkins in Moscow in June. Just as the Big Three had done in Paris, at Potsdam another Big Three made seemingly insignificant decisions in the shadow of seemingly much more important decisions that would affect the lives of millions for decades to come.[38]

Conclusion

I N 1919, THE ITALIAN FOREIGN MINISTER, Sidney Sonnino, expressed his anger with Woodrow Wilson, shouting, "Is it possible to change the world from a room, through the actions of some diplomats? Go to the Balkans and try an experiment with the Fourteen Points." Like most of his fellow European diplomats, Sonnino was exasperated with American ideals and frustrated by the lack of real power the Americans put behind those principles. He and many other Europeans were equally angry with Herbert Hoover, who was then in charge of food relief for Europe, for the contrast between America's beliefs and its actions. Hoover had saved unknown thousands (maybe millions) of Europeans from starvation, but in 1919 he warned Europe that there were limits to what America could and would do. Despite its wealth and protestations of generosity, America, Hoover told Europe, would soon go back to its own shores and leave Europe to an uncertain fate. Europeans found reasons to criticize America both for the failure to back up its ideals and its unwillingness to pay the price required of the great power it now thought it had become.[1]

The end of World War II threatened a repetition of that same gap between ideals and action. Even before the Americans entered the war, Franklin Roosevelt had issued the Atlantic Charter, a Wilsonian statement of principles agreed to with Winston Churchill. Throughout the war years, the United States had combined idealistic rhetoric with promises of support for the reconstruction of Europe. At the end of the war, however, Harry Truman echoed Hoover when he said at Potsdam that the US government would not foot the bill to feed Italy through the winter of 1945–1946. He and James Byrnes had also declared that the only aid forthcoming would be Lend-Lease assistance specifically linked to the military defeat of Japan. Truman then said that "the United States was rich, but it could not forever pour out its resources for the help of others." When Byrnes heard an adviser tell Truman upon his arrival in Europe that it was time for "Uncle Sam to quit playing Santa Claus to the world," Byrnes observed that "this was the kind of talk the President wanted to hear."[2]

But if Truman's generation seemed to find itself stuck once again between the ideals of Wilson and the unwillingness to support those ideals with actions, by 1945 the picture had changed quite dramatically. Between the signing of the Atlantic Charter in August 1941 and the opening of the Potsdam Conference four short years later, the United States had come a long way. Although Truman acknowledged the limits that existed on American resources, the country he led stood in a far stronger position to turn its principles into reality than it had in 1919. New instruments of power now backed American talk in the form of the Bretton Woods economic agreements, the United Nations, and, not least, the atomic bomb. Truman the poker player had far more cards to play in his hand in 1945 than Woodrow Wilson could ever have imagined.

Potsdam symbolized how far the United States had come in thirty years in its understanding of itself and its role in the world. Neither isolation nor Wilsonian idealism had served the nation well in the interwar years. This time, the Americans also intended to demobilize their armed forces as quickly as possible, but in the years to follow 1945 they planned to control or influence events overseas through other instruments of national power. Soon, they would add more cards to their hand, including the North Atlantic Treaty Organization (NATO) military alliance, the strings that came with Marshall Plan aid, and the lure of trade with an economic superpower. The (often self-serving) ideals remained, but now American leaders had both hard and soft power behind them.[3]

The American leaders of 1945 hoped to use that power to reshape Europe, largely in their own image. A democratic Europe with markets open to global trade, they presumed, would provide the necessary foundation for a future of stability and peace. Although they knew that their goals did not always line up with those of the Soviet Union (or, for that matter, those of Great Britain and France), US officials did not leave Potsdam thinking that a future of conflict with the Russians was either inevitable or even likely. Truman later said that at Potsdam he had been an "innocent idealist" in his dealings with Stalin, but he had gotten what he had wanted at the conference, and he left Germany feeling both confident and pleased. Although he knew that the Russians would make more demands, and that those demands might well interfere with American interests, Potsdam confirmed in his mind, at least for the time being, that a future of cooperation remained possible. As he told his press secretary, "Stalin and I were able to get along all right. We had no disagreement whatever except over the treatment of our [diplomatic representatives] in Bulgaria and Rumania." In a letter to his wife, Bess, on July 29, Truman wrote, "I like Stalin. He is straightforward, knows what he wants, and will compromise when he can't get it." Truman then notably added, "His foreign minister isn't so forthright." Like the other leaders at Potsdam, Truman did not yet see the West and the Soviet Union on a collision course to an inevitable future of conflict.[4]

Although some insiders, such as Clement Attlee and George Kennan, predicted a future of increased East-West conflict, more people came out of Potsdam optimistic than pessimistic. Truman thought that the years after 1945 would feature widely expanded American trade with the Russians and the redevelopment of Germany as a single economic and political unit. James Byrnes believed that dividing Germany for the purposes of reparations ensured a future of cooperation, not conflict, with the Soviet Union by removing reparations as a potential area of friction. He left Potsdam optimistic about the future of US-Soviet relations, even though he knew that several areas of disagreement remained. At that time, Byrnes saw bigger problems in American relations with Britain, whose leaders he thought were more interested in the recovery of their empire than in doing the difficult and expensive work necessary to ensure the reconstruction of continental Europe. He also guessed that France, Italy, and maybe even Great Britain would become difficult allies, because their strategic goals and those of the United States did not always overlap. America's closest and most reliable partner for peace in Europe, he presciently predicted, might turn out to be Germany, if America's two-time enemy could somehow develop a democratic government and a functional economy.[5]

Byrnes's observation underscores the fundamental importance of the Potsdam Conference: it did solve the central problems of the 1914–1945 period as the leaders of 1945 understood them. Those issues, notably Franco-German relations, the ethnic makeup of Eastern Europe, the borders of Poland, and the role of Germany in a new Europe, did not drive the problems that came after 1945. The dynamic of the Cold War—with its bipolarity, the role of superpower-based alliance systems, and the concomitant decolonization of Africa and Asia—still carried legacies of the 1914–1945 period, of course, but they sprang from an essentially different dynamic. Europe—what Churchill called at Potsdam "the volcano from which war springs"— has not yet seen a World War III. The volcano has thus far remained dormant. The agreements at Potsdam do not deserve all of the credit for that happy circumstance, but those same agreements show that the leaders of 1945 thought in terms of solving the problems of the past thirty years, not in terms of dealing with a new rivalry among the victors.[6]

Contemporaries saw Potsdam in much the same way. We must be careful with the recollections of the key participants years after the event who retroactively saw Potsdam as the start of the Cold War. By the time they wrote their memoirs, they knew about events like the Berlin airlift, Kennan's so-called Long Telegram, the Chinese Civil War, the Korean War, and other major events of what became the Cold War. In 1945, by contrast, most observers saw the conference as a success, specifically because the problems of the past thirty years seemed to be on the road to a solution, even if that same solution carried with it some flaws. Truman saw that the future relationship with the Soviet Union would present problems, but he had, he thought, avoided the far greater problems of Versailles. Most importantly, the United States would escape the damaging reparations cycle of the 1920s thanks to the division of Germany, and the borders of Europe at long last had a consistency to them that should, Truman thought, promote peace.[7]

Most unofficial observers agreed that despite flaws in the final Potsdam agreements, the Big Three had produced a far better result than their predecessors had in 1919. The criticisms that emerged from the media in 1945 centered not on the fear of a budding rivalry with the Soviet Union, but on the fear that France might not support agreements made without its diplomats' participation. Without French support, contemporaries on both sides of the Atlantic worried, no long-term agreement on Europe would hold.

Some media outlets, such as the British-based *Economist* and the American popular weekly *Time*, wanted the agreements to go further in upholding the ideals of the Atlantic Charter, but virtually all observers saw Potsdam as a massive improvement on the mess that came out of Versailles. They also recognized that Potsdam had achieved the two most important immediate objectives: the destruction of German power, and Russian agreement to help end Japanese military power. In August 1945, Russia remained an ally, and Stalin, in the words of Secretary of the Navy James Forrestal, showed himself to be "not difficult to do business with." The Big Three seemed well placed to carry out a joint program of denazifying, demilitarizing, and rebuilding Germany so that it would never again pose a threat to the peace of Europe.[8]

Germany remained a problem for some time, underscoring the need for the Big Three (and France) to stay on good terms. The military occupation remained in place until 1948; at the time of Potsdam, some observers spoke of an occupation government lasting decades or even a full generation. Columbia University psychologist Richard Brickner, an adviser to both the State and War departments, captured the prevailing mood with his popular 1943 book, *Is Germany Incurable?* In it, he argued that Germany had undergone centuries of paranoid behavior that had twisted and warped its views. It would take generations, he argued, to reeducate and normalize the country.

The revelations of the myriad horrors of the Nazi regime, and the fears of many occupation officials that Germans had not yet accepted their collective guilt, led to a sense that the great powers would need to work together either to rebuild Germany, or, depending on one's view, keep it down so that it never again posed a threat.[9]

Not calling Potsdam a peace conference suited everyone's interests. No peace conference meant no treaty for the new president to press through the Senate. Although Truman faced far less opposition than Wilson had, he did not relish the idea of tangling with his old colleagues in the Senate over details. Like his British and Soviet counterparts, he was content to pass the heavy diplomatic work of negotiating the details onto the Council of Foreign Ministers. The council finalized treaties with Italy, Finland, Romania, Hungary, and Bulgaria in a series of meetings held from September 11, 1945, to December 12, 1946. Although Byrnes was frustrated with the length of time it took professional diplomats to get the wording just right, the ability of the superpowers to work together sent a positive message, as did the symbolism of the four main meetings taking place in Moscow, London, New York, and, notably, Paris. The Paris meeting showed that France had begun to buy in to the general outlines of the new Europe.[10]

The Big Three had carefully avoided discussing some key issues at Potsdam, although none of these issues directly affected their core interests. They did not mention the Holocaust or the future of the Jews of Europe at all during their deliberations. Truman's briefing books contained 163 separate topical briefs; only one of those briefs mentioned Palestine, and none of them discussed the genocide of Europe's Jews. The State Department advised Truman to discuss Palestine "in general terms only" and to agree to nothing that the British or the Soviets might propose. Either the State Department was trying to buy time or it was trying not to entangle the United States in a difficult part of the world that still sat on the periphery of American interests.[11]

The British had a more vested interest in keeping the issue of Palestine off the table at Potsdam, as they did not want outside interference in their already unmanageable prewar dilemma between the

Scylla of Arab nationalism and the Charybdis of Jewish desires for a Palestinian homeland. Eden advised Churchill to keep the Zionist leader Chaim Weizmann as far away from Soviet officials as possible in order that he not convince the Russians to support Jewish emigration to the Middle East. "Such a development could only make it more difficult for us in deciding our policy," he warned Churchill, "a hard enough task as it is." Neither did he want Arab officials to get the ear of the Russians. Palestine, he argued, was Britain's problem alone. Any mention of Jewish suffering might invite outside attention to British interests in the region.[12]

By the time of Potsdam, moreover, the full extent of the Holocaust had not yet revealed itself. Nor did officials yet connect the mass suffering they saw exclusively to the plight of the Jews of Europe. Neither Martha Gellhorn's report nor Edward R. Murrow's broadcast from Dachau used the words "Jews" or "Jewish." The diaries, memoirs, and papers of many of the key actors at Potsdam make no mention of the concentration camps at all, and none of them separated the suffering of the Jews from that of any other group impacted by the war. Most officials showed far more sympathy for German refugees than they did for the survivors of the death camps. The Soviet Union's senior leaders, while showing some sympathy for the Jewish plight, especially resisted the notion that the Jews, or any other class of Soviet citizen, deserved particular recognition for their suffering.[13]

Anti-Semitism and abiding stereotypes about Jews also kept discussions about Jewish suffering off the table, and not just among the notoriously anti-Semitic Soviet inner circle. One American worker for the United Nations Relief and Rehabilitation Administration said that Jewish survivors were "demanding, arrogant, [and] have played upon their concentration camp experience to obtain ends." Several American leaders, notably Secretary of War Henry Stimson, had barely contained anti-Semitic views. George Patton, whose own anti-Semitism was well-known, called Jewish camp survivors "lower than animals," and a senior British official called the Jewish victims of Nazi camps "criminal looking." In most places, German prisoners of war had far better living conditions and received more food than did Jewish displaced persons, consistent with Patton's observation that the conquered Germans "were the only decent people left in Europe." Truman's envoy to Europe, Earl Harrison, told the president in a damning report compiled while the Big Three were meeting at Potsdam that, "as matters now stand, we appear to be treating the Jews as the Nazis treated them except that we do not exterminate them."[14]

To his credit, when Truman saw the Harrison report in late August, he ordered major changes. He told Eisenhower to correct the imbalance in resources by taking supplies away from the German prisoner-of-war camps and sending them to displaced-persons camps. He also took the crucial step of ordering that Jews be identified and registered as Jews, not by their prewar nationality. That step recognized the cold reality that some states did not want their Jews to return and that Jewish refugees had no state of their own. At Harrison's urging, and against British wishes, Truman advocated the immediate relocation of 100,000 Jews to Palestine. Harrison told Truman that the Jews of Europe "definitely and preeminently" sought Palestine as their future home, reinforcing Truman's own growing sympathy for Zionism.[15]

Still, none of these discussions happened at Potsdam itself. Although the Harrison report undoubtedly influenced Truman's support for the creation of the state of Israel, it came about a month too late to have played any role at Potsdam. The Big Three never discussed the Holocaust or Jewish refugees or Palestine. With other subjects pressing for their attention, perhaps their unwillingness to raise the issue of Palestine and the Jews is not surprising, but they clearly missed an opportunity to exchange views on an issue of critical importance to Europe and beyond.

Palestine and the Jews seemed a peripheral issue to the central problems of Potsdam, most importantly the maintenance of good relations among the Big Three. Almost before the statesmen returned to their capitals, however, the Grand Alliance, always tenuous, had begun to erode. To be sure, suspicions from the war itself and disagreements over Poland threatened future Western-Soviet cooperation. But the Americans and the British had been willing to sacrifice

Poland in the interests of that cooperation, however distasteful it appeared to most of them, and the abiding wartime issues were solvable. Moreover, the United States and the Soviet Union still had strategic interests in common, including the final destruction of Japanese military power, the stabilization of China, and the dismantling of the European empires.

As the fate of Poland showed, Eastern Europe paid the price of the Potsdam agreement. As the Western statesmen at Potsdam knew, they could do nothing to stop the Soviets from dominating the region short of starting another war. They recognized the tragedy and their own weakness on that issue, but they also knew that their victory over Germany had been a coalition victory. The Russians, as one of three senior members of that coalition, expected to receive security in exchange for their suffering. As Byrnes recalled, Potsdam had left a lot to be desired on Eastern Europe, but it had, he believed, "established a basis for maintaining our war-born unity" with the Soviet Union and "provide[d] a basis for the early restoration of stability to Europe." And that, more than anything else, had been the goal all along.[16]

EVEN BEFORE TRUMAN returned to the United States, the winds had begun to shift. Everyone in on the secret at Potsdam knew that the atomic bomb would forever change the West's relationship with Russia. Joseph Davies, still one of America's most important Soviet specialists, sent a memo to Truman in September on the deterioration in American relations with the Soviets since Potsdam. He noted that the American use of the atomic bomb against Japan had had a deleterious effect on the Soviet mindset. Molotov had told Davies, "I have only persuasion to rely upon; but Secretary Byrnes has a little atomic bomb." Davies thought that the atomic bomb, not policy disagreements, sat at the root of the deterioration in great-power harmony in the months after Potsdam. American possession of the bomb had aggravated Soviet "suspicion and fear" about what its increasingly erstwhile allies in the West would do to them now that the war had ended. "They have been burned too often," Davies told Truman, "and they won't take a chance" in the future. Stalin called the Hiroshima and Nagasaki bombings "superbarbarity," and was convinced that although the Americans had dropped the bombs on Japan, their true target was Russia. The Japanese, he felt, had been ready to surrender without Hiroshima. Using the weapon proved to him that the West intended to take away the physical security for which the Soviets had just lost more than 20 million people. A third world war, Stalin now believed, had become inevitable. "Hiroshima has shaken the whole world. The balance has been destroyed," Stalin warned. "That cannot be."[17]

Truman still saw the bomb primarily as a way to end the war with Japan as quickly as possible, but the Americans also knew that it would change the power dynamic between the United States and the Soviet Union. After a brief stop on the south coast of England to meet King George VI, Truman had returned to the United States aboard the USS *Augusta*. As the ship moved out into the high seas, Walter Brown watched Byrnes and Truman "hit the bourbon bottle rather heavy" as they celebrated their success at Potsdam. They may also have been contemplating the change that they knew was coming. Three days later, with the *Augusta* still 700 nautical miles east of the Virginia coast, a naval officer interrupted Truman's lunch to give him the first report of the atomic bomb's success over Hiroshima.[18]

As most serious strategists who heard the news instantly recognized, a new era in the history of the world had opened. Although the end of World War II did not close the book on the problems unleashed by the events of 1914, it did surely begin a new chapter in European, and world, history. Potsdam was the final paragraph of the chapter that began on a street corner in Sarajevo in that fateful year. In the next chapter of that ongoing story, Berlin, Poland, and Yugoslavia appeared less as actors in their own right than as pawns in a new game of superpower rivalry. If the men who met at Potsdam in the summer of 1945 could not predict the future, they at least knew the past they were desperately trying not to repeat.

ACKNOWLEDGMENTS

I started thinking about this project on a cold, blustery day in Potsdam. I had spent the day wandering the palaces and shops of this charming town while waiting for Christian Stachelbeck, who had kindly agreed to give me a tour of the MGFA, the German Army's library and archive. While I was waiting I thought I might pick up a book or two on Potsdam, and so I wandered into a few bookshops. To my surprise, I saw nothing in the shops about the conference held there in 1945. That struck me as unusual. At the MGFA I did some more digging but still found almost nothing.

That night over a wonderful dinner in Potsdam I mentioned to Christian and historian Annika Mombauer that I was surprised at the absence of any serious research on the Potsdam Conference. Our conversation about why that might be piqued my curiosity. Once back home, I made two discoveries: that the existing books on Potsdam simply recounted the conversations between the Big Three, and that the Army Heritage and Education Center (AHEC) had a mountain of material to support a much more serious book. My first thanks therefore go to Christian and Annika as well as the phenomenal staff of AHEC, most notably Richard Sommers and Louise Arnold-Friend, who helped me find sources. Thanks also to Steve Bye, Gary Johnson, Matt Dawson, and everyone at AHEC. That place is a treasure.

Thanks next go to my agent, Geri Thoma of Writer's House, and to Lara Heimert of Basic Books, who saw the value of this book and encouraged me at every step. Thank you also to Roger Labrie, who did a marvelous job with the line editing. I am fortunate to have wonderful friends who heard out my ideas and helped me shape this book. They include Tami Davis Biddle, Craig Nation, Bill Allison, Bill Astore, Paul Kan, Frank Jones, Partha Mazumdar, and Rob Citino. Each of these good friends made this book better; Rob, Craig, and the two Bills were kind enough to take the time to read parts of the manuscript. Thanks also to Lance Betros and Richard Lacquement, the provost and dean of the US Army War College, respectively, for their support. Jim McDougall, Major General Anthony Cucolo, and my fellow AHEC researcher Ginger Cucolo also deserve my sincere thanks for all their support.

This book would have been far less rich without the help of the University of Birmingham's Michael Snape, who helped me gain access to Anthony Eden's papers. Indeed, the entire Cadbury Research Library at Birmingham deserves thanks for taking pity on a researcher who arrived with little time and a lot to see. The Harry S. Truman Presidential Library provided me with a grant to do research there and gave me a fascinating glimpse into the life of Mr. Truman.

I have also to thank the staffs of the following libraries and archives for their help: National Archives II in College Park, Maryland; the Library of Congress Manuscript Division; the National Archives, the Imperial War Museum, and the Liddell Hart Centre for Military Archives in the London area; the Franklin D. Roosevelt Presidential Library in Hyde Park, New York; the New York Public Library; Dickinson College's Waidner-Spahr Library; the US Army War College Library; and the Special Collections Department of Clemson University's Library. The ideas in this book, however, are mine, and I take full responsibility for them and for any errors contained herein. The views herein, moreover, do not represent the views of the US Army War College, the US Army, or the Department of Defense.

Above all, thanks go to my family: my parents, Phyllis and Larry Neiberg, first of all; my wife, Barbara, and my daughters, Claire and Maya, who have had to put up with hearing about how everything relates sooner or later back to World War I (and for that I am sorry, especially when school assignments are due); and my in-laws, starting with Michele, Brian, Justin, and Sydney Lockley, for all of the support they have given me over the years. I would like to dedicate this book to Susan and John Lockley, the best mother-in-law and father-in-law anyone could have ever hoped to have. Thank you.

NOTES

ABBREVIATIONS

CLEM. Clemson University Special Collections, Clemson, South Carolina

CRL. Cadbury Research Library, University of Birmingham, United Kingdom

FDR. Franklin Roosevelt Presidential Library, Hyde Park, New York

FRUS. Foreign Relations of the United States Series

HSTL. Harry S. Truman Library, Independence, Missouri

IWM. Imperial War Museum, London

LHCMA. Liddell Hart Centre for Military Archives, King's College, London

LOC. Library of Congress Manuscript Division, Washington, DC

NARA. National Archives and Records Administration II, College Park, Maryland

NYPL. New York Public Library, New York City

SMOF. Staff Member Office Files

USAHEC. United States Army Heritage and Education Center, Carlisle, Pennsylvania

INTRODUCTION

1. David McCullough, *Truman* (New York: Simon and Schuster, 1992), 143–144; Aida D. Donald, *Citizen-Soldier: A Life of Harry Truman* (New York: Basic Books, 2012), 67.

2. James W. Muller, "The Aftermath of the Great War," in James W. Muller, ed., *Churchill as Peacemaker* (Cambridge, UK: Cambridge University Press, 2002),

178; Martin Gilbert, *Winston S. Churchill*, vol. 4, *The Stricken World, 1916–1922* (Boston: Houghton Mifflin, 1975), 427; Alan Wood, *The Origins of the Russian Revolution* (London: Routledge, 2003), 49.

3. Charles Mee, *Meeting at Potsdam* (New York: M. Evans, 1975), 7; Robert Betzell, *Teheran, Yalta, Potsdam: The Secret Protocols* (Hattiesburg, MS: Academic International, 1970), 141.

4. The Big Three at Versailles were American President Woodrow Wilson, French Prime Minister Georges Clemenceau, and British Prime Minister David Lloyd George. Italian Prime Minister Vittorio Orlando thought of himself as part of a Big Four, but clearly he played a secondary role in the conference, in part because he did not speak French or English very well but disliked relying on interpreters out of a fear of appearing weak. In April 1919 he stormed out of the conference, but he returned in June; his terrible showing at the conference contributed significantly to his resignation at the end of the month.

5. Charles à Court Repington, *The First World War, 1914–1918* (Boston: Houghton Mifflin, 1920); Private Alexander Clay, 33rd (US) Infantry Division, 131st Regiment, Veterans Survey, USAHEC.

6. Jacqueline Lévi-Valensi, *Camus at Combat: Writing, 1944–1947* (Princeton, NJ: Princeton University Press, 2006), 111; William Leahy, diary entry for August 14, 1945, William Leahy Papers, Diary Box 6, Reel 4, p. 144, LOC. In Repington's more global conception, the era also included the 1911 revolution in China and the humiliating Russian defeat at the hands of the Japanese in 1904–1905, both of which radically altered the strategic picture in Asia as well as in Europe. Repington, *First World War*.

7. Mee, *Meeting at Potsdam*, 97.

8. Bela Grünewald Ivanyi and Alan Bell, *Route to Potsdam: The Story of the Peace Aims, 1939–1945* (London: Allan Wingate, 1946), 45.

9. "Suggestions for a Peace Settlement," Lord Avon (Anthony Eden) Papers, FO 954, Pal/45/2, folio 103, CRL.

10. "Some Considerations on the Guidance to Be Obtained from the Procedure of the Peace-Making of 1918–20," Lord Avon (Anthony Eden) Papers, FO 954, Pea/43/1, folio 2, CRL.

11. James Byrnes, *Speaking Frankly* (New York: Harper and Brothers, 1947), 234.

12. Harry Hopkins to President Truman, May 30, 1945, Map Room Messages of President Truman, *2H-726, Reel 2, NYPL. Stalin made the observation

about the Senate possibly rejecting agreements made at Potsdam to American diplomat and senior United Nations official Alger Hiss. Within a few weeks of the end of the war, rumors began to spread that Hiss was working as a Soviet spy. Robert Messner, *The End of an Alliance: James F. Byrnes, Roosevelt, Truman, and the Engines of the Cold War* (Chapel Hill: University of North Carolina Press, 1982), 45.

13. McCullough, *Truman*, 415–416.

14. William Leahy, diary entry for April 12, 1945, William Leahy Papers, Diary Box 6, Reel 4, p. 55, LOC.

15. Mee, *Meeting at Potsdam*, 48.

16. I would like to acknowledge the intellectual debt this book owes to two studies: Graham Allison and Philip Zelikow, *Essence of Decision: Explaining the Cuban Missile Crisis*, 2nd ed. (New York: Longman, 1999), and Yuen Foong Khong, *Analogies at War: Korea, Munich, Dien Bien Phu and the Vietnam Decisions of 1965* (Princeton, NJ: Princeton University Press, 1992).

17. Simon Sebag Montefiore, *Stalin: The Court of the Red Czar* (New York: Vintage, 2003), 5, 30.

18. Winston Churchill, *Triumph and Tragedy* (Boston: Houghton Mifflin, 1953), 497.

CHAPTER ONE
"Jesus Christ and General Jackson"

1. Antony Beevor, *The Fall of Berlin, 1945* (New York: Penguin, 2003).

2. Rick Atkinson, *The Guns at Last Light: The War in Western Europe, 1944–1945* (New York: Henry Holt, 2013), 608.

3. Jean Edward Smith, *FDR* (New York: Random House, 2008), 622–626. For more on Roosevelt's health problems, see Smith, 600ff.

4. Ibid., 629.

5. Lord Moran, *Churchill: Taken from the Diaries of Lord Moran: The Struggle for Survival, 1940–1965* (Boston: Houghton Mifflin, 1966), 242; S. M. Plokhy, *Yalta: The Price of Peace* (New York: Penguin, 2010), 3, 76.

6. Charles Bohlen, *Eyewitness to History, 1929–1969* (New York: Norton, 1973), 205–206.

7. George McKee Elsey, *An Unplanned Life* (Columbia: University of Missouri Press, 2005), 77; James Byrnes, *Speaking Frankly* (New York: Harper and Brothers, 1947), 48.

8. William Leahy, diary entry for April 12, 1945, William Leahy Papers, Diary Box 6, Reel 4, p. 55, LOC.

9. Robert Messner, *The End of an Alliance: James F. Byrnes, Roosevelt, Truman, and the Origins of the Cold War* (Chapel Hill: University of North Carolina Press, 1982), 19, 32.

10. J. Robert Moskin, *Mr. Truman's War: The Final Victories of World War II and the Birth of the Postwar World* (Lawrence: University Press of Kansas, 2002), 25; David McCullough, *Truman* (New York: Simon and Schuster, 1992), 245.

11. Allen Drury, *A Senate Journal* (New York: McGraw-Hill, 1965), 219.

12. Ibid., 220.

13. Smith, *FDR*, 618; McCullough, *Truman*, 314.

14. Exhibit from Harry S. Truman Museum, Independence, Missouri. Emphasis in original.

15. McCullough, *Truman*, 291.

16. Drury, *Senate Journal*, 410.

17. Moskin, *Mr. Truman's War*, 10.

18. McCullough, *Truman*, 339.

19. Smith, *FDR*, 582–583.

20. Bohlen, *Eyewitness to History*, 210–211.

21. Robert Skidelsky, *John Maynard Keynes, 1883–1946: Economist, Philosopher, Statesman* (London: Penguin, 2003), 761. Keynes had been Britain's chief economist at the Paris Peace Conference. He published a stinging critique of the failures of the economic aspects of that conference in *The Economic Consequences of the Peace* (New York: Harcourt Brace, 1920), available at Project Gutenberg, www.gutenberg.org/ebooks/15776.

22. See George Kennan, *Russia Leaves the War* (Princeton, NJ: Princeton University Press, 1956); David S. Fogelsong, *America's Secret War Against Bolshevism* (Chapel Hill: University of North Carolina Press, 2001); and William T. Allison, *American Diplomats in Russia* (Westport, CT: Praeger, 1997).

23. For more on East Asia, see Chapter 11.

24. Karen Petrone, *The Great War in Russian Memory* (Bloomington: Indiana University Press, 2011), 5, 190.

25. See Erez Manela, *The Wilsonian Moment: Self-Determination and the International Origins of Anticolonial Nationalism* (New York: Oxford University Press, 2007), esp. Chapter 2.

26. Madhusree Mukerjee, *Churchill's Secret War: The British Empire and the Ravaging of India During World War II* (New York: Basic Books, 2010).

27. Milovan Djilas, *Conversations with Stalin* (New York: Harcourt Brace, 1963), 117.

28. McCullough, *Truman*, 340–342.

29. Simon Sebag Montefiore, *Stalin: The Court of the Red Czar* (New York: Vintage, 2003), 486; Eden to Lord Halifax, April 13, 1945, Lord Avon (Anthony Eden) Papers, FO 954, vol. 30, US/45/86, folio 731, CRL; Andrew Roberts, *Masters and Commanders: How Four Titans Won the War in the West* (New York: Harper Perennial, 2009), 567.

30. Elsey, *Unplanned Life*, 80; Byrnes, *Speaking Frankly*, 48–49; William Leahy, diary entry for April 12, 1945, William Leahy Papers, Diary Box 6, Reel 4, p. 55, LOC.

31. Drury, *Senate Journal*, 412, 419, 422.

32. Elsey, *Unplanned Life*, 78.

CHAPTER TWO

"The Most Terrible Responsibility Any Man Ever Faced"

1. Allen Drury, *A Senate Journal* (New York: McGraw-Hill, 1963), 413.

2. David McCullough, *Truman* (New York: Simon and Schuster, 1992), 375; Henry Lewis Stimson, *Stimson Diaries in the Yale University Library*, microform, Reel #9, entry for April 12, 1945, USAHEC; Charles Bohlen, *Witness to History, 1929–1969* (New York: Norton, 1973), 212.

3. For more information on this topic, see Richard Breitman and Allan Lichtman, *FDR and the Jews* (Cambridge, MA: Belknap Press of Harvard University Press, 2013).

4. Harry Butcher, *My Three Years with Eisenhower: The Personal Diary of Captain Harry C. Butcher, Naval Aide to General Eisenhower* (New York: Simon and Schuster, 1946), 816. The text of Murrow's full, emotional broadcast and Gellhorn's article can be found in *Reporting World War II, Part Two, American Journalism, 1944–1946* (New York: Library of America, 1995), 681–685, 730.

5. James Byrnes to James K. Vardaman, August 25, 1945, and "Dismemberment of Germany," July 11, 1945, Papers of George M. Elsey, Map Room Records, Elsey Papers Folder; Berlin Conference, July-August 1945, Folder 2, HSTL;

McCullough, *Truman*, 349–350; George McKee Elsey, *An Unplanned Life* (Columbia: University of Missouri Press, 2005), 81; James Byrnes, *Speaking Frankly* (New York: Harper and Brothers, 1947), 48; Nigel Hamilton, *American Caesars: Lives of the Presidents from Franklin D. Roosevelt to George W. Bush* (New Haven, CT: Yale University Press, 2010), 54; J. Robert Moskin, *Mr. Truman's War: The Final Victories of World War II and the Birth of the Postwar World* (Lawrence: University Press of Kansas, 2002), 159.

6. William Hillman, ed., *Mr. President: The First Publication from the Personal Diaries, Private Letters, Papers, and Revealing Interviews of Harry S. Truman* (New York: Farrar, Strauss, and Young, 1952), 10, 110–111; Robert Messner, *The End of an Alliance: James F. Byrnes, Roosevelt, Truman, and the Origins of the Cold War* (Chapel Hill: University of North Carolina Press, 1982), 53, 67.

7. There appears to be some disagreement among Truman and Churchill biographers. Some suggest that the two men had never met before Potsdam. It hardly matters. The key point is that the two men did not know one another.

8. Butcher, *My Three Years with Eisenhower*, 816. Following Pearl Harbor, Senator Truman had approached Marshall about reenlisting. Marshall responded by telling him that "we don't need old stiffs like you. This will be a young man's war." Hamilton, *American Caesars*, 53.

9. Truman to Churchill, April 14, 1945, Lord Avon (Anthony Eden) Papers, FO 954, vol. 30, US/45/89, folio 734, CRL.

10. Halifax to Eden, April 16, 1945, Lord Avon (Anthony Eden) Papers, FO 954, vol. 30, US/45/93, folio 738, CRL.

11. Walter J. Brown Papers, Journals, MSS 243, Box 8, Folder 10, CLEM.

12. Walter J. Brown, *James F. Byrnes of South Carolina: A Remembrance* (Macon, GA: Mercer University Press, 1992), 254.

13. Michael Dobbs, *Six Months in 1945: From World War to Cold War* (New York: Knopf, 2012), Kindle location 5918; Walter J. Brown Papers, Journals, MSS 243, Box 8, Folder 12, CLEM. Harriman may have believed that Byrnes (or someone close to him) had been spreading rumors of his affair with Churchill's daughter-in-law, Pamela. The two ended the affair in 1943, but later rekindled the romance and married in 1971. Pamela Harriman eventually served as US ambassador to France.

14. Halifax to Eden, April 16, 1945, Lord Avon (Anthony Eden) Papers, FO 954, vol. 30, US/45/93, folio 738, CRL; William Leahy, diary entry for June 30,

1945, William Leahy Papers, Diary Box 6, Reel 4, p. 102, LOC; Messner, *End of an Alliance*, 78. Truman and Byrnes would begin to fall out before the end of the year. In December, the two had a sharp meeting in the White House. Truman recalled having to say that he would "not tolerate a repetition" of Byrnes's perceived insubordination and grandstanding. The rift was soon out in the open, and Byrnes resigned in 1947, delaying his departure a few months so that George Marshall could replace him. McCullough, *Truman*, 479.

15. Walter J. Brown Papers, Journals, MSS 243, Box 8, Folder 10, CLEM.

16. Hillman, ed., *Mr. President*, 116; Moskin, *Mr. Truman's War*, 164. Hull was seventy-three years old in 1945, Davies was sixty-eight, and Hopkins was fifty-four, but Hopkins was dying of stomach cancer.

17. Messner, *End of an Alliance*, 77; Walter J. Brown Papers, Journals, MSS 243, Box 8, Folder 10, CLEM. Later in the year, at Truman's urging, Congress put the Speaker of the House and president pro tempore of the Senate as numbers one and two in the succession order so that a president could not effectively select his own successor.

18. Russia still celebrates Victory Day on May 9, whereas France, Britain, and the United States mark the day on May 8. That George Elsey mentioned the issue of the German surrender in his diary might also suggest that he was the one who found out about the State Department's intransigence and told Truman, but here I am speculating. Elsey, *Unplanned Life*, 83.

19. "Outline and Notes," entry for August 19, 1945, Wallace Deuel Papers, Box 61, Potsdam Conference Folder, Box 61, LOC.

20. Messner, *End of an Alliance*, 78. For more on the drift in their relationship, see McCullough, *Truman*, 478–480.

21. Truman did name Henry Wallace secretary of commerce, perhaps small compensation for missing out on the presidency by just three months. He named Stettinius the first American ambassador to the United Nations.

22. Messner, *End of an Alliance*, 6; for a reporter's view of the transition, see Drury, *Senate Journal*, 410–419.

23. Deuel Papers, August 19, 1945, LOC; Bohlen, *Witness to History*, 226.

24. Halifax to Eden, Lord Avon (Anthony Eden) Papers, FO 954, vol. 30, US/45/95 and US/45/100, folios 741 and 747, CRL.

25. Hillman, *Mr. President*, 117, 382.

26. Drury, *Senate Journal*, 424 and 439.

27. Madhusree Mukerjee, *Churchill's Secret War: The British Empire and the Ravaging of India During World War II* (New York: Basic Books, 2010), 246.

28. Frederick J. Dobney, ed., *Selected Papers of Will Clayton* (Baltimore: Johns Hopkins University Press, 1971), 136.

29. I am grateful to Professor Michael Snape of the University of Birmingham for a wonderful explanation of how Wilson's Presbyterian worldview made him reluctant to use economic instruments for political gains.

30. See Victoria de Grazia, *Irresistible Empire: America's Advance through 20th Century Europe* (Cambridge, MA: Harvard University Press, 2005).

31. Keith M. Heim, *Hope Without Power: Truman and the Russians, 1945*, PhD Thesis, University of North Carolina at Chapel Hill, 1973, D748.H45, 4.

32. Robert J. Donovan, *Conflict and Crisis: The Presidency of Harry S. Truman, 1945–1948* (New York: Norton, 1977), 40; Heim, *Hope Without Power,* 75n2 and 103.

33. Wilson D. Miscamble, *From Roosevelt to Truman: Potsdam, Hiroshima, and the Cold War* (Cambridge, UK: Cambridge University Press, 2007), 120; "Memorandum of Conversation, 23 April," in FRUS, vol. 5, *Europe* (Washington, DC: Government Printing Office, 1967), 256–257.

34. Heim, *Hope Without Power,* 103; Moskin, *Mr. Truman's War,* 84; Bohlen, *Witness to History,* 213; McCullough, *Truman,* 373.

35. FRUS, vol. 5, *Europe,* 257.

36. McCullough, *Truman,* 262; Oral History of Valentin Berezhekov, 12/8, vol. 2, 6–10, LHCMA.

37. Heim, *Hope Without Power,* 89–93.

38. Andrew Roberts, *Masters and Commanders: How Four Titans Won the War in the West, 1941–1945* (New York: Harper Perennial, 2008), 565; Churchill to Eden, May 13, 1945, and Churchill to Roosevelt, quoted in Correlli Barnett, *Lords of War: From Lincoln to Churchill, Supreme Command 1861–1945* (London: Pen and Sword, 2012), 239; SMOF: Naval Aide to the President Files, 1945–1953, Box 7, May 1945 Folder, HSTL.

39. Moskin, *Mr. Truman's War,* 53; Dwight Eisenhower, *Crusade in Europe* (Garden City, NY: Doubleday, 1948), 401.

40. Roberts, *Masters and Commanders,* 565.

41. Churchill to Truman, June 4, 1945, Lord Avon (Anthony Eden) Papers, FO 954, vol. 20, Pol/45/213, folio 787, CRL.

42. Eden to Halifax, May 11, 1945 (US/45/107, folio 756), and Eden to Halifax, May 13, 1945 (US/45/110, folio 759), Lord Avon (Anthony Eden) Papers, CRL.

43. Elsey, *Unplanned Life*, 84.

Chapter Three
May Days

1. Churchill to Truman, May 11, 1945, Papers of Harry Truman, SMOF: Naval Aide to the President Files, 1945–1953, Box 7, Churchill to Truman, May 1945 Folder, HSTL.

2. Dwight Eisenhower, *Crusade in Europe* (Garden City, NY: Doubleday, 1948), 474.

3. Herbert Feis, *Between War and Peace: The Potsdam Conference* (Princeton, NJ: Princeton University Press, 1960), 143; William Leahy, diary entry for June 13, 1945, William Leahy Papers, Diary Box 6, Reel 4, LOC.

4. Michael Dobbs, *Six Months in 1945: From World War to Cold War* (New York: Knopf, 2012), Kindle location 3395; Eden to Halifax, May 13, 1945, US/45/110, folio 759, CRL.

5. Feis, *Between War and Peace*, 143; Lionel Ismay, *The Memoirs of General Lord Ismay* (New York: Viking, 1960), 398.

6. Max Hastings, *Winston's War: Churchill, 1940–1945* (New York: Knopf, 2010), 473. The imagination reels at that statement, but one guesses that Churchill meant that the United States and Great Britain would always be close, but never completely united.

7. William Leahy, diary entry for June 4, 1945, William Leahy Papers, Diary Box 6, Reel 4, LOC.

8. Churchill to Truman, June 17, 1945, US/45/131, folio 785, CRL; Churchill to Truman, May 13, 1945, Papers of Harry Truman, SMOF: Naval Aide to the President Files, 1945–1953, Box 7, Churchill to Truman, May 1945 Folder, HSTL; Charles Ross to Judge Samuel Rosenman, July 20, 1945, Papers of Harry Truman, SMOF: Naval Aide to the President Files, 1945–1953, Box 5, Berlin Conference File, Communications to the Map Room, July 15–25, 1945, Folder 1 of 2, HSTL.

9. James Byrnes, *Speaking Frankly* (New York: Harper and Brothers, 1947), 59.

10. Sir Alexander Cadogan, Permanent Undersecretary for Foreign Affairs, in S. M. Plokhy, *Yalta: The Price of Victory* (New York: Penguin, 2010), 230; Robert Rhodes James, *Anthony Eden: A Biography* (New York: McGraw-Hill, 1987), 306.

11. Hastings, *Winston's War*, 469–471.

12. Joseph Davies, untitled memorandum, Joseph Davies Papers, Chronological File Part I, Box 17, July 1–5 Folder, LOC.

13. Churchill to Truman, May 31, 1945, Papers of Harry Truman, SMOF: Naval Aide to the President Files, 1945–1953, Box 7, Churchill to Truman, May 1945 Folder, HSTL.

14. Keith M. Heim, *Hope Without Power: Truman and the Russians, 1945*, PhD Thesis, University of North Carolina at Chapel Hill, 1973, D748.H45, 134–135, 146, 151.

15. Joseph Davies, diary entry for July 13, 1945, Joseph Davies Papers, Chronological File Part I, Box 17, LOC.

16. Eden to Churchill, July 10, 1945, Lord Avon (Anthony Eden) Papers, FO 954, vol. 2, Conf/45/152, folio 319–321, CRL.

17. James, *Anthony Eden*, 306.

18. Milovan Djilas, *Conversations with Stalin* (New York: Harcourt Brace, 1963), 73.

19. Heim, *Hope Without Power*, 2; Carlo D'Este, *Patton: Genius for War* (New York: Harper Collins, 1996), 735–736. On Stalin's admiration for Roosevelt, see Charles Bohlen, *Witness to History, 1929–1969* (New York: Norton, 1973), 209. Bohlen was Roosevelt and Truman's Russian interpreter and a key adviser on Russian affairs.

20. J. Robert Moskin, *Mr. Truman's War: The Final Victories of World War II and the Birth of the Postwar World* (Lawrence: University Press of Kansas, 2002), 65.

21. Joseph Davies, Memorandum of June 29, 1945, Joseph Davies Papers, Chronological File Part I, Box 17, 6, LOC.

22. Byrnes, *Speaking Frankly*, 57–58; Bohlen, *Witness to History*, 209; "Second Meeting Kremlin—8 pm, May 27, 1945," in Harry Hopkins Papers, Box 338, FDR.

23. Bohlen, *Witness to History*, 215.

24. Dobbs, *Six Months*, Kindle locations 954, 1944; Doris Kearns Goodwin, *No Ordinary Time: Franklin and Eleanor Roosevelt, the Home Front in World War II* (New York: Simon and Schuster, 1994), 255.

25. Simon Sebag Montefiore, *Stalin: The Court of the Red Czar* (New York: Vintage, 2003), 500; Djilas, *Conversations with Stalin*, 73.

26. Jean Edward Smith, *FDR* (New York: Random House, 2008), 588; Moskin, *Mr. Truman's War*, 203, 222; David McCullough, *Truman* (New York: Simon and Schuster, 1992), 418.

27. *Papers of General Lucius D. Clay: Germany, 1945–1949* (Bloomington: Indiana University Press, 1974), entry for July 9, 1945.

28. Dobbs, *Six Months*, Kindle location 5778; Mark Stoler, *George C. Marshall: Soldier-Statesman of the American Century* (Boston: Twain, 1989), 134–136.

29. Dobbs, *Six Months*, Kindle location 2522; Harriman, LHCMA, 27/80, 28. Ironically in light of that observation, Stalin gave Kathleen Harriman Mortimer two prize Russian horses for her estate as a gift upon her departure from Russia. Because Harriman's wife did not accompany him to Russia, Kathleen served as the effective First Lady of the embassy.

30. George Kennan, *Memoirs,* vol. 1, *1925–1950* (Boston: Atlantic–Little Brown, 1967), 257; Bohlen, *Witness to History*, 222.

31. Plokhy, *Yalta*, 382.

32. Heim, *Hope Without Power*, 115.

33. Ibid., 136n70.

34. Albert L. Weeks, *Assured Victory: How 'Stalin the Great' Won the War, but Lost the Peace* (Westport, CT: Praeger, 2011), 134; Montefiore, *Stalin*, 498; Wilson D. Miscamble, *From Roosevelt to Truman: Potsdam, Hiroshima, and the Cold War* (Cambridge, UK: Cambridge University Press, 2007), 121.

35. Ministry of Foreign Affairs of the USSR, *Correspondence Between the Chairman of the Council of Foreign Ministers of the USSR and the President of the USA and the Prime Ministers of Great Britain During the Great Patriotic War of 1941–1945,* vol. 1 (Moscow: Foreign Languages Publishing House, 1957), 344, 360–361.

36. Charles Bohlen, *Witness to History*, 217; "First Meeting, Kremlin 8 pm, May 26, 1945," in Harry Hopkins Papers, Box 338, 2–3, FDR.

37. A fuller version of Ebert's speech is in Wolfgang Schivelbusch, *The Culture of Defeat: On National Trauma, Mourning, and Recovery* (New York: Metropolitan Books, 2001), 203.

38. Plokhy, *Yalta*, 38, 53, 323.

39. Robert Gellately, *Stalin's Curse: Battling for Communism in War and Cold War* (Oxford: Oxford University Press, 2013), 76.

40. Papers of William L. Clayton, Chronological File 1945, June 1945–December 31, 1945, Box 1, Berlin Conference, July-August 1945, Folder 1, HSTL.

CHAPTER FOUR
"Our Troubles Might Not Yet Be Over"

1. Ben Steil, *The Battle of Bretton Woods: John Maynard Keynes, Harry Dexter White, and the Making of a New World Order* (Princeton, NJ: Princeton University Press, 2013), 2. The British emerged from the war with their debt at 240 percent of their gross domestic product (GDP); in 1939 it had been at 29 percent.

2. Christopher Bayly and Tim Harper, *Forgotten Wars: Freedom and Revolution in Southeast Asia* (Cambridge, MA: Belknap Press of Harvard University Press, 2007). Not for nothing did Anthony Eden, then prime minister, embroil Great Britain in the 1956 Suez crisis. He compared Gamal Adbel Nasser, who had been among those Egyptian officers with pro-German sympathies in World War II, to Benito Mussolini, and ordered British forces to join French and Israeli forces as part of a military operation to take the canal back after Nasser nationalized it. When President Eisenhower refused to extend American support, the British withdrew, leaving Eden and members of his government embarrassed and angry. See David A. Nichols, *Eisenhower 1956: The President's Year of Crisis—Suez and the Brink of War* (New York: Simon and Schuster, 2011).

3. S. N. Sen, *History of the Freedom Movement in India, 1857–1947* (New Delhi: New Age International Press, 1997), 323; Sugata Bose, *His Majesty's Opponent: Subhas Chandra Bose and India's Struggle Against Empire* (Cambridge, MA: Belknap Press of Harvard University Press, 2011); Madhusree Mukerjee, *Churchill's Secret War: The British Empire and the Ravaging of India During World War II* (New York: Basic Books, 2010), 247. I'd like to thank my friend Partha Mazumdar for his help over the years in explaining many of the nuances of South Asian history in addition to his extensive knowledge of macroeconomics.

4. Mukerjee, *Churchill's Secret War*, esp. Chapter 4.

5. Lionel Ismay, *The Memoirs of General Lord Ismay* (New York: Viking, 1960), 396–397; Roy Jenkins, *Churchill: A Biography* (New York: Farrar, Straus, and Giroux, 2001), 773; Eden to Churchill, July 12, 1945, Lord Avon (Anthony Eden) Papers, Conf/45/157, folio 328, CRL.

6. Joseph Davies to Truman, June 12, 1945, Papers of Harry Truman, SMOF: Naval Aide to the President Files, Box 4, vol. XI, Miscellaneous Papers, Reports by Joseph E. Davies, HSTL.

7. Steil, *Battle of Bretton Woods*, 110.

8. Robert Skidelsky, *John Maynard Keynes, 1883–1946: Economist, Philosopher, Statesman* (New York: Penguin, 2003), 756, 758, 765, 769; Michael Beschloss, *The Conquerors: Roosevelt, Truman, and the Destruction of Hitler's Germany, 1941–1945* (New York: Simon and Schuster, 2002), 121.

9. Krishan Kumar, "Empire, Nation, and National Identities," in Andrew Thompson, ed., *Britain's Experience of Empire in the Twentieth Century* (Oxford: Oxford University Press, 2012), 318.

10. Skidelsky, *John Maynard Keynes*, 758, 775–783.

11. Jean Edward Smith, *FDR* (New York: Random House, 2008), 562.

12. Milovan Djilas, *Conversations with Stalin* (New York: Harcourt, Brace, and World, 1962), 81; Olivier Wieviorka, *Normandy* (Cambridge, MA: Belknap Press of Harvard University Press, 2008), 288–289.

13. Beschloss, *Conquerors*, 229. Truman's remarks appeared in the June 24, 1941, issue of the *New York Times* and many other newspapers as well.

14. The essay appears in Vasily Grossman, *The Road: Stories, Journalism, and Essays* (New York: New York Review Books, 2010).

15. Richard Bessel, *Germany, 1945* (New York: Harper, 2009), 150–151; Karen Petrone, *The Great War in Russian Memory* (Bloomington: Indiana University Press, 2011), 9–13; Anne Applebaum, *Iron Curtain: The Crushing of Eastern Europe, 1944–1956* (New York: Doubleday, 2012), 27. Grossman, *The Road*, contains a new translation of "The Hell of Treblinka" as well as other wartime writings.

16. Giles MacDonogh, *After the Reich: The Brutal History of the Allied Occupation* (New York: Basic Books, 2007), 46; Bessel, *Germany, 1945*, 71.

17. Oral History of Yevgeni Khaldei, Cold War Collection, 28/1, pp. 1–4, LHCMA; Oral History of Konstantin Koval, 28/5, p. 12, LHCMA; Lord Moran, *Winston Churchill: The Struggle for Survival, 1940–1965* (London: Constable, 1966), 268; Applebaum, *Iron Curtain*, 26; Geoffrey Roberts, *Stalin's General: The Life of Georgy Zhukov* (New York: Random House, 2012), 5.

18. Simon Sebag Montefiore, *Stalin: The Court of the Red Czar* (New York: Vintage, 2003), 479. The figure of 2 million women raped is a rough estimate at best. The true figure will never be known. Oral history of Yevgeni Khaldei, 4,

LHCMA; *A Wartime Journey: The 296th Engineer Combat Battalion (1939–1945)*, ARCH COLL Bay 5, Row 190, Face B, Shelf 6, Box 69, Folder 6, p. 84, USAHEC; J. E. Rhys, *Memoirs of a Soldier*, 12/35/1, 59, IWM.

19. Rhys, *Memoirs of a Soldier*, 58. Three different American soldiers recorded the soap anecdote in *Wartime Journey*, 86. The 296th was one of the first American units into Berlin.

20. Eden to Churchill, July 17, 1945, Lord Avon (Anthony Eden) Papers, FO 954, vol. 26, SU/45/135, folio 708, CRL

21. See Sean McMeekin, *The Russian Origins of the First World War* (Cambridge, MA: Belknap Press of Harvard University Press, 2011), esp. Chapter 5.

22. David Reynolds, *From World War to Cold War: Churchill, Roosevelt, and the International History of the 1940s* (Oxford: Oxford University Press, 2006), 235; Michael Dobbs, *Six Months in 1945: From World War to Cold War* (New York: Knopf, 2012), Kindle location 6303.

23. Djilas, *Conversations with Stalin*, 82, 114–115.

24. Aida D. Donald, *Citizen Soldier: A Life of Harry Truman* (New York: Basic Books, 2012), 156; William Hillman, ed., *Mr. President: The First Publication from the Personal Diaries, Private Letters, Papers, and Revealing Interviews of Harry S. Truman* (New York: Farrar, Straus, and Young, 1952), 115.

25. Harry Truman, *Memoirs*, vol. 1, *Year of Decisions* (Garden City, NY: Doubleday, 1955), 341–342.

26. Ibid., 350; Hillman, *Mr. President*, 83; Nigel Hamilton, *American Caesars: Lives of the Presidents from Franklin D. Roosevelt to George W. Bush* (New Haven, CT: Yale University Press, 2010), 59.

27. Eden to Churchill, July 17, 1945, Lord Avon (Anthony Eden) Papers, FO 954, vol. 26, SU/45/135, folio 708, CRL; Lord Alanbrooke, diary entry for June 11, 1945, 5/1/11, LHCMA. Churchill's allusion to Russia's only further penetration of Western Europe refers to the Russian occupation of Paris following the first capitulation of Napoleon. The figure of twenty divisions is the high end of the estimate that Joseph Davies, the US ambassador to the Soviet Union, relayed to Truman. See Joseph Davies, Memorandum of June 29, 1945, Joseph Davies Papers, Chronological File Part I, Box 17, June 26–30 Folder, 7, LOC.

28. William Leahy, diary entry for April 23, 1945, William Leahy Papers, Diary Box 6, Reel 4, p. 62, LOC.

29. George Kennan, "Russia's International Position at the Close of the War with Germany," in Harry Hopkins Papers, Sherwood Collection, Book 11, Box 338, Hopkins in Moscow (1945) Folder, Harry Hopkins Papers Box 338, n.d., FDR.

30. John Lewis Gaddis, *George Kennan: An American Life* (New York: Penguin, 2011), 200–202. For the text of the Long Telegram, see National Security Archive, George Washington University, www.gwu.edu/~nsarchiv/coldwar/documents/episode-1/kennan.htm.

31. Winston Churchill, *The Second World War, Triumph and Tragedy*, Book 2 (London: Bantam, 1962), 489.

32. Applebaum, *Iron Curtain*, xxviii.

CHAPTER FIVE

"A Vast Undertaking": Coming to Potsdam

1. Eden to Churchill, July 17, 1945, Lord Avon (Anthony Eden) Papers, FO 954, vol. 26, SU/45/135, folio 708, CRL.

2. Michael Dobbs, *Six Months in 1945: From World War to Cold War* (New York: Knopf, 2012), Kindle location 589.

3. Helen Rappaport, *Joseph Stalin: A Biographical Companion* (Santa Barbara, CA: ABC CLIO, 1999), 118; Antony Beevor, *Stalingrad: The Fateful Siege* (New York: Penguin, 1998), 407.

4. Dmitri Volkogonov, *Stalin: Triumph and Tragedy* (New York: Grove Weidenfeld, 1991), 504.

5. Robert van Hallberg, "Translation," in Sacman Bercovitch, ed., *The Cambridge History of American Literature*, vol. 8 (Cambridge, UK: Cambridge University Press, 1996), 181; Anne Applebaum, *Iron Curtain: The Crushing of Eastern Europe, 1944–1956* (New York: Doubleday, 2012), 18.

6. Nicklaus Thomas-Symonds, *Attlee: A Life in Politics* (London: I. B. Taurus, 2010), 124.

7. Joseph Davies, "Potsdam: Prelude," Joseph Davies Papers, Chronological File Part I, Box 17, July 6–10 Folder, LOC.

8. Martin Gilbert, *Churchill: The Power of Words* (Boston: Da Capo Press, 2012), 360.

9. Roy Jenkins, *Churchill: A Biography* (New York: Farrar, Straus, and Giroux, 2001), 792–793.

10. Robert Rhodes James, *Anthony Eden* (New York: McGraw-Hill, 1986), 306; Jenkins, *Churchill*, 774.

11. James Byrnes noted at Yalta that Roosevelt and Churchill had each "worried about how the other looked." Walter J. Brown Papers, Journals, MSS 243, Box 8, Folder 10, CLEM; Robert Rhodes James, *Anthony Eden* (New York: McGraw-Hill, 1986), 310.

12. Joseph Davies to Truman, June 12, 1945, Papers of Harry Truman, SMOF: Naval Aide to the President Files, Box 4, vol. XI, Miscellaneous Papers, Reports by Joseph E. Davies, HSTL.

13. William Leahy, diary entry for July 31, 1945, William Leahy Papers, Diary Box 6, Reel 4, LOC.

14. Walter J. Brown Papers, Journals, MSS 243, Box 8, Folder 13, CLEM; Herbert Feis, *Between War and Peace: The Potsdam Conference* (Princeton, NJ: Princeton University Press, 1960), 138.

15. Charles Mee, *Meeting at Potsdam* (New York: M. Evans, 1975), 83; Max Hastings, *Winston's War: Churchill, 1940–1945* (New York: Knopf, 2010), 473.

16. "Terminal Administrative Arrangements, June 27, 1945," in Mrs. O. M. Margerison Papers, IWM 99/40/1.

17. Prime Minister to President Truman, June 4, 1945, Harry Hopkins Papers, Box 338, Message number 72, FDR.

18. Anthony Eden, *The Reckoning: The Memoirs of Anthony Eden, Earl of Avon* (Cambridge, UK: Riverside Press, 1965), 631.

19. Eden, *Reckoning*, 629.

20. Papers of Lord Ismay, 2/3/284/2a, LHCMA; Clement Attlee, *As It Happened* (New York: Viking, 1954), 204.

21. Scrapbook of Colonel J. W. E. Gainher, Spec Misc C10, IWM.

22. "Potsdam Symphony" and Brigadier O. M. Wales, "Report on Operation Terminal," in Papers of Lieutenant Colonel Evelyn Lindsay-Young, Potsdam Conference, Germany, July 1945 Folder, LHCMA.

23. Eden, *Reckoning*, 634.

24. Harry Truman, *Memoirs*, vol. 1, *Year of Decisions* (Garden City, NY: Doubleday, 1955), 331–332.

25. Robert Moskin, *Mr. Truman's War: The Final Victories of World War II and the Birth of the Postwar World* (Lawrence: University Press of Kansas, 2002), 234;

Truman to Alben Barkley, July 5, 1945, WHCF: OF 190, Potsdam Conference, Folder 1 of 2, HSTL. Barkley soon became Truman's vice president. On Senate reservations to both treaties, see Allen Drury, *A Senate Journal* (New York: McGraw-Hill, 1963), 464–466. Drury was the United Press's Capitol Hill bureau chief.

26. Walter J. Brown Papers, Journals, MSS 243, Box 16, Folder 12, CLEM.

27. Robert Messner, *The End of an Alliance: James F. Byrnes, Roosevelt, Truman, and the Engines of the Cold War* (Chapel Hill: University of North Carolina Press, 1982), 80–83.

28. William Hillman, ed., *Mr. President: The First Publication from the Personal Diaries, Private Letters, Papers, and Revealing Interviews of Harry S. Truman* (New York: Farrar, Strauss, and Young, 1952), 123.

29. James Byrnes, *Speaking Frankly* (New York: Harper and Brothers, 1947), 66.

30. Ibid., 68.

31. John R. Deane, *The Strange Alliance: The Story of Our Efforts at Wartime Collaboration with Russia* (New York: Viking, 1947), 273.

32. David McCullough, *Truman* (New York: Simon and Schuster, 1992), 403.

33. Moskin, *Mr. Truman's War*, 68; Walter J. Brown Papers, Journals, MSS 243, Box 16, Folder 12, CLEM.

34. Walter J. Brown Papers, Journals, MSS 243, Box 16, Folder 12, CLEM.

35. Charles Ross to Eben Ayers, July 19, 1945, Papers of Harry Truman, SMOF: Naval Aide to the Presidential Files, 1945–1953, Box 5, Berlin Conference File, Communications to the Map Room Folder, HSTL.

36. Dwight Eisenhower, *Crusade in Europe* (Garden City, NY: Doubleday, 1948), 442; McCullough, *Truman*, 430.

37. Mee, *Meeting at Potsdam*, 15.

38. Volkogonov, *Stalin*, 497–499; Simon Sebag Montefiore, *Stalin: The Court of the Red Czar* (New York: Vintage, 2003), 480, 498.

39. Lord Moran, *Winston Churchill: The Struggle for Survival, 1940–1965* (London: Constable, 1966), 267; Oral History of George McKee Elsey, 27/11, 5–6, LH-CMA; Lucius Clay, *Decision in Germany* (Garden City, NY: Doubleday, 1950), 37.

CHAPTER SIX

"What a Scene of Destruction"

1. John R. Deane, *The Strange Alliance: The Story of Our Efforts at Wartime Cooperation with Russia* (New York: Viking, 1947), 269.

2. Nigel Hamilton, *American Caesars: Lives of the Presidents from Franklin D. Roosevelt to George W. Bush* (New Haven, CT: Yale University Press, 2010), 57. See also Tony Judt, *Postwar: A History of Europe Since 1945* (New York: Penguin, 2005), and Tami Davis Biddle, *Rhetoric and Reality in Air Warfare, 1914–1945* (Princeton, NJ: Princeton University Press, 2004).

3. Martha Gellhorn, "Dachau," in *Reporting World War II*, Part Two, *American Journalism, 1944–1946* (New York: Library of America, 1995), 724. See also Peter Schrijvers, *The Crash of Ruin: American Combat Soldiers in Europe During World War II* (New York: New York University Press, 2001).

4. James Byrnes, *Speaking Frankly* (New York: Harper and Brothers, 1947), 68.

5. Flight Lieutenant A. H. Coleman, 09/69/1, and L. M. I. Marston, 93/18/1, IWM.

6. J. E. Rhys, 12/35/1, IWM, and Walter J. Brown Papers, MSS 243, Box 8, Folder 12, CLEM.

7. Lionel Ismay, *The Memoirs of General Lord Ismay* (New York: Viking, 1960), 401–402; Lord Alanbrooke, diary entries for July 16 and July 19, 1945, 5/1/11, LHCMA.

8. Floyd Parks, Diary entry for July 16, 1945, Floyd Parks Papers, Box 1, "Diary, July-August 1945" Folder, USAHEC; President's Trip to the Berlin Conference, MSS 90, James F. Byrnes Papers, Series 5, Box 16, Folder 12, CLEM; Harry Truman, *Memoirs*, vol. 1, *Year of Decisions* (Garden City, NY: Doubleday, 1955), 341.

9. "Potsdam Prelude," Joseph Davies Papers, Chronological File Part I, Box 17, July 6–10 Folder, LOC.

10. Ibid.; Ismay, *Memoirs*, 402; Oral History Interview with Richard R. Beckman, July 5, 1991, HSTL, downloaded from Truman Library, Independence, Missouri, http://trumanlibrary.org/oralhist/beckmanr.htm, 62; David Roll, *The Hopkins Touch: Harry Hopkins and the Forging of the Alliance to Defeat Hitler* (New York: Oxford University Press, 2013), 392; Floyd Parks, diary entry for July 26, 1945, Floyd Parks Papers, Box 1, "Diary, July-August 1945 Folder," USAHEC.

11. Lord Moran, *Churchill, Taken from the Diaries of Lord Moran* (Boston: Houghton Mifflin, 1966), 289; Ismay, *Memoirs*, 402.

12. "Narrative, Lille, September, 1944 to Berlin, 1945," in Lieutenant Colonel Evelyn Lindsay-Young Papers, LHCMA; Evelyn Lindsay-Young, entries for June 25 and July 28, 1945, ibid., LHCMA; Alan Brooke, diary entry for July 16, 1945, 5/1/11, LHCMA.

13. William Leahy, diary entry for July 16, 1945, William Leahy Papers, Box 6, Reel 4, LOC.

14. A. H. Colman, 09/69/1, IWM.

15. Anne Applebaum, *Iron Curtain: The Crushing of Eastern Europe, 1944–1956* (New York: Doubleday, 2012), 23; Alfred de Zayas, *Nemesis at Potsdam: The Expulsion of the Germans from the East* (Lincoln: University of Nebraska Press, 1977), 60.

16. Zayas, *Nemesis at Potsdam*, 1, 8.

17. See Richard Bessel, *Germany, 1945* (New York: Harper, 2009), 67–68; Giles MacDonogh, *After the Reich: The Brutal History of the Allied Occupation* (New York: Basic Books, 2007), 1.

18. Keith Lowe, *Savage Continent: Europe in the Aftermath of World War II* (New York: St. Martin's Press, 2012), 31, 58–59.

19. Ben Shephard, *The Long Road Home: The Aftermath of the Second World War* (New York: Anchor Books, 2010), 40–52.

20. Ibid., 65–73.

21. Bessel, *Germany, 1945*, 9, 235.

22. Beckman oral history, 60–61, HSTL.

23. Deane, *Strange Alliance*, 270; Walter J. Brown Papers, Box 8, Folder 12, CLEM.

24. Richard Beckman to his wife, August 2, 1945, Papers of Richard Beckman, "An Accounting of Time to Scrapbook, 1942–1945 [1 of 2]," Box 1, Correspondence, 1945, Folder 2 of 2, HSTL.

25. Bessel, *Germany, 1945*, 134.

26. Carlo D'Este, *Eisenhower: A Soldier's Life* (New York: Henry Holt, 2002), 686. Eisenhower ordered all American units able to make the trip to see the camp for themselves. "We are told the American soldier does not know what he is fighting for," Eisenhower said. "Now, at least, he will know what he is fighting against."

27. Lucius Clay, *Papers of Lucius Clay*, vol. 1, *Germany 1945–1949* (Bloomington: Indiana University Press, 1974), 47.

28. O. M. Margerison to her husband, August 2, 1945, 99/40/1, IWM; Richard Beckman to his father, August 4, 1945, Papers of Richard Beckman, "An Accounting of Time to Scrapbook, 1942–1945 [1 of 2]," Box 1, Correspondence, 1945, Folder 2 of 2, HSTL.

29. Deane, *Strange Alliance*, 268.

30. Papers of A. H. Colman, 09/69/1, and O. M. Margerison, 99/40/1, IWM.

31. Papers of O. M. Margerison, 99/40/1, IWM; Papers of Harry S. Truman, President's Secretary's Files, Box 283, August 5, 1945, Folder, HSTL.

32. Robert Moskin, *Mr. Truman's War: The Final Victories of World War II and the Birth of the Postwar World* (Lawrence: University Press of Kansas, 2002), 216.

33. William Leahy, diary entries for July 15 and 16, 1945, William Leahy Papers, Box 6, Reel 4, LOC; Truman to Churchill, April 19, 1945, Papers of Harry Truman, SMOF: White House Map Room Files, April 1945–January 1946, Outgoing Messages, Box 2, Top Secret File, April 1945, HSTL.

34. Geoffrey Roberts, *Stalin's General: The Life of Georgy Zhukov* (New York: Random House, 2012), 235.

CHAPTER SEVEN

"In Seventeen Days You Can Decide Anything"

1. J. E. Rhys, *Memoirs of a Soldier*, 12/35/1, IWM.

2. *Die Villa Ingenheim* (Berlin: be.bra wissenschaft, 2005).

3. L. M. I. Marston to her mother, July 4, 1945, 93/18/1, IWM; "Information Bulletin, Tripartite Conference," Papers of Harry S. Truman, SMOF: President's Secretary Files, Box 141, Potsdam, Germany, Trip [July-August, 1 of 2] Folder, HSTL.

4. Anne Applebaum, *Iron Curtain: The Crushing of Eastern Europe, 1944–1956* (New York: Doubleday, 2012), 105.

5. John Deane, *The Strange Alliance: The Story of Our Efforts at Wartime Cooperation with Russia* (New York: Viking, 1947), 269; Joseph Davies, diary entry for July 15, 1945, Joseph Davies Papers, Chronological File Part I, Box 17, July 14 Folder, LOC.

6. Truman to Hopkins, May 28, 1945, White House Cable No. 281558, Harry Hopkins Papers, Hopkins 338, FDR; David L. Roll, *The Hopkins Touch: Harry Hopkins and the Forging of the Alliance to Defeat Hitler* (New York: Oxford University Press, 2013), 390.

7. O. M. Margerison to her husband, August 2, 1945, 99/40/1, IWM; C. R. Attlee, *As It Happened* (New York: Viking, 1954), 205. Today Cecilienhof is a hotel and also a UNESCO World Heritage Site.

8. "The Potsdam Conference," July 22, 1945, Papers of Richard Beckman, "An Accounting of Time to Scrapbook, 1942–1945 [1 of 2]," Box 1, Potsdam Folder, HSTL.

9. Ibid.

10. Floyd L. Parks, diary entry for July 9, 1945, Floyd L. Parks Papers, Box 1, "Papers, 1944–1945," "Diary, July-August 1945" Folder, USAHEC; Herbert Feis, *Between War and Peace: The Potsdam Conference* (Princeton, NJ: Princeton University Press, 1960), 151; "The Potsdam Conference."

11. Lucius Clay, *Decision in Germany* (Garden City, NY: Doubleday, 1950), 38.

12. Lieutenant Colonel Evelyn Lindsay-Young, "Narrative, Lille, Sept. 1944, to Berlin, 1945," entries for July 8, 9, and 15, 1945, LHCMA; George McKee Elsey, *An Unplanned Life* (Columbia: University of Missouri Press, 2005), 88; Richard Beckman to his father, August 5, 1945, Papers of Richard Beckman, "An Accounting of Time to Scrapbook, 1942–1945 [1 of 2]," Box 1, Correspondence, 1945 [2 of 2] Folder, HSTL.

13. L. M. I. Marston to her mother, July 6, 1945, 93/18/1, IWM.

14. Brigadier O. M. Wales, "Report on Operation Terminal," LHCMA; Richard Beckman to his father, July 15, 1945, Papers of Richard Beckman, "An Accounting of Time to Scrapbook, 1942–1945 [1 of 2]," Box 1, Correspondence, 1945 [2 of 2] Folder, HSTL; MSS 90, "Report on the Tripartite Conference of Berlin," James F. Byrnes Papers, Series 5, Box 16, Folder 10, CLEM.

15. V. Biriskov, Nuclear Age 12/9, LHCMA; Charles Bohlen, *Witness to History* (New York: Norton, 1973), 227.

16. Harry Truman, *Memoirs*, vol. 1, *Year of Decisions* (Garden City, NY: Doubleday, 1955), 350, 364.

17. Michael Dobbs, *Six Months in 1945: From World War to Cold War* (New York: Knopf, 2012), Kindle location 3286.

18. Halifax to Eden, April 23, 1945, Lord Avon (Anthony Eden) Papers, FO 954, vol. 30, US/45/101, folio 748, CRL; Joseph Davies, diary entry for July 13, 1945, Joseph Davies Papers, Chronological File Part I, Box 17, July 11–13 Folder, LOC.

19. Map Room Messages of President Truman, *2H-726, Reel 2, NYPL, June 8, 1945.

20. Truman, *Memoirs*, 386.

21. Floyd L. Parks, diary entries for July 31 and August 1, 1945, Floyd L. Parks Papers, Box 1, "Papers, 1944–1945" "Diary, July-August 1945" Folder, USAHEC; Walter J. Brown Papers, MSS 243, Box 8, Folder 12, CLEM.

22. Papers of L. M. I. Marston, 93/18/1, IWM; Scrapbook of Colonel J. W. E. Gainher, Spec Misc C10, IWM; O. M. Margerison to her husband, August 2, 1945, 99/40/1, IWM.

23. Floyd L. Parks, diary entry for July 14, 1945, Floyd L. Parks Papers, Box 1, "Papers, 1944–1945," "Diary, July-August 1945" Folder, USAHEC.

24. Truman, *Memoirs*, 370.

25. David McCullough, *Truman* (New York: Simon and Schuster, 1992), 406. Canfil gave Harry Truman his famous plaque reading "The Buck Stops Here."

26. Clay, *Decision in Germany*, 45; Robert Moskin, *Mr. Truman's War: The Final Victories of World War II and the Birth of the Postwar World* (Lawrence: University Press of Kansas, 2002), 234; Truman to Alben Barkley, July 5, 1945, WHCF: OF 190, Potsdam Conference, Folder 1 of 2, HSTL. Barkley soon became Truman's vice president; on Senate reservations to both treaties, see Allen Drury, *A Senate Journal* (New York: McGraw-Hill, 1963), 464–466.

27. Lord Avon (Anthony Eden) Papers, FO 954, vol. 389, folio 63, and vol. 30, US/45/157, folio 813, CRL; Ministry of Foreign Affairs of the USSR, *Correspondence Between the Chairmen of the Council of Foreign Ministers of the USSR and the Presidents of the USA and the Prime Ministers of Great Britain During the Great Patriotic War of 1941–1945* (Moscow: Foreign Languages Publishing House, 1957), 370; Charles Ross to Eben Ayers, July 13, 1945, Papers of Harry Truman, SMOF: Naval Aide to the President Files, 1945–1953, Box 5, Berlin Conference File, Communications to the Map Room, July 7–14, 1945, Folder 1 of 2, HSTL.

28. Acting Secretary of State to Secretary of State, July 21, 1945, "Outgoing Potsdam" Folder, Entries 307 and 308, Box 8b, Record Group 43, NARA.

29. "The Berlin Conference," *Life*, August 6, 1945, 15–28; Robert Ferrell, ed., *Truman in the White House: The Diary of Eben A. Ayers* (Columbia: University of Missouri Press, 1991), 55. Ayers served as Truman's assistant press secretary.

30. Acting Secretary of State to Secretary of State, July 20, 1945, "Outgoing Potsdam" Folder, Entries 307 and 308, Box 8b, Record Group 43, NARA; Lindsay-Young, "Narrative," entry for July 19, 1945; Charles Ross to Eben Ayers, July 19 and July 24, 1945, Papers of Harry Truman, SMOF: Naval Aide to the President Files, 1945–1953, Box 5, Berlin Conference File, Communications to the Map Room, July 15–25, 1945, Folder 1 of 2, HSTL; and Ross to Ayers, July 24, 1945, Papers of Harry Truman, SMOF: Naval Aide to the President Files,

1945–1953, Box 5, Berlin Conference File, Communications to the Map Room, July 7–14, 1945, Folder 2 of 2, HSTL.

31. Ferrell, ed., *Truman in the White House*, 204.

32. Truman, *Memoirs*, 349.

33. Ibid., 394; Robert J. Donovan, *Conflict and Crisis: The Presidency of Harry S. Truman, 1945–1948* (New York: Norton, 1977), 84, 88.

34. Margaret Macmillan, *Paris 1919: Six Months That Changed the World* (New York: Random House, 2003), 58.

35. Italy sent a corps to support the German invasion of Russia in 1941. The 130,000-man strong Italian Eighth Army fought with the Germans at the Battle of Stalingrad. See MacGregor Knox, *Hitler's Italian Allies: Royal Armed Forces, Fascist Regime, and the War of 1940–43* (Cambridge, UK: Cambridge University Press, 2000).

36. See Michael S. Neiberg, *The Blood of Free Men: The Liberation of Paris, 1944* (New York: Basic Books, 2012), Chapter 9.

37. Truman to Churchill, June 5, 1945, Papers of Harry Truman, SMOF: White House Map Room Files, April 1945–January 1946, Outgoing Messages, Box 2, Top Secret File, June 1945 Folder, HSTL.

38. Joseph Davies, diary entry for July 14, 1945, Joseph Davies Papers, Chronological File Part I, Box 17, July 11–13 Folder, LOC; Irwin Gellman, *Secret Affairs: Franklin Roosevelt, Cordell Hull, and Sumner Wells* (Baltimore: Johns Hopkins University Press, 1995), 401.

39. Roll, *The Hopkins Touch*, 379; Walter J. Brown Papers, Box 8, Folder 13, CLEM.

40. Churchill headed the British government, but King George VI was its head of state. Stalin held the official title of general secretary of the Central Committee of the Communist Party of the Soviet Union, which was not the equivalent of a head of state.

Chapter Eight
"I Dreamed That My Life Was Over"

1. Albert L. Weeks, *Assured Victory: How 'Stalin the Great' Won the War but Lost the Peace* (Santa Barbara: ABC-CLIO, 2011), 139. For more on Hopkins and his impressions, see Matthew B. Wills, *Wartime Missions of Harry L. Hopkins* (Bloomington, IN: Author House, 2004), and David I. Roll, *The Hopkins Touch:*

Harry Hopkins and the Forging of the Alliance to Defeat Hitler (New York: Oxford University Press, 2013).

2. "Conversation, 30 July, 1945, 4:30 pm," in Potsdam Conference Minutes, Record Group 43, Entry 307, Box 8a, p. 11, NARA; Averill Harriman to Truman, June 8, 1945, *Map Room Messages of President Truman*, *2H-726, Reel 2, NYPL; Joseph Davies, untitled document, Joseph Davies Papers, Chronological File Part I, Box 17, July 1–5 Folder, LOC; David McCullough, *Truman* (New York: Simon and Schuster, 1992), 347–348.

3. Simon Sebag Montefiore, *Stalin: The Court of the Red Czar* (New York: Vintage, 2003), 491. In 1970, the KGB ordered Hitler's remains removed from the grave at Magdeburg, the body cremated, and the ashes scattered.

4. James Byrnes, *Speaking Frankly* (New York: Harper and Row, 1947), 68; "First Meeting, Kremlin 8 pm, May 26, 1945," in Harry Hopkins Papers, Box 338, 7, FDR. This might well be the origin of the popular myth that Hitler had somehow escaped to South America after the war.

5. Montefiore, *Stalin*, 497–498; Oral History of Valentin Berezhekov, prepared for the documentary *The Nuclear Age*, 12/8, vol. 2, 8, LHCMA.

6. Ben Macintyre, *A Spy Among Friends: Kim Philby and the Great Betrayal* (New York: Crown, 2014).

7. Robert Rhodes James, *Anthony Eden* (New York: McGraw-Hill, 1986), 307–308; Walter J. Brown Papers, Journals, MSS 243, Box 8, Folder 12, CLEM. These were not new patterns for Churchill, as previously unpublished World War I diaries from Lewis Harcourt and Margot Asquith will demonstrate. Harcourt, a cabinet member, wrote of Churchill, "I think he has gone mad." Asquith, the wife of Prime Minister H. H. Asquith, called Churchill, "insolent" and said that his "vanity is septic." See Hannah Furness, "Revealed: War Diary Meant to Stay Secret," The Telegraph, June 8, 2014, www.telegraph.co.uk/news/10883656 /Revealed-war-diary-meant-to-stay-secret.html; Dalya Alberge, "'Insolent' Churchill, 'Ignorant' Kitchener: Waspish Wartime Diaries of Margot Asquith," *The Guardian*, June 7, 2014, www.theguardian.com/world/2014/jun/08/margot -asquith-diaries-insolent-churchill-ignorant-kitchener; and Michael Brock, ed., *Margot Asquith's Great War Diary* (Oxford: Oxford University Press, 2014).

8. Max Hastings, *Winston's War: Churchill, 1940–1945* (New York: Knopf, 2010), 475.

9. Michael Dobbs, *Six Months in 1945: From World War to Cold War* (New York: Knopf, 2012), Kindle location 6186.

10. Nigel Hamilton, *American Caesars: Lives of the Presidents from Franklin D. Roosevelt to George W. Bush* (New Haven, CT: Yale University Press, 2010), 85.

11. Charles Mee, *Meeting at Potsdam* (New York: M. Evans, 1975), 96, 100; Harry Truman, *Memoirs*, vol. 1, *Year of Decisions* (Garden City, NY: Doubleday, 1955), 363; Herbert Feis, *Between War and Peace: The Potsdam Conference* (Princeton, NJ: Princeton University Press, 1960), 189.

12. Feis, *Between War and Peace*, 188; William Leahy, diary entry for July 20, 1945, William Leahy Papers, Diary Box 6, Reel 4, 1945, LOC.

13. Lord Alanbrooke, diary entry for July 23, 1945, 5/1/11, LHCMA.

14. Eden to Cadogan, June 17, 1945, in Anthony Eden (Lord Avon) Papers, Conf/45/126, folio 287, CRL.

15. Anthony Eden, *The Reckoning: The Memoirs of Anthony Eden, Earl of Avon* (Cambridge, UK: Riverside Press, 1965), 630, 632.

16. Walter J. Brown Papers, Journals, MSS 243, Box 8, Folder 12, CLEM.

17. Field Marshal Brooke was one British leader who told Churchill to resist Labour's demands for an early election. After Churchill's defeat, Brooke complained to his diary "What was my advice to him, a mere soldier!!!" Lord Alanbrooke, diary entry for July 26, 1945, 5/1/11, LHCMA.

18. Mrs. O. M. Margerison to her husband, August 2, 1945, 99/40/1, IWM (emphases in original).

19. Martin Gilbert, *Winston S. Churchill*, vol. 3 (Boston: Houghton Mifflin, 1998), 101; Churchill, after all, is the man who said, "History will be kind to me for I intend to write it." On Churchill and his memoirs, see David Reynolds, *In Command of History: Churchill Fighting and Writing the Second World War* (New York: Random House, 2005).

20. Eden, *Reckoning*, 635.

21. Ibid., 636.

22. Clement Attlee, *Twilight of Empire: The Memoirs of Prime Minister Clement Attlee* (New York: A. S. Barnes, 1962), 69; Eden, *Reckoning*, 638.

23. Clement Attlee, *As It Happened* (New York: Viking, 1954), 207; William Leahy, diary entry for July 26, 1945, William Leahy Papers, Diary Box 6, Reel 4, LOC.

24. McCullough, *Truman*, 446; Dmitri Volkogonov, *Stalin: Triumph and Tragedy* (New York: Grove Weidenfeld, 1988), 501.

25. Attlee, *Twilight of Empire*, 71.

26. Mee, *Meeting at Potsdam*, 233; Hastings, *Winston's War*, 476; Lord Alanbrooke, diary entry for July 26, 1945, LHCMA.

27. James, *Anthony Eden*, 311; Mee, *Meeting at Potsdam*, 232.

28. Attlee, *Twilight of Empire*, 9.

29. Walter J. Brown Papers, MSS 243, Box 7, Folder 5, CLEM; Hastings, *Winston's War*, 478.

30. Mee, *Meeting at Potsdam*, 232; James, *Anthony Eden*, 311.

31. Lieutenant General Burrows to General Lionel Ismay, August 17, 1945, in Burrows Papers, 4/4/1–9, LCHMA.

32. Mee, *Meeting at Potsdam*, 45, 254.

33. McCullough, *Truman*, 447–448.

34. Lieutenant General Burrows to General Ismay, August 17, 1945, in Burrows Papers, 4/4/1–9, LHCMA; Mee, *Meeting at Potsdam*, 251.

35. Truman, *Memoirs*, 395; Lucius Clay, *Decision in Germany* (Garden City, NY: Doubleday, 1950), 39.

36. "Clement Richard Attlee," *Life*, August 6, 1945, 27; Truman, *Memoirs*, 389.

37. Walter J. Brown Papers, Journals, MSS 243, Box 8, Folder 12, CLEM.

38. Byrnes, *Speaking Frankly*, 79.

39. Andrew Roberts, *Masters and Commanders: How Four Titans Won the War in the West, 1941–1945* (New York: Harper Perennial, 2008), 567.

40. Eden, *Reckoning*, 635.

CHAPTER NINE

"Dismemberment as a Permanent Fate"?
Solving the Problem of Germany

1. See David Kennedy, *Freedom from Fear: The American People in Depression and War, 1929–1945* (New York: Oxford University Press, 1999), Chapter 3.

2. Lucius Clay, *Decision in Germany* (Garden City, NY: Doubleday, 1950), 38; Harry Truman, *Memoirs*, vol. 1, *Year of Decisions* (Garden City, NY: Doubleday, 1955), 367.

3. S. M. Plokhy, *Yalta: The Price of Peace* (New York: Penguin, 2010), 111; Truman, *Memoirs*, 370; FRUS, vol. 2 (Washington, DC: US Government Printing Office, 1945), 795–797.

4. George Kennan, "Russia's International Position at the Close of the War with Germany," n.d. [but almost certainly May 1945], Harry Hopkins Papers, Sherwood Collection, Book 11, Box 338, Hopkins in Moscow Folder, 10, FDR.

5. "Wilson's War Message to Congress," April 2, 1917, World War I Document Archive, http://wwi.lib.byu.edu/index.php/Wilson's_War_Message _to_Congress.

6. Henry Stimson, *On Active Service in Peace and War* (New York: Harper and Brothers, 1948), 583; Herbert Feis, *Between War and Peace: The Potsdam Conference* (Princeton, NJ: Princeton University Press, 1960), 57; Joseph Grew to James Byrnes, July 21, 1945, NARA II, Record Group 43, entries 307 and 308, Box 8b, "Outgoing Potsdam" Folder; Proposal by the Soviet Delegation, July 23, 1945, FRUS, 755–756.

7. Proposal by the Soviet Delegation, July 23, 1945, FRUS, 810.

8. Ibid., 802–804.

9. Ben Shephard, *The Long Road Home: The Aftermath of the Second World War* (New York: Anchor Books, 2010), 132, 134.

10. Charles Bohlen, *Witness to History, 1929–1969* (New York: Norton, 1973), 231.

11. Floyd L. Parks Papers, Box 1, "Papers, 1944–1945," "Diary July-August, 1945," Folder 1, USAHEC.

12. Lord Avon (Anthony Eden) Papers, FO 954, vol. 31, WARC/45/5, folios 67–73, CRL.

13. Interview with Dick Hottelet, Parks Papers, Box 1, Folder 1, USAHEC.

14. Jean Edward Smith, *Lucius D. Clay: An American Life* (New York: Henry, Holt, 1990); Jennifer Fay, *Theaters of Occupation: Hollywood and the Reeducation of Postwar Germany* (Minneapolis: University of Minnesota Press, 2008).

15. Plokhy, *Yalta*, 92, 109; "Dismemberment of Germany," July 11, 1945, Papers of William L. Clayton, Chronological File 1945, June 1945–December 31, 1945, Box 1, Berlin Conference, July-August 1945, Folder 2, HSTL.

16. Benn Steil, *The Battle of Bretton Woods: John Maynard Keynes, Harry Dexter White, and the Making of a New World Order* (Princeton, NJ: Princeton University Press, 2013), 283.

17. Jean Edward Smith, *FDR* (New York: Random House, 2008), 624; Steil, *Battle of Bretton Woods*, 287.

18. "Third Meeting, Kremlin, 8 pm, May 28, 1945," in Harry Hopkins Papers, Box 338, FDR; Steil, *Battle of Bretton Woods*, 283, 286.

19. James Byrnes, *Speaking Frankly* (New York: Viking, 1947), 82; Truman to Joseph Davies, July 20, 1945, Joseph Davies Papers, Chronological File Part II, Box 42, Correspondence, June-July 1945 Folder, LOC.

20. Robert Skidelsky, *John Maynard Keynes, 1883–1946: Economist, Philosopher, Statesman* (New York: Penguin, 2003), 771.

21. Averill Harriman to the Secretary of State, July 6, 1945, NARA II, Record Group 43, entries 307 and 308, Box 8b, "Outgoing Potsdam" Folder.

22. Recommendations from the Joint Chiefs of Staff, June 26, 1945, Papers of Harry Truman, SMOF: Naval Aide to the President Files, 1945–1953, Box 2, vol. V, HSTL.

23. Anne Applebaum, *Iron Curtain: The Crushing of Eastern Europe, 1944–1956* (New York: Doubleday, 2012), 34; Clement Attlee, *Twilight of Empire: Memoirs of Prime Minister Clement Attlee* (New York: A. S. Barnes, 1962), 77.

24. Thomas Lamont, quoted in Margaret Macmillan, *Paris, 1919: Six Months That Changed the World* (New York: Random House, 2003), 180; Foreign Ministers Meeting, July 27, 1945, Record Group 43, Entry 307, Box 8a, NARA.

25. Pauley to Molotov, July 27, 1945, FRUS, 896.

26. Potsdam Conference Minutes, entries for July 23 and July 27, 1945, NARA II; FRUS, 876, 889; "Russian Machinery Removals from Berlin," July 25, 1945, Papers of Harry Truman, SMOF: Naval Aide to the President Files, Box 4, vol. XI, Miscellaneous Papers, Reparations, HSTL.

27. Byrnes, *Speaking Frankly*, 83–84; Bohlen, *Witness to History*, 233; Shephard, *Long Road Home*, 149; Truman, *Memoirs*, 357; FRUS, 918, 927.

28. Truman, *Memoirs*, 360; FRUS, 809, 837, 961.

29. Potsdam Conference Minutes, Foreign Ministers Meeting, July 23, 1945, 4 pm, Record Group 43, Entry 307, Box 8a, NARA; Memorandum, July 18, 1945, Record Group 43, entries 307 and 308, Box 8b, NARA.

30. "Proposal for the Establishment of a Council of Foreign Ministers," Harry Hopkins Papers, Box 171, "Big Three Conference Agenda (Potsdam)," July 1945, tabs 1, 2, 9, 14, 15, FDR; FRUS, 896.

31. FRUS, 993–997.

CHAPTER TEN
"The Bastard of Versailles"

1. Halik Kochanski, *The Eagle Unbowed: Poland and the Poles in the Second World War* (Cambridge, MA: Harvard University Press, 2012), 96.

2. Timothy Snyder, *Bloodlands: Europe Between Hitler and Stalin* (New York: Basic Books, 2010), 128.

3. For more on Soviet crimes against Poles, see Snyder, *Bloodlands*. Zaolzie had a plurality of ethnic Poles, but not a majority. It also had a key rail juncture and valuable coal mines. The Germans were happy to give Poland a piece of Czechoslovakia at the Munich conference in order to make the point that Germany was not solely responsible for the dismemberment of Czechoslovakia.

4. John Owens, editorial from the *Baltimore Sun* "sent to the President for Potsdam," Joseph Davies Papers, Chronological File Part I, Box 17, June 26–30 Folder, LOC.

5. Margaret Macmillan, *Paris 1919: Six Months That Changed the World* (New York: Random House, 2003), 226. The main difference in the two lines existed around the town of Bialystok, which lay west of the Curzon Line but east of the Molotov-Ribbentrop Line.

6. Kochanski, *Eagle Unbowed*, 439, 445; Arthur Bliss Lane, *I Saw Poland Betrayed: An American Ambassador Reports to the American People* (Indianapolis: Bobbs-Merrill, 1948), 60; Churchill to Truman, April 29, 1945, Papers of Harry Truman, SMOF: Naval Aide to the President Files, 1945–1953, Box 7, Churchill to Truman, April 1945 Folder, HSTL.

7. Bela Grünwald Ivanyi and Alan Bell, *Route to Potsdam: The Story of the Peace Aims, 1939–1945* (London: Allan Wingate, 1946), 72, 96; Lane, *Poland Betrayed*, 84. Lane estimated that in fact 12 million Poles then lived between the Curzon and Riga lines, although this number may be too high.

8. Snyder, *Bloodlands*, 307; "The Polish Problem, 1943–1945," April 25, 1945, Papers of William L. Clayton, Chronological File 1945, June 1945–December 31, 1945, Box 1, Historical Reports and Research Notes—Poland Folder, HSTL.

9. *Henry Lewis Stimson Diaries in the Yale University Library*, microfilm reel 9, entry for April 2, 1945, USAHEC; Recommendations from the Joint Chiefs of Staff, June 26, 1945, Papers of Harry Truman, SMOF: Naval Aide to the President Files, 1945–1953, Box 2, vol. V, HSTL.

10. Kochanski, *Eagle Unbowed*, 331.

11. S. M. Plokhy, *Yalta: The Price of Peace* (New York: Penguin, 2010), 177–178; David L. Roll, *The Hopkins Touch: Harry Hopkins and the Forging of the Alliance to Defeat Hitler* (New York: Oxford University Press, 2013), 371; July 18 Meeting of the Heads of State, MSS 90, James F. Byrnes Papers, Series 5, Box 16, Folder 6, CLEM.

12. Kochanski, *Eagle Unbowed*, 452, 455; Alfred M. de Zayas, *Nemesis at Potsdam: The Expulsion of the Germans from the East* (Lincoln: University of Nebraska Press, 1977), 47–49; "Summary of the Views Expressed by the Polish Delegation," July 24, 1945, Papers of Harry Truman, SMOF: Naval Aide to the President Files, Box 4, vol. XI, Miscellaneous Papers, Poland, HSTL.

13. Roll, *Hopkins Touch*, 371.

14. "Summary of the Views Expressed by the Polish Delegation," HSTL.

15. Michael Dobbs, *Six Months in 1945: From World War to Cold War* (New York: Knopf, 2012), Kindle location 1919; "The Polish Problem, 1943–1945."

16. Ben Shephard, *The Long Road Home: The Aftermath of the Second World War* (New York: Anchor Books, 2010), 152, 167; FRUS, vol. V, 362.

17. Lane, *Poland Betrayed*, i; George Kennan, *Memoirs*, vol. 1, *1925–1950* (Boston: Atlantic–Little Brown, 1967), 263; Robert Dallek, *Franklin D. Roosevelt and American Foreign Policy, 1932–1945* (New York: Oxford University Press, 1995), 515.

18. Truman to Stalin, May 4, 1945, Papers of Harry Truman, SMOF: White House Map Room Files: April 1945–January 1946, Outgoing Messages, Box 2, Top Secret File, May 1945 Folder, HSTL; Draft Submitted by the Soviet Delegation, July 18, 1945, MSS 90, James Byrnes Papers, Series 5, Box 16, Folder 6, CLEM.

19. Richard Bessel, *Germany, 1945* (New York: Harper, 2009), 69–70, 214; Kochanski, *Eagle Unbowed*, 545; FRUS, vol. V, 277; Joseph Grew to James Byrnes, July 25, 1945, Record Group 43, Entry 307, Box 8b, NARA.

20. For more on this issue, see Kochanski, *Eagle Unbowed*, 514–515.

21. Messages of June 3 and June 6, 1945, Map Room Messages of President Truman, *2H-726, Reel 2, NYPL; J. Robert Moskin, *Mr. Truman's War: The Final*

Victories of World War II and the Birth of the Postwar World (Lawrence: University Press of Kansas, 2002), 85. In the end three of the men were acquitted; one was sentenced to ten years in prison, another to eight years, and three men to five years; the rest received sentences of between four months and one year. Three of the men died in prison. See Kochanski, *Eagle Unbowed*, 534–536.

22. Halifax to Eden, Lord Avon (Anthony Eden) Papers, FO 954, May 14, 1945, US/45/114, folio 765, CRL; Clement Attlee, *Twilight of Empire: Memoirs of Prime Minister Clement Attlee* (New York: A. S. Barnes, 1962), 76; Joseph Davies, Memorandum of June 29, 1945, Joseph Davies Papers, Chronological File Part I, Box 17, June 26–30 Folder, LOC; Robert Messner, *The End of an Alliance: James F. Byrnes, Franklin Roosevelt, Harry Truman, and the Origins of the Cold War* (Chapel Hill: University of North Carolina Press, 1982), 50; FRUS, vol. V, 252; Harry Hopkins to Truman, June 3, 1945, Papers of Harry Truman, SMOF: White House Map Room Files, Incoming Messages, Top Secret File, June 1945 Folder, HSTL.

23. Halifax to Eden, May 14, 1945; "Second Meeting, Kremlin—8 pm, May 27, 1945," and "Fifth Meeting, Kremlin—6 pm, May 31, 1945," Harry Hopkins Papers, Sherwood Collection, Box 338, Hopkins in Moscow Folder, FDR.

24. "Territorial Studies," July 6, 1945, Papers of Harry Truman, SMOF: Naval Aide to the President Files, 1945–1953, Berlin Conference File, Box 1, vol. III, Tabs 12, 17–24, HSTL.

25. Charles Mee, *Meeting at Potsdam* (New York: M. Evans, 1975), 171; "President's Trip to the Berlin Conference," James F. Byrnes Papers, MSS 90, Series 5, Box 16, Folder 12, CLEM; Anthony Eden, *The Reckoning: The Memoirs of Anthony Eden, Earl of Avon* (Cambridge, UK: Riverside Press, 1965), 630–631; Dobbs, *Six Months in 1945*, Kindle location 1214.

26. Eden, *Reckoning*, 630–631; Martin Gilbert, *Winston Churchill: A Life* (New York: Henry Holt, 1991), 819; Harry Truman, *Memoirs*, vol. 1, *Year of Decisions* (Garden City, NY: Doubleday, 1955), 369.

27. Herbert Feis, *Between War and Peace: The Potsdam Conference* (Princeton, NJ: Princeton University Press, 1960), 232; Mee, *Meeting at Potsdam*, 177, 179.

28. Bessel, *Germany, 1945*, 232; Kochanski, *Eagle Unbowed*, 538.

29. Oral History of Kathleen Harriman Mortimer, Cold War 27/80, 22, 29–30, LHCMA; Charles Bohlen, *Witness to History, 1929–1969* (New York: Norton, 1973), 211.

30. John Lewis Gaddis, *George Kennan: An American Life* (New York: Penguin, 2011), 202.

31. Zayas, *Nemesis*, 53; William Leahy, diary entry for July 31, 1945, William Leahy Papers, Diary Box 6, Reel 4, LOC; Bessel, *Germany, 1945*, 228, 234–237, 240.

32. Joseph Grew to James Byrnes, July 25, 1945, Record Group 43, Entry 307, Box 8b, NARA.

33. FRUS, vol. V, 257.

34. Ibid., 263.

35. Feis, *Between War and Peace*, 229; Dobbs, *Six Months in 1945*, Kindle locations 6160, 6168.

36. FRUS, vol. V, 254, 265; Churchill to Truman, April 29, 1945, Papers of Harry Truman, SMOF: Naval Aide to the President Files, 1945–1953, Box 7, Churchill to Truman, April 1945 Folder, HSTL.

37. "Second Draft of Speech by President Truman on Berlin Conference," n.d., Papers of William L. Clayton, Chronological File 1945, June 1945–December 31, 1945, Box 1, Berlin Conference, July-August 1945, Folder 1, HSTL.

38. Anne Applebaum, *Behind the Iron Curtain: The Crushing of Eastern Europe, 1944–1956* (New York: Doubleday, 2012), 17.

CHAPTER ELEVEN
Dr. Groves's Son and the Fate of East Asia

1. See Guoqi Xu, *Strangers on the Western Front: Chinese Workers in the Great War* (Cambridge, MA: Harvard University Press, 2011).

2. Margaret Macmillan, *Paris, 1919: Six Months That Changed the World* (New York: Random House, 2003), 338.

3. A Chinese version of these events is in Hu Sheng, *From the Opium War to the May Fourth Movement*, vol. 2 (Beijing: Foreign Languages Press, 1991), 646ff.

4. Joseph Davies Papers, Chronological File Part I, Box 17, July 6–10 Folder, LOC.

5. "Third Meeting, Kremlin—8 pm, May 28, 1945," Harry Hopkins Papers, Box 338, 6, FDR. See also Odd Arne Westad, *Restless Empire: China and the World Since 1750* (New York: Basic Books, 2012), 263–265, and Zhang Baijia, "China's Quest for Foreign Military Aid," in Mark Peattie, Edward Drea, and Hans van de Ven, eds., *The Battle for China: Essays on the Military History of the Sino-Japanese War of 1937–1945* (Stanford, CA: Stanford University Press, 2010), 283–307.

6. "Third Meeting, Kremlin—8 pm, May 28, 1945"; Hopkins to Truman, May 29, 1945, Map Room Messages of President Truman, *2H-726, Reel 2, NYPL; Baijia, "China's Quest for Foreign Military Aid," 292.

7. ALUSNA [American Legation United States Naval Attaché, the office responsible for coding and sending secret messages] Moscow to Truman, July 9, 1945; Harriman to Truman, July 11, 1945; and COMNAVGROUP China to Byrnes, July 19 and 20, 1945, "Potsdam to Babelsberg (From Other Sources)" Folder, Record Group 43, Box 8b, NARA; FRUS 1945, vol. II (Washington, DC: US Government Printing Office, 1945), 1223.

8. James I. Matray, "Fighting the Problem: George C. Marshall and Korea," in Charles F. Brower, ed., *George C. Marshall: Servant of the American Nation* (London: Palgrave Macmillan, 2011), 81; *Henry Lewis Stimson Diaries in the Yale University Library*, microfilm reel 9, entry for April 5, 1945, USAHEC; Papers and Minutes of Meetings of the Combined Chiefs of Staff, Papers of Harry Truman, SMOF: Naval Aide to the President Files, 1945–1953, Box 2, vol. VI, 33, HSTL.

9. George Kennan to Truman, April 23, 1945, and Harry Hopkins to Truman, May 30, 1945, Papers of Harry Truman, SMOF: White House Map Room Files, Incoming Messages, Top Secret File, April 1945–May 1945, HSTL.

10. Harry Truman, *Memoirs*, vol. 1, *Year of Decisions* (Garden City, NY: Doubleday, 1955), 382; Lionel Ismay, *The Memoirs of General Lord Ismay* (New York: Viking, 1960), 401.

11. [Joseph] Grew to [James] Byrnes, July 21, 1945, "Outgoing Potsdam" Folder, Record Group 43, Box 8b, NARA; USS Augusta Morning Press, August 5, 1945, Presidential Secretary's Files, Box 141, Potsdam Germany Trip, July-August 1945, Folder 1 of 2, and Frank Boykin to Truman, July 25, 1945, WHCF: OF 190, Miscellaneous (1945), Folder 1 of 2, HSTL.

12. Stimson Diary, entry for July 23, 1945, USAHEC.

13. Dmitri Volkogonov, *Stalin: Triumph and Tragedy* (New York: Grove Weidenfeld, 1988), 493.

14. John R. Deane, *The Strange Alliance: The Story of Our Efforts at Wartime Cooperation with Russia* (New York: Viking, 1947), 272–276; Walter Millis, ed., *The Forrestal Diaries* (New York: Viking, 1951), 74.

15. Truman, *Year of Decisions*, 382, David McCullough, *Truman* (New York: Simon and Schuster, 1992), 424; Gar Alperovitz, *The Decision to Use the Atomic*

Bomb (New York: Vintage, 1995), 268; Meeting of Heads of Government, July 19, 1945, 5 pm, MSS 90, James F. Byrnes Papers, Series 5, Box 16, Folder 6, CLEM.

16. J. Robert Moskin, *Mr. Truman's War: The Final Victories of World War II and the Birth of the Postwar World* (Lawrence: University Press of Kansas, 2002), 224; Stimson Diary, entry for July 24, 1945, USAHEC; Millis, *Forrestal Diaries*, 80.

17. Cordell Hull, *The Memoirs of Cordell Hull*, vol. 2 (New York: Macmillan, 1948), 1594.

18. State [Department] to Babelsberg, July 21, 1945, "Outgoing Potsdam" Folder, Record Group 43, Box 8b, NARA; Millis, *Forrestal Diaries*, 53; Background Information, Papers of Harry Truman, SMOF: Naval Aide to the President Files, 1945–1953, Berlin Conference Files, Box 1, vol. II, 63, HSTL.

19. Harry Hopkins to Truman, May 30, 1945, Map Room Messages, HSTL; Walter J. Brown Papers, MSS 243, Box 8, Folder 12, CLEM.

20. Millis, *Forrestal Diaries*, 52, 69–71.

21. J. David Kidwell to Truman, May 10, 1945, Fred Burdick to Truman, July 14, 1945, and *New York Times*, May 11, 1945, in WHCF: OF 190, Miscellaneous (1945), Folder 1 of 2, HSTL.

22. Ferenc Szasz, *The Day the Sun Rose Twice: The Story of the Trinity Site Nuclear Explosion, July 16, 1945* (Albuquerque: University of New Mexico Press, 1984), 145. The full text of Groves's two notes and the much longer reports that followed are in FRUS, vol. II, 136off.

23. Tsuyoshi Hasegawa, *Racing the Enemy: Stalin, Truman, and the Surrender of Japan* (Cambridge, MA: Harvard University Press, 2005), 149; Michael Dobbs, *Six Months in 1945: From World War to Cold War* (New York: Knopf, 2012), Kindle location 4429; Stimson Diary, entry for July 21, 1945, USAHEC.

24. Walter J. Brown Papers, MSS 243, Box 8, Folder 12, CLEM. See also Barrett Tillman, *Whirlwind: The Air War Against Japan* (New York: Simon and Schuster, 2010).

25. Robert H. Ferrell, *Off the Record: The Private Papers of Harry S. Truman* (New York: Harper and Row, 1980), 55–56.

26. Lord Alanbrooke, diary entry for July 23, 1945, 5/1/11, LHCMA (emphasis in original).

27. McCullough, *Truman*, 393; Clement Attlee, *Twilight of Empire: Memoirs of Prime Minister Clement Attlee* (New York: A. S. Barnes, 1962), 73.

28. Mee, *Meeting at Potsdam*, 206, 289; Ismay, *Memoirs*, 401.

29. Gideon Rose, *How Wars End: Why We Always Fight the Last Battle* (New York: Simon and Schuster, 2011), 112; McCullough, *Truman*, 444.

30. Anthony Eden, *The Reckoning: The Memoirs of Anthony Eden, Earl of Avon* (Cambridge, UK: Riverside Press, 1965), 634; Dobbs, *Six Months in 1945*, Kindle location 4454; Charles Mee, *Meeting at Potsdam* (New York: M. Evans, 1975), 110.

31. Simon Sebag Montefiore, *Stalin: The Court of the Red Czar* (New York: Vintage, 2003), 498.

32. Montefiore, *Stalin*, 499. Curiously, Anthony Eden, who was standing nearby, said that Stalin only replied "Thank you." A Russian aide later said that Stalin only shook his head. See David Holloway, *Stalin and the Bomb: The Soviet Union and Atomic Energy, 1939–1956* (New Haven, CT: Yale University Press, 1994), 117.

33. Charles Bohlen, *Witness to History, 1929–1969* (New York: Norton, 1973), 237; Messner, *End of an Alliance*, 112; Herbert Feis, *Between War and Peace: The Potsdam Conference* (Princeton, NJ: Princeton University Press, 1960), 177.

34. Oral histories of Valentin Berezhkov and V. Biriskov, Nuclear Age, 12/8 and 12/9, LHCMA; Montefiore, *Stalin*, 500; Messner, *End of an Alliance*, 104.

35. Charles Ross to Eben Ayers, July 24, 1945, Papers of Harry Truman, SMOF: Naval Aide to the President Files, 1945–1953, Box 5, Berlin Conference, Communications to the Map Room, July 15–25, 1945, Folder 1 of 2, HSTL.

36. The full declaration is available at National Diet Library, Birth of the Constitution of Japan, Text of the Constitution and Other Important Documents, Potsdam Declaration, www.ndl.go.jp/constitution/e/etc/c06.html.

37. FRUS, vol. II, 1293.

38. McCullough, *Truman*, 785–786; Feis, *Between War and Peace*, 115. Rusk, of course, went on to become secretary of state from 1961 to 1969.

CONCLUSION

1. Margaret Macmillan, *Paris 1919: Six Months That Changed the World* (New York: Random House, 2003), 62, 285.

2. MSS 90, James F. Byrnes Papers, Series 5, Box 16, Folder 6, CLEM; MSS 243, Walter J. Brown Papers, Box 8, Folder 10, CLEM.

3. Victoria De Grazia, *Irresistible Empire: America's Advance Through Twentieth Century Europe* (Cambridge, MA: Harvard University Press, 2005), Jennifer Fay,

Theaters of Occupation: Hollywood and the Reeducation of Postwar Germany (Minneapolis: University of Minnesota Press, 2008), and Christopher Endy, *Cold War Holidays: American Tourism in France* (Chapel Hill: University of North Carolina Press, 2004) all show the far more aggressive role of US government agencies in using soft and hard power to influence events in Europe in the 1940s compared to the 1920s.

4. Nigel Hamilton, *American Caesars: Lives of the Presidents from Franklin D. Roosevelt to George W. Bush* (New Haven, CT: Yale University Press, 2010), 59; Truman to Eben Ayers, Papers of Harry S. Truman, SMOF: President's Secretary's Files, Box 197, Potsdam Conference, 1945 Folder, HSTL; Alonzo Hamby, *Man of the People: A Life of Harry Truman* (New York: Oxford University Press, 1995), 331.

5. Walter J. Brown Papers, Box 8, Folder 12, CLEM; Hamilton, *American Caesars*, 59. Debates over sharing the atomic bomb show the continued tensions between the United States and Great Britain. In the fall of 1946, after a meeting with Byrnes on the subject, Ernest Bevin told Clement Attlee: "I don't want any other Foreign Secretary of this country to be talked at, or to, by the Secretary of State in the United States as I just have in my discussions with Mr. Byrnes. We've got to have this thing [the atomic bomb] over here, whatever it costs. We've got to have the bloody Union Jack on top of it." Gerard de Groot, *The Bomb: A Life* (London: Pimlico, 2005), 219.

6. MSS 90, James F. Byrnes Papers, Series 5, Box 16, Folder 6, CLEM.

7. George McKee Elsey, *An Unplanned Life* (Columbia: University of Missouri Press, 2005), 91; Harry Truman, *Memoirs*, vol. 1, *Year of Decisions* (Garden City, NY: Doubleday, 1955), 410–412.

8. Lukas E. Hoska, *A Critical Analysis of the Summit Conferences of Tehran, the Crimea, and Berlin* (Cambridge, MA: Center for International Affairs, 1960), 173–179, USAHEC; Lucius Clay, *Decision in Germany* (Garden City, NY: Doubleday, 1950), 39–43; James Forrestal, *The Forrestal Diaries* (New York: Viking, 1951), 78.

9. Richard M. Brickner, *Is Germany Incurable?* (Philadelphia: J. B. Lippincott, 1943). Brickner saw some hope, noting that the very different attitudes of ethnic Germans in the United States proved that the problem was societal, not racial. See Fay, *Theaters of Occupation*, 17–26.

10. Papers of Wallace R. Deuel, Box 61, Potsdam Conference Folder, LOC.

11. Vol. II, Background Information, and vol. IV, Papers Prepared by the Department of State for Discussion, Papers of Harry Truman, SMOF: Naval Aide to the President Files, 1945–1953, Box 1, HSTL.

12. Eden to Churchill, February 2, 1945, Lord Avon (Anthony Eden) Papers, FO 954, vol. 19, Pal/45/2, folio 72–73, Palestine 1936–1945 and Peace Settlement, CRL.

13. Peter Novick, *The Holocaust in American Life* (New York: Mariner Books, 2000), Chapter 4. For more on the extremely complex reactions of the Soviet Union to the Holocaust, see Simon Sebag Montefiore, *Stalin: Court of the Red Czar* (New York: Vintage, 2003), 545–547.

14. Ben Shephard, *The Long Road Home: The Aftermath of the Second World War* (New York: Anchor Books, 2010), 103, 110–114; Alex Grobman, *Rekindling the Flame: American Jewish Chaplains and the Survivors of European Jewry, 1945–1948* (Detroit: Wayne State University Press, 1993), 81.

15. Shephard, *Long Road Home*, 113–118; David McCullough, *Truman* (New York: Simon and Schuster, 1992), 595. Harrison was then dean of the law school at the University of Pennsylvania and a former senior official with the US Immigration Department.

16. James Byrnes, *Speaking Frankly* (New York: Harper and Brothers, 1947), 86–87.

17. Joseph Davies Papers, Chronological File Part I, Box 17, 28, LOC; Montefiore, *Stalin*, 502; Student Research File, Potsdam Conference, Folder 1, HSTL.

18. Walter J. Brown Papers, MSS 243, Box 8, Folder 13, CLEM; McCullough, *Truman*, 454.

INDEX